Religion and Politics Series
John C. Green, Ted G. Jelen, and Mark J. Rozell, series editors

The Christian Right in American Politics: Marching to the Millennium
John C. Green, Mark J. Rozell, and Clyde Wilcox, Editors

Of Little Faith: The Politics of George W. Bush's Faith-Based Initiatives
Amy E. Black, Douglas L. Koopman, and David K. Ryden

School Board Battles: The Christian Right in Local Politics
Melissa M. Deckman

School Board Battles

The Christian Right in Local Politics

Melissa M. Deckman

Georgetown University Press
Washington, D.C.

Georgetown University Press, Washington, D.C.
© 2004 by Georgetown University Press. All rights reserved.
Printed in the United States of America

10 9 8 7 6 5 4 3 2 1   2004

This book is printed on acid-free paper meeting the
requirements of the American National Standard for
Permanence in Paper for Printed Library Materials.

Library of Congress Cataloging-in-Publication Data
Deckman, Melissa M. (Melissa Marie), 1971–
   School board battles : the Christian right in local politics / Melissa
M. Deckman.
       p. cm. — (Religion and politics series)
Includes bibliographical references and index.
   ISBN 1-58901-000-0 (cloth : alk. paper) — ISBN 1-58901-001-9 (pbk. :
alk. paper)
   1. Religion in the public schools—United States.   2. School board
members—United States.   3. Christians—United States—Political
activity.   I. Title.   II. Religion and politics series (Georgetown
University)
   LC111.D42   2004
   379.2′8′0973—dc22
                                                      2003019465

To Sean

Contents

List of Tables

Acknowledgments

Undertaking this book project on the Christian Right and school boards has been a rewarding experience. I would first like to thank the many school board candidates who took the time to be interviewed for my project. Without their cooperation, this book would not be possible.

I also wish to thank Patricia Sykes, who chaired the dissertation out of which this project grew. While she offered essential advice on various aspects of the study, I am especially grateful for her enthusiasm for the project, as well as her confidence in my abilities to see it through. I am also thankful for the helpful comments of Jeff Fishel and Karen O'Connor, who also served on my dissertation committee.

Several people offered advice on conducting the survey, including Jim Lynch and John Shapard. I wish to thank the School of Public Affairs and the Graduate Student Association at American University for funding part of the survey research. Mark Rozell and Clyde Wilcox were also helpful in the early phases of the project, both giving me feedback on drafts of my survey and dissertation proposal. I would also like to thank David Rosenbloom for his encouragement at various stages of the study. I wish to acknowledge the librarians at the National School Boards Association and People for the American Way, who made their private libraries available for me to use and who were always quick to answer my questions.

My colleagues at Washington College, including John Taylor, Dan Premo, Tahir Shad, and Andrew Oros, have also been supportive of my work. I also appreciate the encouragement Joachim Scholz, provost and dean of Washington College, has given me.

I wish to thank the editors of the Georgetown Series on Religion and Politics—Ted Jelen, Mark Rozell, and John Green—for their unwavering support and interest in the project. Their suggestions for revisions have improved the manuscript greatly. I am also grateful for the comments of an anonymous reviewer. It has been an absolute pleasure working with Richard Brown, the director of Georgetown University Press, who also offered useful suggestions on how to improve this book.

I owe a special debt of gratitude to Laura Olson and Sue Crawford. Laura, Sue, and I have been involved in a research project on the politics of women clergy during much of the time I have worked on this book. That project has given me a welcome reprieve from this book and has "recharged" my creative energies.

I wish to thank my family. My parents, Lloyd and Diann Deckman, have always been a source of comfort and support to me, as have my parents-in-law, Andrew and Lesley Fallon. I would like to thank the Fallon clan, who helped me on several occasions with the unglamorous—but vital—aspects of survey research, such as stuffing envelopes. In that vein, I would also like to thank my friend Elaine Cummins. I am especially grateful to my sister-in-law, Seannon Fallon Meeks, who helped enter data from the survey and read early drafts of some chapters. I would also like to acknowledge Scott Deckman and Malcolm Meeks.

Finally, I wish to thank my husband Sean Fallon for his love and support during the long process of completing this book. In addition to being a wonderful sounding board, he fixed every computer problem that I encountered. He also provided a welcome and needed distraction at many points along the way. For that, I am grateful.

Introduction

In a move that sent shockwaves through the nation's scientific community, in August 1999 the Kansas State Board of Education (led by several outspoken conservative Christians) voted to eliminate the subject of evolution from the state's science curriculum and standardized tests. Although individual school districts could elect to continue to teach evolution, the board's critics believed that the practical effect of the decision would be to remove evolution theory from the classroom because teachers generally design their lesson plans to enable students to pass the mandatory state exams. Board supporters, however, praised the move, including one local school board president in Pratt, Kansas, who hoped that the decision would lead to the teaching of creationism in her district: "I don't think it's relegated to Sunday school. If you present material to students with critical thinking, and they come to you with a paper supporting creationism, or arguing against evolutionary theory from a creationist point of view, you should accept that."[1]

The decision to remove evolution, however, was short lived. The high-profile decision cost two of the conservative Christian board members their seats in primary elections the following year. Moderate members replaced them and rescinded the decision that had received such notoriety. This scenario—in which conservative Christians are elected to school boards, make controversial policy changes, and then are voted out of office—is one that has also taken place on several local school boards as Christian Right activists have tried to influence education politics at the grassroots level. During the past decade, in school districts such as Vista, California; Merrimack, New Hampshire; and Lake County, Florida, conservative Christian majorities have voted to place limits on sexual education, remove references to homosexuals from the classroom, and promote American culture as superior to other cultures—only to have these decisions revoked after losing their reelection bids (Arocha 1993; Brooks 1995; Wald 1995; Ammis 1996, Granberry 1996, and Detwiler 1999). These controversial policy decisions have sometimes come after contentious school board campaigns, in which critics of conservative Christian candidates accused them of using unfair, "stealth" campaign practices promoted by Christian Right organizations such as the Christian Coalition. Such campaigns had Christian Right candidates mobilizing sympathetic voters in conservative churches while avoiding mainstream audiences or downplaying their ties to Christian Right groups to the general public, an appealing strategy that can be successful given that voter turnout in school board elections, particularly in those that do not coincide with federal or state elections, is very low (Townley, Sweeney, and Schneider 1994). National media attention on such elections has heightened concerns among progressive educators and others opposed to the Christian Right's political agenda.

The school board campaigns of conservative Christians, as well as the campaigns of conservative Christians running for higher office, are just one piece of a larger political phenomenon that has captured the attention of political scientists in the past twenty years: the rise of Christian Right participation in American politics. In his study of the role of the Christian Right in American politics, *Onward Christian Soldiers*, Clyde Wilcox defines politicized conservative Christianity as a "social movement that attempts to mobilize evangelical Protestants and other orthodox Christians into conservative political action" (Wilcox 2000, 5). Although leaders of the Christian Right have tried to recruit conservative Catholics, conservative black Protestants, and Orthodox Jews to their ranks, the movement is primarily made up of white, evangelical Christians. Having first gained national attention early in the Reagan administration under the leadership of the Reverend Jerry Falwell and his Moral Majority, the "profamily" movement (the term that movement participants themselves prefer) today is more multifaceted. While maintaining a national presence in politics through groups such as the Family Research Council, Christian Right organizations such as the Christian Coalition, Eagle Forum, and Concerned Women for America work just as hard at influencing public policy at the state and grassroots levels.

Although political scientists have analyzed various aspects of Christian Right political participation at length—including its members' attitudes on political and social issues (Jelen 1991; Jelen, Smidt, and Wilcox 1993; Wilcox 2000), their voting behavior (Brudney and Copeland 1984; Rothenberg and Newport 1984; Guth and Green 1991; Green, Rozell, and Wilcox 2000), and the development of national and state interest groups (Guth 1983; Moen 1989, 1992; Rozell and Wilcox 1996)—little is known about conservative Christians who run for political office, especially at the local level of government. This omission by scholars is surprising, in light of the salience of education to the Christian Right, the controversy that surrounds many of the races in which conservative Christians have participated, and the fact that a major goal of prominent Christian Right interest groups is to elect conservative Christians to local offices such as school boards (Reed 1994, 1996).

Despite such well-publicized incidents as those in California, New Hampshire, and Florida, political scientists know little about the overall impact of the movement on local elections. For instance, we have insufficient empirical evidence that documents why conservative Christians run for local school boards or how they go about campaigning. Further, the strength and nature of the ties between conservative Christian candidates and Christian Right organizations—several of which have attempted to recruit and train activists to run for local offices such as school board—are unclear. We also do not know whether Christian Right candidates are more likely to win their elections than other candidates. If the "stealth" theory offered by critics of the movement is to be believed, then Christian Right candidates might have an advantage in such elections; however, no empirical data exist to support such theories. Finally, although the media have highlighted several notable cases in the 1990s, there has been little thoughtful analysis of how effectively conservative Christians govern on school boards once they are elected.

This book fills this gap by studying the motivation, strategies, and electoral success of Christian Right school board candidates by use of a national survey of candidates and case studies of two school districts in which conservative Christians ran for and served on local school boards. I address the following questions: Why do conservative Christians run for school board, and how do their decisions differ from candidates who are not part of the Christian Right? Do they campaign differently than other candidates? What role do churches and Christian Right organizations play in these decisions? Are Christian Right candidates more successful in their bids to become members of school boards than non–Christian Right candidates? Once elected, in what ways (if any) do the deep religious convictions of conservative Christian board members conflict with the practical demands of governing and the compromising nature of politics? Does their status as a majority or minority on the board affect their ability to influence education policy? Finally, what consequences do the campaigns of conservative Christians have for school board policy and on the political system more generally?

The issues at stake—for both supporters of the movement and its detractors—are huge. Serious worries about the health of the U.S. education system, from violence and safety in schools to the lagging academic performance of many American students, have prompted Americans to say that education is among their most pressing political concerns.[2] Politicians have proposed innumerable solutions to fix what ails American schools, from trying to enforce stricter accountability among individual schools and school districts (through the use of regular testing and standards) to mandating curriculum changes (such as experimenting with new ways to teach reading and math) and changing the physical environment of classrooms (such as reducing class sizes). But many of these solutions, according to Christian Right leaders, will not address what they see as the real problems with American schools—an increasing acquiescence of control by local schools to the federal government and a hostility among the public schools toward their religious and moral values.

Yet concern about public education among conservative Christians is nothing new. Conservative Christians have had an interest in public education throughout American history. The first public schools were started more than 350 years ago to teach children to read the Bible, and religion continued to play a major role in American public education until the twentieth century. The nature of the relationship between conservative Protestants and education, however, has changed dramatically in the past eighty years, beginning with the debate about evolution theory in the 1920s. Changes in the public school curriculum that contradict the religious beliefs of conservative Christians have propelled the Christian Right toward political action at various times this century. The widespread attempt to recruit and train conservative Christians to run for school board in recent years is just the latest attempt by the Christian Right to influence the direction of public education.

Looking Ahead

This study analyzes the impact of the Christian Right on school board elections, by use of both quantitative and qualitative methods, including a survey of school board candidates drawn from a random sample of school districts nationwide and two diverse case studies in which conservative Christians ran for and later served on school boards. Focusing on the historical roots of the movement, chapter 1 examines earlier waves of Christian Right activism directed toward education politics. That chapter considers the political activism centered on the evolution debate in the 1920s, the move to stop the spread of communism in the public schools in the 1950s, and the response by conservative Christians toward sex education and multiculturalism that was spreading in public schools during the 1960s and 1970s. Chapter 1 also examines the education issues that currently concern the Christian Right, as well as the leading conservative Christian political organizations and actors now engaged in the battle over public education.

Chapter 2 discusses the methods used in the book in more detail, as well as the system I use for categorizing whether an individual is part of the Christian Right. Christian Right classification—who is a member and who is not—is a topic of many debates among scholars of the movement, and these debates are revisited here. Chapter 2 examines the socioeconomic status of school board candidates nationally, their religious makeup and behavior, and how religion affects their views on various education issues.

Chapters 3–5 offer new, substantive findings about Christian Right school board candidates and their campaigns. Chapter 3 analyzes the motivation behind candidates' decisions to run for school board office, including the role that religion and religious interest groups play in these decisions. Chapter 4 evaluates the nature of the campaigns themselves, comparing and contrasting the strategies behind the school board campaigns of Christian Right and non–Christian Right candidates. The role of Christian Right interest groups in the elections (as well as their opposing groups) is examined. Chapter 4 also addresses the issue of "stealth" campaigns. Chapter 5 determines how successful Christian Right candidates are in their campaigns. Using the survey data, chapter 5 employs regression analysis to determine whether Christian Right candidates are more or less likely than non–Christian Right candidates to win their school board elections.

The impact Christian Right board members have on school board policy is discussed in chapter 6, with special emphasis placed on participant-observation data and newspaper coverage of school boards in Fairfax County, Virginia, and Garrett County, Maryland. The case studies demonstrate that Christian Right board members face the same constraints and opportunities that other governing coalitions endure in other types of legislatures. At the same time, these cases have interesting implications for priestly versus prophetic politics.

The conclusion of the book summarizes the study's major findings about the impact of the Christian Right on school board elections and local education policy. The chapter also reflects on the future of the Christian Right as it relates to political participation at the school board level. In light of the very recent push by some conservative Christian organizations to promote homeschooling and the recent troubles experienced by the Christian Coalition, once the flagship organization of the movement, how will the Christian Right approach school board elections in years to come? Will conservative Christian activists return to a more isolationist stand, or will they instead employ prophetic or priestly forms of religious politics?

Chapter One

The Christian Right and Education Politics

Past History and Current Concerns

The Christian Right and Education Politics Historically

The first public schools—started more than 350 years ago when Massachusetts became the first colony to establish compulsory education for all children, in 1642—were founded on religious principles (Berkeley and Fox 1978). The Olde Deluder Satan Act mandated that teachers should be appointed for every fifty households in the Bay Colony. The express purpose of public education was to teach children to read the Bible, because the law states that a chief trick of "ye olde deluder, Satan," was to "keepe men from the knowledge of ye Scriptures" (Berkeley and Fox 1978, 258). Puritan leaders in Massachusetts viewed a public school system as the primary vehicle to pass their religious values from one generation to the next. Moreover, these religious values were tied to the belief that the new nation would play a role in human and divine history. In *American Education: The National Experience*, Lawrence Cremin writes, "If America was to be the setting for the building of God's Kingdom on Earth, the values and aspirations that Americans needed to share could not be left to chance; they would have to be carefully defined and nurtured" through the schools (1980, 17). The first "textbook" used in Massachusetts and the rest of the colonies was the *New England Primer*, which was based almost exclusively

1

on Bible stories. Further, local school committees (the first school boards), whose members were appointed by religious leaders in the community, ensured the religious purity of schoolmasters (Deighton 1971).

The role of sectarian religion remained important in many schools even after the ratification of the First Amendment to the United States Constitution, in 1791, which nominally called for the separation of church and state. Both sectarian and nondenominational public schools continued to foster religious values and to use textbooks with religious themes (Rippa 1976). As the population of the United States expanded westward and an increasing number of Catholics and Jews immigrated to the country during the nineteenth century, however, there was a shift in the way that religion was incorporated into the public schools. Between 1820 and 1850, the common school movement, which sought to ensure every child access to free education in a system of publicly supported common schools, viewed education as a moral activity conceived in part as an attack on poverty, crime, and other social ills. Leaders of the movement, including Horace Mann, feared that teaching a particular sectarian creed would jeopardize the cause of public education. Instead, they drew common doctrinal elements from various Christian denominations to help guide their curriculum, such as honesty, fairness, and truth. Mann even supported daily Bible reading, as long as teachers made no remarks or comments on the passages (Cremin 1980). As Cremin notes, Mann's ideas were not far from general evangelical concepts of the day: "A common piety rooted in Scripture, a common civility revolving around the history and the state documents of a Christian Republic, and a common intellectual culture conveyed via reading, writing, spelling, arithmetic, English grammar, geography, singing, and some health education." Mann's efforts helped define a generalized "Protestant piety" that became part of the American vernacular by the mid-nineteenth century (Cremin 1980, 17). Further, it is largely due to Mann's belief that the Bible could be used as a nonsectarian text in inculcating moral values that Bible reading at the beginning of the school day remained in many public schools until the Supreme Court banned the practice with its 1963 decision in *School District of Abington v. Schempp*.

Conservative Protestants did not organize politically to effect changes within the public schools during the nineteenth century, mainly because there was little substance being taught in the public school to which they could object. It was not until schools faced the introduction of Darwin's theory of evolution into the classroom that the religious views of conservative Protestants were directly challenged, sparking the first widespread political mobilization of Christian fundamentalists. The evolution battles in the 1920s, led by William Jennings Bryan, mark the first of four discernible waves of political activism among conservative Christians this century. The next wave of activity occurred in the 1950s, when Christian Right organizations joined the outspoken anticommunist Senator Joseph McCarthy's efforts to stem the tide of communism and other, noncommunist ideas that McCarthyites considered "subversive." Although the primary target of the anticommunist movement was foreign affairs, aspects of the Christian Right's involvement had important ramifications for education policy and personnel matters in school districts around the country. Throughout the 1960s and 1970s, conservative Christians led grassroots battles nationwide against sex education and other "value-less" curricula, including in Kanawha County, West Virginia, where protests led to widespread violence. Finally, these grassroots initiatives alerted many conservative Christian leaders to problems in the public schools, and education became a major focus for the New Christian Right, led by the Reverend Jerry Falwell and others in the early 1980s. The movement started by Falwell has progressed into a sophisticated network of individuals and organizations dedicated to restoring traditional values in the public schools.

Evolution: The First Challenge to Conservative Christian Beliefs

In the early 1920s, fundamentalist Christians organized to fight the introduction of Darwin's theory of evolution into public classrooms. Although history best remembers the Scopes trial as the most important defeat of the fundamentalist crusade against evolution (at least in the court of public opinion), the movement achieved some success in keeping Darwin's ideas from being taught in public schools. Between 1921 and 1929, opponents of evolution succeeded in proposing forty-five antievolution bills (all supported by fundamentalist groups) in twenty-one different state legislatures (Lienisch 1997). Five of these bills ultimately passed. Moreover, Christian fundamentalists swayed many state and local boards of education. Perhaps most important, however, is that this conservative Christian movement succeeded in influencing the content of many science textbooks, published by companies who, afraid of the controversy that might ensue, opted to omit references to evolution.

The start of the antievolution movement is best understood in the context of religious denominational politics that occurred among major Protestant denominations shortly after the turn of the century. Societal changes brought about by immigration and industrialization, as well as the growing secularization of many universities, challenged the religious orthodoxy of many Protestant traditions. Factions ensued between modernists—who began to embrace a more liberal view of biblical interpretation and the role of religion in addressing societal problems—and fundamentalists, the conservative defenders of a more orthodox tradition—who labeled the modernist's beliefs "New Christianity." Fundamentalists viewed evolution theory as antithetical to their own beliefs in the inerrancy of the Bible, whereas modernists began to accommodate evolution within their own religious doctrines.

The most famous opponent of evolution was William Jennings Bryan, who began speaking and writing about the dangers of evolution in 1920 in his syndicated newspaper column "Bryan Bible Talks," which was published in hundreds of small-town newspapers. Recruited by fundamentalist organizations to lead the effort against evolution, Bryan charged that evolutionists were leading individuals away from God and that Darwinism had a chilling effect on college students exposed to the theory. Bryan was especially troubled by Darwin's theory of natural selection, which he believed went against the basic teachings of Christ by teaching that "might makes right" (Colletta 1969, 272). Bryan spent much of his time speaking before state legislatures and with governors across the country about the evils of evolution. In conjunction with the World's Christian Fundamentals Association (WCFA), led by evangelist William Bell Riley, Bryan appeared in a series of public debates about evolution with leading scientists of the day. These debates never failed to attract large crowds and publicity.

Bryan's efforts drew much support for the antievolution cause from Democrats and Democratic politicians nationwide, especially in the South. In Florida, his adopted home state, Bryan was instrumental in getting allies to introduce an antievolution bill into the Tallahassee legislature. The bill passed in 1923, due largely to Bryan's lobbying efforts and his insistence that the bill be phrased in terms that would attract the most political support possible, by applying only to the teaching of evolution as fact and carrying no legal penalties (Lienisch 1997).

Many fundamentalist ministers and revivalists, such as Mordecai Ham and Billy Sunday, took to denouncing evolution theory in their revivals. These popular traveling ministers often had a strong impact on the beliefs of powerful state politicians. For example, Michael Lienisch (1997) reports that Ham persuaded North Carolina governor Cameron Morrison to become an early champion of the antievolution cause. In 1924, the governor persuaded the state board of education to reject two biology books that contradicted the Genesis account of creation (Lienisch 1997).

Besides sponsoring debates and directly contacting important state politicians, the movement used other tactics to stop the spread of evolution in the public schools. Lienisch (1997) notes that, in the South, conservative Christian churches emerged as powerful contributors to the cause and were instrumental in mobilizing their members to lobby legislatures and local school boards. Large denominations and organizations that dominated Southern religion, such as the Southern Baptist Convention, played a vital role by providing foot soldiers and sponsoring forums about evolution at organizational meetings (Larson 1989). These denominations produced many declarations, reports, and resolutions denouncing the teaching of evolution, all of which many politicians took seriously (Lienisch 1997). These religious groups also organized letter-writing campaigns to local newspapers, denouncing Darwin's theories.

Proevolution forces were for the most part made up of scientists and academics, who believed that the efforts of the antievolution movement constituted an attack on academic freedom. In his study on the evolution battle in North Carolina, Gatewood (1966) notes that many religious leaders, both liberal and conservative, also opposed efforts to pass an antievolution resolution in the state legislature, citing their belief that the state should play no part in dictating religious beliefs of any sort. The bill in question would have outlawed any teaching that "links man in blood relationship between any lower form of life" (Gatewood 1966, 126). Despite strong support from Governor Morrison and strong lobbying efforts from William Bell Riley and the WCFA, the bill was defeated in 1925, largely because of the efforts of the charismatic president of the University of North Carolina, Harry W. Chase. Chase successfully convinced enough state legislators that the bill in question was an affront to academic freedom.

In that same year, the famous *Scopes* trial was held in Dayton, Tennessee. Troubled by some early legislative successes for the antievolution forces in Oklahoma, Florida, and Tennessee, the American Civil Liberties Union (ACLU) decided to initiate a case that would test the constitutionality of antievolution statutes. ACLU officials placed ads in local newspapers in Tennessee to recruit a teacher who was willing to admit he or she had taught evolution theory in deliberate violation of a Tennessee statute. The ACLU found such a test case in John Scopes, a science teacher who had once taught Darwinism in the classroom. Scopes was willing to be put on trial by the state of Tennessee because he believed such legislation infringed on academic license.

This was to be no ordinary criminal trial. Clarence Darrow, the famed liberal defense attorney, agreed to lead the defense on behalf of Scopes, while Bryan assisted local prosecutors (Colletta 1969). The legal question in the trial involved the state legislature's right to establish the school curriculum. The trial itself attracted hundreds of reporters from around the world, in what Garry Wills describes as one of the first true media events (Wills 1990). The

judge gave concessions to the influx of media by letting radio lines and pho-
tographers be brought into the courtroom. Many observers believed the resulting "monkey trial" was a comedy of errors, highlighted by the testimony of
Bryan, who agreed to testify on whether evolution was irreconcilable with the
biblical account in Genesis. Under Darrow's relentless cross-examination,
Bryan looked foolish, particularly in his description of how Jonah ended up in
the belly of a whale. Despite the ridiculous nature of Bryan's testimony, Scopes
was ultimately found guilty of violating the new Tennessee law, and the right of
the state of Tennessee to write curriculum was upheld.

Both sides, however, claimed victory after the verdict was handed down.
For Darrow and the ACLU, the real purpose behind the trial was to discredit
the fundamentalists in their crusade against evolution. For leaders of the
antievolution movement, however, the guilty verdict legitimized their efforts
in state legislatures. The decision in Dayton proved that antievolution legislation passed in state legislatures could be upheld in courts of law. Although
Bryan's death shortly after the trial was related to diabetes, many in the movement attributed it to the humiliation he suffered at the hands of Darrow.
Bryan's "martyrdom" further galvanized leaders in the movement, whose
efforts reached a peak in 1927, when antievolution bills were introduced in fifteen states (Lienisch 1997).

By 1928, however, the fundamentalist crusade against evolution was
winding down. Despite legislative successes in Mississippi and Arkansas the
previous year, most anti-Darwin legislation stalled in committees. State legislators looked less favorably on such proposed bills, mainly because the scientific
and academic community had persuasively argued that antievolution statutes
were little more than censorship of academic freedom. Many fundamentalists
grew disenchanted with politics. Those who remained politically active shifted
their attention to the 1928 presidential election, in hopes of defeating the first
Catholic to be nominated for president, Al Smith.

Conventional wisdom holds that fundamentalists were mostly unsuccessful in their attempts to stop the spread of evolution in the classroom and that
they retreated from the antievolution movement largely because of the public's
ridicule of their beliefs. Yet the movement did succeed in passing five pieces of
antievolution legislation, and at the local level there was "quiet success" for
antievolutionists achieved by the "subtle manipulation of local political strings
and public opinion" (Gatewood 1966, 151). The result of this manipulation
was the eviction of evolution from many public classrooms. Further, many
textbook companies decided to omit references to evolution in science books
altogether, for fear of further controversy and reduced textbook sales (Wills
1990). Until the 1960s, when the federal government sought stricter science

standards in high schools because of the space race with the Soviet Union, many students never learned about evolution theory in public schools. One study estimates that close to 70 percent of high schools omitted the teaching of evolution from the 1920s through the 1960s (Larson 1989).

Anticommunist Struggles within the Schools

After the evolution controversy, fundamentalist Christians largely retreated from public life. Many fundamentalist leaders instead concentrated on forming their own institutions of higher learning, such as Bob Jones University and the Dallas Theological Seminary. It was not until the McCarthy era that some conservative Christian leaders participated in politics again, nearly twenty-five years after the *Scopes* trial. Initially, the chief concern of the Christian Right's anticommunism crusade involved the alleged infiltration of communists into mainline Protestant denominations. Fundamentalist leaders also became concerned about America's foreign policy in the fight against communism. Nonetheless, some groups within the conservative Christian anticommunism movement did take stands on domestic issues that related to communism. Chief among these domestic concerns was the relationship between communism and the public schools.

One of the first fundamentalist leaders to become involved with the anticommunism crusade was the Reverend Carl McIntire, who founded the American Council of Christian Churches (ACCC) in 1941. Prior to his work with the ACCC, McIntire was best known for leading a breakaway, fundamentalist sect from the Presbyterian Church, dividing the denomination into a modernist faction, the Presbyterian Church USA, and a fundamentalist faction, the Presbyterian Church in America (Jorstad 1970). McIntire formed the ACCC to counter the ecumenical social work of the Federal Council of Churches (later the National Council of Churches), an organization of mainline denominations. In the heyday of the McCarthy era, the ACCC's accusations that communists were infiltrating churches involved with the Federal Council of Churches garnered much media attention.

McIntire set out his arguments against communism in his 1946 book *Author of Liberty*, in which he maintained that the United States' free market prosperity and its political system were instruments of God's purpose. McIntire believed that the nation had begun to lose sight of that purpose and that communism was exploiting this "loss of purpose" for Satan (Clabaugh 1974). Other organizations, such as the Christian Anti-Communism Crusade, founded by Australian physician Fred Schwartz, and preacher Billy James Hargis's Christian Crusade, shared McIntire's philosophy. These groups believed the expanded role of government in social issues was part of a communist effort to undermine the United States (Wilcox 2000). Sex education in the schools in particular was viewed as a communist plot to undermine the moral fiber of the nation's young people, making the next generation of Americans more susceptible to communist ideology.

Although conservative Christian anticommunist groups such as the ACCC attracted a great deal of attention in the media, often through their own radio broadcasts, they were unable to amass large numbers of members or to coordinate political efforts at the grassroots effectively, compared with antievolution leaders in the 1920s. Part of the reason might be because the anticommunist leaders lacked the charisma and nationwide respect of a William Jennings Bryan. Some critics claimed that the anticommunist groups were led by mere "figurehead" leaders, who, as George Marsden points out, were "loudly calling for political action but [who] found little hearing in the mainstream" (1993, 13). This does not mean that mainstream America was in favor of communism, but rather that these Christian Right anticommunist groups were unable to form alliances or persuade many conservative Christians to join their national organizations.

Some anticommunist political activism did occur, however, in local venues, especially among parents concerned about the possible infiltration of communism into their school's personnel and curriculum. One case in Houston, Texas, made national headlines and is illustrative of the type of tactics local anticommunist organizations, both secular and religious, used to achieve their goals. Organized activity in the McCarthy era did not occur in Houston until the fall of 1950, when local groups, such as the Minute Women and the Committee for the Preservation of Methodism, formed and began to scrutinize the actions of local churches. Group members monitored sermons of local ministers, censored Sunday school materials, proselytized their political views among church members, and "generally kept local churches stirred up" (Carleton 1985, 151). These organizations then turned their attention to curriculum and activities in the local schools that dealt with potentially "subversive influence": discussions about world politics and the United Nations; school desegregation; and federal aid to education. For example, in 1952, members of these groups protested an annual school essay contest about the United Nations.

The disapproval of the anticommunist groups led to their use of the usual pressure group tactics within the Houston school district. Joining forces, the local groups devised telephone chain systems, instituted a massive letter-writing campaign, brought in outside speakers, and distributed pamphlets to influence local school affairs (Carleton 1985). At the height of the McCarthy era, four of seven board seats were open in the fall 1952 elections. Conservative Christian groups formed a local alliance—the Committee for Sound American Education (CSAE)—and ran a slate of candidates whose main platform consisted of opposition to the "creeping socialism" within the public schools. CSAE distributed flyers and pamphlets, asking voters whether they were aware that a socialist plot existed in the schools "for the purpose of eradicating the fundamental principles of learning and the spiritual concepts upon which America was founded" (Carleton 1985, 170). The anticommunists went on to win two of the four seats.

The greatest "accomplishment" of the anticommunists in the Houston school district, however, was the forced removal of the district's assistant superintendent, George Ebey, who had been hired in 1951. Anticommunist forces in the community had been suspicious of Ebey for his liberal stand on racial integration. When they found out he had received his doctorate in education at Columbia University (considered sympathetic to communism by conservatives), the anticommunists decided to leak charges that Ebey was a communist sympathizer. With the backing of several board members, the school administration agreed to perform a detailed background check into Ebey's life. Anticommunist supporters looked for any small detail to nail Ebey on his alleged communist ideas. For example, while serving as a professor in California, Ebey voluntarily headed the California chapter of the American Veterans' Committee. (Ebey had served at the Pentagon during World War II). Ebey's critics believed that the group's slogan—"Citizens First, Veterans Second"—was supportive of communist ideology. Ebey pointed out that the slogan really just meant to imply that veterans did not want special privileges. Despite protests from Ebey and other administrators in the Houston schools, and, despite a lack of proof that Ebey had ever been a member of a communist organization or a supporter of communist ideology, the school board ultimately voted four to three to not renew his contract, largely because they believed that Ebey was not "vocal enough" about his anticommunist views. Ebey's firing made national headlines in both *Time* magazine and the *Nation*, which called the incident "the zaniest of the poison-pen attacks on public education since they began in 1949" ("Ebey Story" 1953, 242 [quoted in Carleton 1985, 219]).

The Ebey affair is perhaps the most prominent example of grassroots, anti-communist activism in the 1950s directed toward the public schools, although it is not the only one. Similar to the case in Houston, other grassroots initiatives were led by both religious and secular activists who wished to protect children from the "evil," godless influences of communism; however, the activities of Christian Right anticommunist organizations—both local and national—toned down after Senator Joseph McCarthy began to lose credibility at the national level.

Continued Battles about Sex Education and Secular Humanism

Many conservative Christian parents in school districts around the country became increasingly upset about the content of sex education courses during the 1960s and early 1970s, which marks the third wave of Christian Right activism in education politics. Battles emerged in school districts across the country between educators who saw the need to address shifting sexual attitudes and practices among Americans with a comprehensive sex education curriculum and conservative, religious parents who believed such doctrines went against their teachings and violated their authority as parents. In much the same way as the evolution debate began, the struggles of parents with local and state education agencies concerning the introduction of sex education in their local schools were largely a defensive reaction to the kinds of values that their children were being taught.

Sex Education Battles in Anaheim

One of the first big battles concerning sex education occurred in Anaheim, California. In 1965, the Anaheim school district implemented a family life and sexual education (FLSE) curriculum, which caused little stir in its first three years. A conservative Catholic parent, Eleanor Howe, first raised objections in 1968, after she discovered the content of the program from her two teenage sons. Howe obtained a copy of the FLSE curriculum and was disturbed at its explicitness. She explained, "After I went through all of that [curriculum], I just refused to believe what they were doing. And I was angry. I was angry that no love attachment was mentioned anywhere. No closeness, no love, no marriage, nothing that depicted my values. I resented it because . . . because they didn't have to know all that they were told. It wasn't so much the information. It was the shift in values" (Martin 1996, 104).

Howe photocopied parts of the curriculum and distributed it to her friends, which set off a chain reaction among other parents in the conservative religious community. Some conservative Christian parents were particularly upset with the course's treatment of homosexuals, which taught that homosexuality was a variant rather than a deviant behavior. At a meeting she hosted to discuss the curriculum, Howe met a former Goldwater campaign activist, James Townsend, who used his connections to the media to help publicize the concerns of the conservative parents. It was Townsend's personal belief that homosexuality was sinful rather than merely variant that spurred much of his involvement. He later charged that "there were more homosexuals made in that sex-education classroom than would have ever been here today if they hadn't told them, 'If you haven't tried it, don't knock it; it's just an alternative lifestyle'" (Martin 1996, 106).

Howe and her followers attended board meetings in Anaheim to protest the FLSE curriculum, often reading aloud parts of it at the podium, a move meant to pressure the board to have a special hearing about the curriculum. Eventually, Howe was allowed to make a presentation, where she showed a film titled *Pavlov's Children*, which argued that Russian communists, through the United Nations Education, Scientific, and Cultural Organization, were "using Pavlovian conditioning techniques, in sex education and elsewhere, to render American youth susceptible to totalitarianism" (Martin 1996, 107). In addition to the board presentation, Howe, Townsend, and others produced fliers containing excerpts from the books used in the FLSE courses, which they later put on windshields and handed out at Anaheim churches on Sunday mornings. Townsend also began a small antisex education newspaper, the *Educator*, which was sent to hundreds of subscribers throughout the state.

These efforts by the conservative Christians paid off, both within the Anaheim school district and throughout the state. In the 1969 Anaheim school board elections, the anti–sex education forces were able to elect two of three contested positions, joining one current member on the five-member board who had opposed the curriculum from its inception. Ultimately, the FLSE curriculum was rewritten in a more conservative tone. Conservative Christian parents in Anaheim also organized a successful campaign to force the resignation of Anaheim's school superintendent, who had supported the original FLSE curriculum. At the state level, conservative legislators in Sacramento successfully backed a law that made sex education voluntary—not mandatory—in local districts.

The scene in Anaheim was replayed in other communities across the country, spurred on largely by the grassroots efforts of conservative Christians, who viewed sex education as a threat to their own values and beliefs about sexual behavior. Particularly offensive to Christian Right parents was the curriculum's refusal to instruct children that any sexual activity outside of the marriage covenant was morally wrong. This defensive reaction expanded from sex education to larger areas of the curriculum during the early 1970s, as conservative Christian parents began to raise objections to the content of literature, history, and reading textbooks. In particular, parents were concerned that their children were being sent a subtle message that "absolute truth" did not exist. Similar to earlier reactions concerning sexual education, these parents complained that this newer curriculum did not teach their children that some behaviors were always right and others were always wrong. Rather, children were led to believe that "situation ethics" were acceptable. These parents believed that religion—particularly Christianity—was not only ignored in many history and reading books, but was ridiculed in some instances. Further, some parents even claimed that a new religion—secular humanism—was being introduced into the classroom.

These arguments were all present in the textbook controversy that took place in Kanawha County, West Virginia, in the mid-1970s, perhaps the most famous controversy of its kind to occur that decade. The controversy in West Virginia, which eventually led to book burning, school boycotts, and widespread violence, had national ramifications. The case illustrates the vital importance of education issues to conservative Christian parents—issues that continue to be salient to Christian Right activists more than two decades later.

The Kanawha County Textbook Controversy

In some respects, the "Battle of Anaheim" led to the textbook controversy in Kanawha County, where Alice Moore, the wife of a fundamentalist minister, became concerned about sex education in the county schools after reading an article about the situation in California. She decided to investigate the county's own proposed sex education curriculum in 1970 and found the proposed course of study objectionable, not just for its discussion of sex. According to Moore, "What concerned me was that this wasn't just a sex education course. It dealt with every aspect of a child's life. It dealt with their attitudes. In fact, the stated purpose of the course was to teach children how to think, to feel, to act. And it covered everything, from their relationship with their parents, to their attitudes toward the use of drugs and social drinking, to their attitudes toward sexual conduct. So that concerned me" (Martin 1996, 118).

After Moore met resistance from the school board regarding her concerns, she ran for, and won, a seat on the school board later that year. After taking office, Moore was successful in passing what she considered were appropriate changes in the sex education courses, largely by arguing that it was anti-Christian and anti-American and that it indoctrinated students in "atheistic and relativistic views of morality" (Martin 1996,119).

Four years later, the school board sought to adopt 325 new titles for its K–12 language arts courses as recommended by an appointed, language arts advisory committee. Many of the books stressed multicultural themes and were deliberately chosen because African American, Latino, and other minority writers wrote them. Alice Moore objected to the various themes in the books, including their "growing tolerance of non-standard English, among other things" (Martin 1996).

Moore contacted Mel and Norma Gabler of Longview, Texas, for help in fighting against the recommended texts. The Gablers are fundamentalist Christians who run a nonprofit organization called Educational Research Analysts, Inc., dedicated to reviewing the content of textbooks for improper or objectionable content. The Gablers and their staff review books as acceptable or objectionable based on their ideological views and compile lists of reviewed books available to parents embroiled in textbook battles nationwide. They are sometimes called the two most powerful people in education because their reviews have enormous influence on textbook sales in Texas, one of the nation's largest purchasers of textbooks. Subsequently, the production of books that are not bought in Texas is often halted, making the books largely unavailable to other school districts throughout the United States.

The Gablers believe that the goal of modern education is to transform children from an older, traditional, moral way of thinking (which distinguishes good from evil) to a new, relativistic way (in which good and bad principles change according to the situation). According to Mel Gabler, "Allowing a student to come to his own conclusion about abstracts and concepts creates frustration. Ideas, situation ethics, values, anti-God humanism—that's what the schools are teaching. And concepts. Well, a concept never will do anyone as much good as a fact" (Parker 1979, 23).

The Gablers also object to textbooks that downplay patriotism or question American heroes (for example, a history text that notes that Thomas Jefferson owned slaves). They argue that school children often receive lessons in despair when novels and books are chosen that stress suicide, death, or lawbreaking. Finally, they believe that many texts routinely assault or belittle the beliefs of Christians and that some even advocate other religions such as New Age religious teachings or expose children to the occult (Gabler and Gabler 1985).

With the Gablers' help, Moore was able to raise hundreds of objections to many of the recommended textbooks. Echoing their views, Moore charged that many of the controversial books were negative, morbid, and depressing, especially those written by black authors such as Alice Walker and James Baldwin. Critics, in turn, argued that these objections were a thinly veiled effort to keep white children away from black influences, even in books. Moore and her supporters argued that many of the books lacked moral conviction. Instead, students were being taught that there were no right or wrong answers to life's problems. The fundamentalists also disliked books that contained symbolism, irony, satire, or role playing, because they could invite interpretations that diverge from a literal reading of the text. As William Martin points out, these parents believed that "cultivating a taste and talent for multiple interpretations can only increase the likelihood of thought and behavior that call into question the settled and dependable nature of one's community and religion" (1996, 125).

Moore's tenacity pushed the other board members to display the controversial books at the public libraries. Moore sought support for her convictions by writing letters to the editors of local newspapers, speaking at churches and community meetings, and recruiting local fundamentalist ministers to her cause. These ministers, who stirred up members of their own congregations, later formed an antitext group, Concerned Citizens of Kanawha County. Shortly thereafter, a local conservative newspaperman started an organization of business leaders opposed to the adoption of the controversial texts.

At the school board meeting in August 1974, the board voted (three to two) in favor of adopting all but a few of the books originally recommended by the textbook adoption committee, despite the appearance of more than one thousand protesters from Kanawha's fundamentalist churches. Moore began to urge parents to keep their children home at the beginning of the school year in September if the board tried to force them to use the new books. Concerned Citizens and other groups wrote letters to the editor, held rallies, and picketed a board member's company. The day before school began, Concerned Citizens sponsored a rally to persuade parents to participate in the school boycott. The rally, which drew a crowd of more than eight thousand parents, was a success—more than 20 percent of the school children stayed at home the first day of school, most from rural communities. Boycotters received a boost the next day, when the coal miners in Kanawha County decided to strike in a show of solidarity (Page and Clelland 1978).

After a week of boycotts and strikes, the school board agreed to withdraw the controversial books and submit them for review by a special citizen's committee. This partial victory was not enough for many of the protesters, some of whom initiated violence. Vandalism of school property became commonplace, two schools were firebombed, and two men were wounded by gunfire at the picketing sites. The lives of school administrators and board members (including Moore) were threatened.

The battle in Kanawha attracted national attention and drew new adversaries into the arena. One organization that became involved was the Heritage Foundation, an upstart conservative group founded by Paul Weyrich, who would be instrumental in the formation of the New Christian Right several years later. (Weyrich is credited with coining the term "moral majority" and in 1979 helped Jerry Falwell form the [now defunct] organization of the same name.) The Heritage Foundation sent attorneys to Kanawha to provide legal assistance to jailed antitextbook protesters. Antitext forces, led by the fundamentalist ministers, sponsored a day-long rally to try to persuade committee members to vote against the controversial textbooks. Featured speakers included Robert Dornan (later a conservative congressman from California), Mel and Norma Gabler, and members of the John Birch Society.

The special citizens review committee was divided about the materials. The majority ultimately recommended that all but thirty-five of the 325 textbooks be reinstated. The minority faction issued its own report, urging that 180 of the books be banned permanently. Shortly after the announcement of the committee's recommendations, the county board of education's office building was partially destroyed by a firebomb. One week later, the board voted four to one to endorse the majority committee's recommendations. The board said, however, that each school could make individual decisions regarding which texts to use in the classroom, helping to discourage some of the violence that previously marked the protest movement. Still, some protesters continued to keep their children from the public schools despite the conciliation of local control, opting instead to start their own private, Christian academies. By the start of the new school year in 1975, 2,000 students enrolled in these fundamentalist Christian schools, siphoning off many of the hard-core protesters (Page and Clelland 1978).

The New Christian Right and Its Fight against Public Education

The case in Kanawha County, West Virginia, was an important predecessor to the current political movement of conservative Christians. As Wilcox notes, this controversy and similar grassroots movements opposing gay rights legislation and the Equal Rights Amendment in many states and localities showed that "evangelicals can be enthusiastic and effective political actors" (2000, 35). Combined with the election of Jimmy Carter, a born-again Christian whose campaign mobilized many evangelicals into first-time political action, these events helped to usher in a new wave of Christian Right activity in the late 1970s, often referred to as the "New" Christian Right (Wilcox 2000).

Various conservative Christian groups that formed in this era, such as the Reverend Jerry Falwell's Moral Majority and the Religious Roundtable, grew disenchanted with Carter's presidency and disavowed what they viewed as his liberal policies, many of which were linked to education. Especially disturbing to Christian Right leaders was the Carter administration's attempt in 1978 to revoke the tax-exempt status of newly formed Christian academies for not meeting certain standards of racial integration (Martin 1996). As Weyrich argues, conservative Christians were politically mobilized to an unprecedented level by this proposed action by the federal government: "What caused the [Christian Right] movement to surface was the federal government's moves against Christian schools; this absolutely shattered the Christian community's notion that Christians could isolate themselves inside their own institutions and teach what they pleased" (Marsden 1993, 26). Weyrich further says that evangelicals were propelled into action when this realization was "linked up with the long-held conservative view that government is too powerful and intrusive" (Marsden 1993, 26).

Although the Moral Majority, the Religious Roundtable, and a few other early Christian Right groups disbanded by the late 1980s, others, such as the Eagle Forum, Concerned Women for America, the Christian Coalition, the Family Research Council, and Focus on the Family, still actively promote a conservative Christian political agenda. And although these groups draw most of their support from conservative evangelical Protestants, their issue agenda also appeals to conservatives within some mainline Protestant denominations, black Protestant denominations, and Catholics. In many ways, these groups are leaders in the "culture war" as described by James Davison Hunter. Hunter's (1991) culture wars theory maintains that a major cleavage dividing American public opinion exists between those who support "traditional values" and those who adopt more liberal political stances. In terms of American religion, the culture wars thesis maintains that such a cleavage transcends even religious denominations and identities so that the divide between conservative and liberal Catholics, for example, is pronounced and carries over into political behavior. Although a fuller exploration of the culture wars theory is beyond the scope of this study (and there are critics who complain that the theory is either wrong or too imprecise [see Wald 1997, 188–91]), if applied to public education, it may help explain the breadth of the education issues that the Christian Right now addresses and the diversity of tactics it uses, which helps to set apart this movement from previous waves of conservative Christian movements.

Another distinction between the New Christian Right and other conservative Christian movements in the past century concerns the variety of interest
groups that make up the movement. No one organization dominates the movement, and although they often work together to speak out against education
policies they deem ineffectual or damaging to their beliefs, there are also varia-
tions among them. Some groups, such as the Family Research Council, concentrate more heavily on national and federal education policy, whereas groups
such as Citizens for Excellence in Education and the Gablers' Educational
Research Analysts, Inc., have concentrated their efforts at the local level, with
more of an emphasis on overtly religious themes such as secular humanism.

Regardless of the distinctions between groups, however, the education
concerns of the Christian Right can be placed into two general categories. First,
many conservative Christians struggle to attain increased autonomy and
greater local control of schools. Many Christian Right activists advocate
vouchers, charter schools, a "back-to-basics" curriculum, and parental rights
(as well as its disapproval of the federal Department of Education) out of a
desire for greater parental control of education. Several movement leaders
believe that an improvement in academics can come only from local leadership, because local teachers and administrators know best how to address the
needs of their students. These concerns often correspond with calls by other
conservatives, Christian or otherwise, who believe the federal government is
too large and powerful and that education is a policy area best left to the states.

Second, many in the Christian Right are concerned about issues that deal
with more overtly religious themes and what they deem anti-Christian bigotry.
Conservative Christian leaders often focus on current educational ideas, curricula, and teaching methods that offend their religious values. Some Christian
Right activism revolves around moral issues that have involved the movement
at previous times in the last century, such as sex and family education, creationism, and school prayer. More recently, the movement has shifted some of
its attention to the negative portrayal of religion in United States history and
English textbooks. Some Christian Right leaders allege that there is a widespread conspiracy by leaders in the "liberal" education establishment to
change the religious values of their children, through various curricula, teaching methods, and behavior-modification programs. Concern about the teaching of Islam in public schools has emerged in wake of the September 11 terror-
ist attacks on the World Trade Center in New York City and the Pentagon in
Washington, D.C. (Henry 2002). Convinced that educators routinely expose
children to New Age techniques, occult practices, and the "religion" of secular
humanism, these conservative Christians believe that their children are virtually "abused" in the classroom (Schlafly 1984).

Local Control: The Christian Right's Fight against the Department of Education and Federal Education Policies

Much of what is wrong with public education, according to several leaders in the Christian Right, stems from the involvement of the federal government in local schools. Since its creation in 1980, the Department of Education has attracted hostility from Christian Right leaders and organizations, such as the Family Research Council, that describe its conception as dubious—the result of a political payoff to the National Education Association (Marshall and Unsworth 1995). The Family Research Council is not the only Christian Right group to believe that the U.S. Department of Education "has elbowed its way into places it does not belong" (Marshall and Unsworth 1995, 3). Scholars from Regent University (founded by former Christian Coalition president Pat Robertson) believe that federal involvement in education is unconstitutional. J. R. Wynsma, from Regent, writes in the university's political journal *NeoPolitique* that the movement's first goal with respect to education reform "must be to eliminate the federal role in education" and return power to the hands of parents, "where control should be" (1997, 2).

Perhaps no other federal program has been more hated by the Christian Right than the Department of Education's Goals 2000, which was initiated (ironically) by a Republican president (George H. W. Bush) but was carried out by the Clinton administration on the authorization of Congress in 1994. Although Congress eliminated funding for Goals 2000 after passage of President George W. Bush's highly touted No Child Left Behind Act of 2002, many Christian Right activists routinely attacked Goals 2000 during its eight-year existence. Goals 2000 was federal legislation that promoted national education goals for American schools to meet and offered funding through competitive grants to local school districts that had to submit a detailed plan on how to achieve them. The eight goals listed in the legislation included an increased high school graduation rate, having U.S. students rank first in the world in mathematics and science achievement, and having each school promote partnerships that would increase parental involvement and participation in the public schools.[1]

Although many of the goals sounded laudable, Christian Right critics claimed that Goals 2000 was in fact a plan to restructure the American education system drastically, calling for further centralization, federal coercion, and the abandonment of local control. One prominent Christian Right organization, the Family Research Council, wrote regularly about the dangers of Goals

2000. One Family Research Council report states, "The concept of national education goals is based on faulty logic. If the federal government is setting goals, that presupposes that it has the authority and ability to ensure the accomplishment of the goals. Reaching national education goals will require an unprecedented federal intrusion in schools" (Marshall 1995, 2).

Of particular concern to Christian Right critics were the funding mechanisms associated with the Goals 2000 legislation and its linkage with the Elementary and Secondary Education Act (ESEA), which provides most federal funding of public schools (Marshall and Unsworth 1995). States that participated in the program received seed money from the government to launch and sustain reform efforts that fell in line with the eight stated goals, in an application process similar to ESEA. The Department of Education insisted that participation in such programs was voluntary, but conservative Christian organizations such as the Family Research Council did not agree: "Some argue that Goals 2000 is voluntary because states are free to write standards of their own. The catch is that even these state standards must be approved by the U.S. Department of Education in order for the state to receive Goals 2000 funds. What kind of standards are the feds likely to approve? Since there will be federal standards and curriculum for each discipline, no state will be left guessing" (Marshall and Unsworth 1995, 4).

The fear among such groups as the Family Research Council was that states and localities had to conform to the progressive reform ideas touted by the liberal education establishment (of which the Department of Education is supposedly part) before they could be "approved" to receive funding. Phyllis Schlafly, founder of the Christian Right organization Eagle Forum, argues that Goals 2000 is a device to "finance teaching attitudes and outcomes rather than cognitive skills and factual knowledge," requiring grantees to "give special attention to how assessments treat all students in regard to race, gender, ethnicity, [and] disability" (1994, 3).

No other goal received more attention from the Christian Right than the third, which dealt with national standards in core academic subjects such as math, reading, and history. The fear among conservative Christians was that state governments and local school districts would be pressured to adopt "politically correct" standards, as opposed to standards based on "objective" or factual information, to meet the approval of partisan (Democratic) appointees in the Department of Education or implement "progressive" teaching methods in order to qualify for much-needed financial assistance.[2] Schlafly maintained in her monthly *Phyllis Schlafly Report* that Goals 2000 "uses the heavy-handed technique of tying funding to state adaptation of federal standards and mandates. Goals 2000 explicitly rejects private school choice in favor of plowing more tax money into the same dinosaur establishment that has failed our children" (1994, 3).

Ironically, Christian Right opposition to President Bush's call for mandatory testing by all states as a way to measure accountability in public schools in his No Child Left Behind Act has been muted compared with its earlier opposition to Goals 2000. Bush's legislation, which reauthorizes ESEA, actually increases federal funding for local school districts and mandates that such funding be tied to improvement in mandatory standardized tests given in grades 3–8 (Cohen 2002; United States Department of Education 2002). Christian Right organizations such as the Family Research Council have been hesitant to criticize the legislation as vociferously as Goals 2000, although they have not been overtly supportive either. Schlafly, however, has spoken out against the new legislation, calling it a "continuation of a failed strategy" (2002, 1).

Closely linked with its opposition to federal standards in the Goals 2000 legislation is the Christian Right's resistance to a learning system of instruction and management known as outcomes-based education (OBE), which has been implemented in many school districts across the nation. Although OBE is not a federal program, many states have moved toward these learning systems and mandate that local school districts should follow suit. Similar to national goals, OBE involves an attempt to be explicit about what students should know and when. In its most basic form, OBE "is a simple concept: identify what you want your students to learn and then make sure that the curriculum, teaching, and assessment are designed to produce the intended learning or outcome" (Gaddy, Hall, and Marzano 1996, 94). Again, conservative Christian leaders fear that the outcomes that students will be required to learn under this system will not be based on factual information. Instead, they believe that outcomes will measure "politically correct" attitudes, opinions, and values that students must meet before being allowed to advance to another grade. Robert Holland from the Family Research Council writes, "The outcomes that the gurus of OBE have in mind are quite different from the hard-headed pragmatism or TQM's [Total Quality Management's] emphasis on customer satisfaction. They have less to do with whether Johnny can comprehend the Federalist Papers or place the Civil War in the correct half-century than with the acquisition of the desired attitudes on such issues as global resource inequality, multiculturalism, homelessness, alternative lifestyles, and environmentalism. Under OBE, political correctness goes to grade school" (Holland 1994, 1). Rather than basing their opposition to such programs on any sort of empirical evidence, David Berliner notes that resistance by the Christian Right toward OBE "is based on fear of losing control over their children's thinking" (1997, 381).

Christian Right opponents are also concerned that some of the other goals affiliated with many OBE programs, such as fostering collaborative work, will not promote a competitive environment, which many in the movement believe is necessary to push individual students to work hard and achieve their best. Instead, emphasis is placed on group success, which means that an OBE approach "will slow the class to the pace of the slowest student" as smarter students are forced to assist their slower peers in learning the lesson for the day (Schlafly 1993, 1). The result of OBE in the classroom, according to Schlafly, is a "'dumbed-down' egalitarian scheme that stifles individual potential for excellence and achievement" (1993, 2).

Concern about OBE learning systems prompted conservative Christian Robert Simonds, founder and president of Citizens for Excellence in Education, to develop an option to OBE called the Enhanced Basics–Based Education (EBBE) model in the mid-1990s. Simonds writes that the basic design principles of the EBBE model include the following: a "focus on academic curriculum design;" the establishment of "high standards of subject understanding, as a prerequisite to higher-order thinking skills and creative expression;" an assessment of "all basics-based curriculum objectives with factual academic testing, similar to the S.A.T. academic testing program" (noting that testing should be "objective"); and the "establishment of an in-school 'parents and students' partnership for achievement designed for excellence" (Simonds 1995, 2). Although EBBE does not appear to have entered the lexicon of other Christian Right leaders and organizations, the concept of "back to basics" as a teaching method has become a very popular campaign theme among school board candidates, as chapter 4 will demonstrate.

Christian Right activists, led by Eagle Forum, also oppose a federal policy known as School-to-Work, passed by Congress in 1994 as part of the School-to-Work Opportunities Act. Touted as an improved approach to vocational-technical education, School-to-Work is the federal government's initiative to better prepare students for their first jobs after high school through a series of work internships, exposure to various careers, and an integration of academic and occupational learning in the classroom. Conservative Christian leaders believe that the School-to-Work program is yet another attempt by the federal government and the "liberal education establishment" to take over the public schools. According to Schlafly, who calls the legislation too socialistic in nature, School-to-Work would ultimately "change the mission of the public schools from teaching children knowledge and skills to training them to serve the global economy in jobs selected by workforce boards" (1997, 1–2).

While funding for Goals 2000 has already been repealed, the Christian Right would like the same for the School-to-Work Opportunities Act. Some

Christian Right organizations, such as the Christian Coalition and the Family Research Council, believe that the "interference" of the federal government in education is unconstitutional because education is not listed as a federal responsibility under the U.S. Constitution (Marshall and Unsworth 1995). For this reason, many in the Christian Right wish to see the Department of Education abolished. Christian Right organizations have pushed other initiatives that they believe would ensure autonomy for both parents and local school districts from state and federal education agencies. One popular reform is the "parental rights amendment," introduced in more than twenty state legislatures within the past few years as well as Congress in 1995 (Allen 1996). Cathleen Cleaver and Greg Erken of the Family Research Council argue that such legislation at the federal level would "protect parental rights, including directing or providing for the education of the child; making a health or mental health care decision for the child; disciplining the child, including reasonable corporal discipline; and directing or providing for the religious teaching of the child" (Cleaver and Erkin 1996, 6). The Christian Coalition endorsed such legislation in their highly touted "Contract with the American Family" in 1995.[3]

Other reforms pushed by the Christian Right include vouchers, tax credits, and charter schools, broadly conceived of as school choice. Voucher programs would give parents a set amount of money to be spent toward tuition at religious or nonreligious private schools. Tuition tax credits would work largely the same way, with parents being able to take tax deductions for money spent on private education tuition. Both conservatives and liberals often champion the cause of charter schools. Although supported by public funds, charter schools have greater freedom and flexibility in terms of the curricula they choose and the standards that students must meet to graduate. Charter schools exist in many districts around the country, usually in the form of special "math and science" schools. Some parent groups envision the creation of charter schools based on ideological belief systems, which is potentially appealing to many conservative Christians, who could run schools that would omit many so-called progressive programs supported by the federal government. James Dobson, head of the influential conservative Christian organization Focus on the Family, states that school choice "is an idea whose time has come," arguing that such programs, by giving parents a choice, "would improve the quality of education because it would force school personnel to compete for students" (Dobson 2000). The arguments for and against vouchers and charter schools are too numerous to mention here, although the Supreme Court's 2002 ruling in *Zelman v. Simmons-Harris* removed constitutional constraints from consideration after upholding a school voucher program in Ohio. This landmark decision was lauded by Christian Right organizations such as the Family Research Council, whose president Ken Connor stated that the Supreme Court, by supporting the voucher program in Cleveland, "has given parents nationwide the hope that they, too, will soon have the power to rescue their children from failing schools" (Family Research Council, 2002). Further, Schlafly has claimed that the decision sent teachers' unions into a frenzy: "They are squealing because school choice plans divert a tiny fraction of public funds to private schools 'that are not accountable to the public.' Public schools are currently accountable only to the political bureaucracy that unions control" (2002, 1–2).

Conservative Christians have suggested other reforms to improve the academic record of public education as well. Most frequently, Christian Right organizations and individuals routinely call for a "back-to-basics" approach to education, as typified in Robert Simonds's EBBE model. This "back-to-basics" theme is often echoed in the school board campaigns of conservative Christians, as well as the literature published by Christian Right groups such as the Christian Coalition, Eagle Forum, and Citizens for Excellence in Education—all groups that have supported conservative Christians running for office. Largely a response to progressive teaching methods introduced in the 1970s and 1980s, the back-to-basics philosophy emphasizes rote memorization of facts and mathematical equations, spelling bees, intelligence tests, and the use of phonics for reading.

The parental rights amendment, vouchers and charter schools, and a back-to-basics curriculum all represent the Christian Right's attempt to guide the education of their children and to protect them from what the parents consider an obstructive federal government. Like most parents, Conservative Christian parents want to ensure that their children receive a solid education (in a safe environment) that can prepare them adequately for the future. According to these parents, however, their children's prospects for a decent education have been hindered by progressive teaching methods and ideas. Worse yet, they believe these reforms are encouraged by the Department of Education through legislation such as Goals 2000 (now defunct) and School-to-Work.

Improvement of children's academic environment, however, is not the only factor motivating the political activism of conservative Christians. Many conservative Christian parents believe that the content of education curricula in today's classrooms jeopardizes the ideological, moral, and religious beliefs of their children. The struggle to retain autonomy over local schools also involves protecting the community's religious and moral values. Some Christian Right leaders fear that there is a conspiracy among liberal and humanist educators to subtly indoctrinate school children into anti-Christian religions such as the New Age religion, secular humanism, the occult, and, most recently, Islam (Michaelson 1989). According to Simonds—described by Fritz Detwiler as the "single most influential Christian Right activist speaking exclusively to educational issues" during the first half of the 1990s (1999, 73)— Christian children "all across America are quietly sitting in their public school chairs while, unbeknownst to either the church, their parents, or the children themselves, they are being subjected to a subtle but systematic mind-altering and faith-destroying curriculum" (Simonds 1993).

Religious Values under Siege in the Public Schools

Conservative Christian activism geared at the public schools over morality and education is not new in the United States. In the 1960s, the introduction of sex education in public schools, along with the removal of state-sponsored school prayers, turned many school districts around the country into local battle-fields. These two issues remain at the forefront of concern for Christian Right leaders, who now routinely advocate for abstinence-based sex education and "moments of silence" in place of organized prayer, which is unconstitutional.

Christian Right critics such as Simonds of Citizens for Excellence in Education and Mel and Norma Gabler, however, also fear that many of the beliefs they hold as sacred and unchanging—parental authority, the biblical creation of the Earth, unquestionable loyalty to the United States, and innate gender differences—are being undermined by what they see as the underlying "secular humanist" philosophy of public education (Gaddy, Hall, and Marzano 1996; Detwiler 1999). Exact definitions of secular humanism vary, but all focus on the rejection of God. The Gablers maintain that secular humanism is a religion "with an anti-biblical, anti-God bent" that "worships the creature instead of the Creator" (1985, 42). Fundamentalists such as the Gablers and Simonds believe that the National Education Association and other leading educational organizations, textbook publisher and writers, and educational theorists "primarily come from a humanistic world view" (Simonds 1993, 1). Such beliefs on the part of many conservative Christian leaders have led to pitched battles in many school districts about the content of history, English, science, and social studies textbooks.

This humanism, according to Christian Right critics, plays itself out in various forms, such as the recent emphases on multiculturalism and global education in many public classrooms. Kathi Hudson, from Citizens for

Excellence in Education, argues that multicultural programs as they are currently used damage respect for American culture and history. She writes, "Rather than promoting diversity, a good multicultural program should help students understand and overcome diversity. Multiculturalism should promote unity as Americans" (Hudson 1993, 1). Teaching about other cultures has often meant teaching students about other types of non-Judeo-Christian religions, such as Islam, Hinduism, and Buddhism. Many conservative Christians do not necessarily object to books or classes that teach children *about* alternative religions; however, some Christian Right leaders believe that the way these religions are discussed by some texts or presented in class actually *indoctrinate* students in these beliefs. For instance, the Gablers have protested the use of role-playing techniques in teaching about other religions. In their book *What Are They Teaching Our Children*, they disparagingly refer to one world cultures text in which children are assigned to pretend they are Hindus for several days (1985, 39).

In response to the public school's willingness to discuss religions apart from Christianity, conservative Christians often closely monitor the textbooks that their local schools use. Some school districts, spurred by conservative Christian advocates such as Elizabeth Ridenour, president of the National Council on Bible Curriculum in the Public Schools, have even begun to offer Bible history courses in the public schools as an elective. Ridenour maintains that these courses are designed to teach the Bible, among other reasons, in order "to equip students with a fundamental understanding of the influence of the Bible on history, law, American community life, and culture" (National Council on Bible Curriculum in Public Schools, n.d.). The constitutionality of such programs, however, remains questionable.[4]

But conservative Christian activists such as the Gablers do not stop at monitoring textbooks that deal with other cultures and their religions. They also examine the content of American history books to determine how religion is depicted in the Founding period and other historical eras in the United States. Detwiler argues that the Christian Right has developed an exclusionary version of early American history, what he calls the "great American monomyth": "It emphasizes the religious origins of the nation, particularly as represented in the Puritans, and transforms the history of the country into a religious destiny. . . . The myth argues that the principle of separation of church and state is a fiction never intended by the founding figures. By invoking First Amendment establishment arguments, secular humanists have erected an unintended wall that has kept America's teachers from presenting a true picture of the nation and its history" (Detwiler 1999, 188). Moreover, many Christian Right education activists worry that many recent history texts have become too "politically correct." Rather than focusing on patriotic and moralistic themes, some Christian Right activists believe history textbooks now place far too much emphasis on the oppression of women, blacks, homosexuals, and other minority groups in American history (Gaddy, Hall, and Marzano 1996).

Works of literature that challenge the values of the Christian Right have also come under attack, including novels with overt sexual content or themes, such as Maya Angelou's *I Know Why the Caged Bird Sings*. Conservative Christian leaders and activists also worry about novels such as *Of Mice and Men* and *Catcher in the Rye* that use vulgar language and that, in their view, promote "moral relativism." In addition, fictional stories with occult themes have come under attack. In the past few years, the American Library Association reports that the popular Harry Potter series, which deals with wizardry, have been the top books to come under challenge by conservative parents in local school districts (American Library Association 2000). Even the American Library Association's annual "Banned Book Week," which compiles these lists of challenged books, has been derided by Focus on the Family's director of social research and cultural affairs, who has called the event "one of the most popularized, longest-running manufactured crises in America" (Jordahl 2002).

Realizing that local school boards determine the textbooks to be used in public schools, as well as shape the types of courses to be taught, the Christian Right has encouraged its followers to run for office. Having sympathetic school board members on its side would allow the Christian Right to monitor books for material it deems offensive (including science textbooks that discuss evolution) and to promote abstinence-based sexual education and other curriculum more consistent with its values. Some scholars, such as Catherine Lugg, argue that far from merely monitoring books and curriculum for any anti-Christian themes, the goal of conservative Christian candidates is to overtly push a Christian agenda in the schools in hopes of "re-Christianizing" America's public schools (2000). In addition to such value control, Christian Right board members could also work to keep their local school districts as free from federal entanglement as possible.

The Strategies Used by the Movement

Similar to previous waves of conservative Christian mobilization, activists from the Christian Right lobby state legislatures and confront local school boards about curriculum issues. Beyond lobbying state and local government,

Christian Right organizations routinely lobby Congress and the federal government, monitor the textbooks that school districts plan to adopt (for potentially anti-Christian themes), and distribute voter guides in churches to inform parishioners where candidates stand on "profamily" education issues such as vouchers and sex education. But unique to this era of Christian Right activism is the widespread attempt by conservative Christian groups to encourage, recruit, and train candidates to run for school board. In view of the movement's desire to elect conservative Christians to school board, what leading Christian Right organizations have assisted school board candidates in their struggle to win seats on local school boards? What kinds of assistance and advice have these groups offered to conservative Christian candidates?

The two Christian Right organizations most heavily involved with school board elections have been the Christian Coalition and Citizens for Excellence in Education. The apogee of their participation in school board elections, however, appears to have occurred in the 1990s. The Reverend Pat Robertson founded the Christian Coalition in 1989, after his unsuccessful bid for president in 1988. Robertson envisioned an organization that focused on grassroots politics as intensely as national politics. Under the initial leadership of the young political operative Ralph Reed (who resigned as executive director in 1997), the Christian Coalition was once the largest and best-known organization of Christian conservatives in the United States. As recently as 1996, the Coalition claimed close to 2 million members working in 2,000 local chapters with an annual budget of $27 million (Yang and Goodstein 1997). In recent years, the flagship organization of the Christian Right has been plagued by debt, the departures of key staff members, a decision by the Internal Revenue Service to rescind its nonprofit tax status for engaging in partisan activities, and weakened local and state organizations (Goodstein 1999).

Despite its recent troubles, the Christian Coalition still advocates electing conservative Christians to all levels of political office. Nonetheless, school board elections appear to have held a more prominent position in its agenda in years past. For example, in 1994 Ralph Reed remarked that he would "exchange the Presidency for 2,000 school seats in the United States" (Vail 1995, 32). To that effort, the Christian Coalition held several candidate-training seminars specifically catered to individuals desiring a seat on their local school boards. These seminars provided potential candidates with the nuts and bolts of campaigning, including information on how to raise funds, develop a campaign message, canvass local neighborhoods, recruit volunteers from local churches and conservative organizations, and convince potential voters to come to the polls.

Although the Christian Coalition has not held a school board–specific training seminar since the mid-1990s, it began to host activist training schools, which touch on running effective local campaigns, in various states in 2001 (Christian Coalition 2001). Further, local and state Christian Coalition chapters continue to assist school board candidates through the distribution of voter guides in local conservative churches. Voter guides are nonpartisan pamphlets that tell voters how candidates stand on issues of importance to the Christian Coalition. Though these guides do not specifically tell voters how to vote (tax-exempt organizations are not allowed to endorse candidates), the wording of questions leaves little doubt as to which candidates overwhelmingly support the views of conservative Christians.

Whereas the Christian Coalition was founded to be active in local, state, and national politics, the mission of Citizens for Excellence in Education has been geared to the school board level. Founded in 1983 by Dr. Robert L. Simonds (Th.D.), a former high school and college math instructor, its original goal was to develop a local chapter in every American school district to help elect conservative Christians to school boards. As of 2001, Citizens for Excellence in Education reported 1,680 active chapters, involving more than 350,000 parents in all fifty states (Citizens for Excellence in Education 2001). As with the Christian Coalition, there has been a change in emphasis at Citizens for Excellence in Education since 1998. Although Citizens for Excellence in Education continues to advocate for the election of conservative Christians to school boards, as well as work with conservative churches and other local groups to lobby school officials and current board members to make policy and curricula changes, it has begun to promote homeschooling as the preferred alternative for Christian Right parents as part of its Rescue 2010 campaign (Simonds 2002).

Although Citizens for Excellence in Education has never held formal candidate-training seminars, it continues to offer parents interested in running for school board a "Public School Awareness" kit. This kit contains materials designed to inform parents about the problems with public education and provides a checklist for parents to determine how many of these problems currently exist in their own school districts. The kit helps parents to establish a Citizens for Excellence in Education charter in their school district and offers advice on how to lobby local school officials. It also includes a copy of Simonds's book, *How to Elect Christians to Public Office*, which offers inspirational passages to potential candidates. The book contains dozens of Bible passages regarding the necessity of Christian involvement in politics and society, including Proverbs 29:11: "With good men in authority, the people rejoice; but with the wicked in power they groan." Simonds also offers practical suggestions designed for effective participation in school board elections, such as breaking down school districts geographically by precinct to target each block effectively, polling potential voters, raising money, canvassing neighborhoods, and involving local churches and pastors in the campaign. Simonds believes that the strategies he advocates in *How to Elect Christians to Public Office* have been successful, claiming that Citizens for Excellence in Education chapters have "seen 25,300 Christians elected over ten years" (Simonds 1998, 4).

Although Simonds and other Christian Right leaders claim such successes, little empirical evidence exists that determines how widespread Christian Right candidacies for school board are. Further, we know little about the overall impact of Christian Right organizations such as Citizens for Excellence in Education or the Christian Coalition on local school board elections. Have they trained or sponsored many candidates in the past? How closely do conservative Christian candidates rely on these groups when campaigning for school board? Do the reasons that conservative Christians run for school board, and the issues that they campaign on, closely resemble the concerns of Christian Right movement leaders? In view of the negative media attention that sometimes follows the school board candidacies of conservative Christians, are Christian Right candidates more or less likely to win their elections? And once elected, how do conservative Christians try to influence school board policy? Analyzing the impact that the Christian Right is having on school board politics will increase our understanding of one of the most influential political movements in the past two decades.

The Role of Religion in the Public Square: Priestly versus Prophetic Politics

Examining the Christian Right's participation in school board politics also allows for the opportunity to address the broader question of the proper role of religion in the public square. Since the nation's founding, scholars, politicians, and religious adherents have debated the ramifications of allowing religion to influence the tenor of public debate. Some religious adherents have pushed for an isolationist stand, either viewing politics as corrupt or political action as futile. Some say that the price of political clout may be too high, coming at the expense of diminishing spiritual influence. As long as the state guarantees the rights of such individuals to practice their religion as they see fit, these individuals are content to stay out of public debate and concentrate instead on pursuing spiritual goals.

As Daniel Hofrenning notes, however, organized religion has sometimes served to "legitimate politics with a priestly blessing of public policies" (1995,

25). David Leege argues that self-government, democracy, freedom, limited government—the very concepts that have defined American political life since the founding period—not only derive from biblical and theological concepts, but continue today to "get subsumed in a spiritual purpose" (1993, 13). According to Kenneth Wald, this priestly view of civil religion means the "nation is recognized as a secular institution, yet one that is somehow touched by the hand of God" (1997, 60). Adherents who subscribe to this form of religious politics justify their pursuit of political actions and public policies as related to the work of God.

Yet, for others, religion is not best served by justifying the actions of government. Instead, these religious adherents employ a long-standing prophetic form of religious politics, taking a more critical stance of government (Riemer 1996). Like the prophets of the Old Testament, religious activists who follow a prophetic stance call for a radical transformation of the status quo, taking issue with public policies that challenge their moral values. From the abolitionist movement in the nineteenth century to the civil rights and prolife movements in the twentieth, religious activists have dedicated themselves to criticizing government actions that they believe conflict with their religious principles, believing a "higher authority" is calling America to "live up to" its divine purpose (Leege 1993, 13).

This study examines how these conceptions of religious politics—priestly or prophetic—apply to the case of the Christian Right and their involvement with school board politics. In particular, in light of the hostility that Christian Right leaders often hold for public schools, are the campaigns of Christian Right school board candidates marked by prophetic rhetoric? When it comes to governance, do Christian Right school board members employ a prophetic stance or are they likely instead to legitimate their decisions in a priestly manner? Such an examination might allow us to uncover the conditions under which such activists will be successful and those under which they will fail. It will also illuminate the special challenges that face people of religious faith when they encounter politics.

Chapter Two

A Profile of School Board Candidates

Crucial to any analysis of the Christian Right is determining who is a part of the movement, and this chapter discusses in great detail the criteria used to delineate who belongs and who does not. In doing so, I revisit many of the scholarly debates regarding Christian Right classification. This chapter also provides a glimpse of the religious and socioeconomic backgrounds of the school board candidates profiled in the book. What sorts of individuals run for school board, and what sorts of differences exist between Christian Right and non–Christian Right candidates with respect to their backgrounds and religious behavior (if any)?

This chapter also discusses the methods—both the survey and case study research—used to address the impact of the Christian Right on school board elections. Because the methods address similar questions in different ways, the findings offer a more comprehensive look at the impact of the Christian Right on school board elections. Further, the case study research, in particular, allows for the chance to explore the challenges and opportunities faced by people of faith in governing at the local level. Before turning to the details of the cases profiled here, however, we will first look at the national survey of school board candidates employed for this study.

Methods

School Board Candidate Survey

I conducted a cross-sectional, national survey of recent school board candidates drawn from a random sample of school districts in 1998. There are
approximately 15,000 school boards in the United States, 98 percent of which
are elected. The United States Department of Education maintains a list of
each school district in the nation. This list, with a few modifications, was the
sampling frame from which 300 school districts were randomly drawn as the
primary sampling unit.[1] By using the entire list of school districts as its initial
sampling frame, the study can speak quite confidently about the generalizability of the survey results. Because the majority of school districts had relatively
small numbers of students compared with very large districts, the sample was
divided into three groups based on size to account for this disparity: small
school districts (less than 2,000 students; $N = 6,627$); medium school districts
(2,000–9,999 students; $N = 6,275$); and large school districts (10,000 or more
students; $N = 690$). The 300 districts were then drawn randomly in a proportionate manner, with a total of 147 small school districts, 137 medium school
districts, and 16 large school districts selected.[2] In other words, I avoided a
simple random selection because the likely result would have involved selecting more small districts and fewer large districts, which could have been problematic, considering that the largest districts serve more than 48 percent of all
public school students in the United States (National Center for Education
Statistics 1995).

The districts were contacted and asked to provide lists of all candidates
who ran in the most recent school board election held in their particular districts. More than 91 percent of the districts responded, yielding a final list of
1,220 former school board candidates, who represent the secondary sampling
unit. After two waves of mailings, 671 usable responses were received from former candidates (a 55 percent response rate). Sixty-two percent of respondents
won their elections. The generalizability of the survey is further supported by
the fact that almost an equal percentage of nonrespondents—59 percent—also
won their races.[3]

The survey provides important information about why candidates
decided to run for office and how they went about conducting their campaigns. In addition, the survey measures candidates' attitudes about various
education issues that are important to the movement, while it allows the
opportunity to test empirically whether Christian Right candidates are more or

less likely to lose their races than non–Christian Right candidates. Appendix A contains more specific information on how the survey was conducted; appendix B contains a copy of the survey.

The School Board Case Studies

The two case studies featured in this book involve the school boards in Garrett County, Maryland, and Fairfax County, Virginia. These cases offer an alternative venue to research the larger implications of Christian Right school board campaigns for local education policy. By studying the phenomenon of school board elections involving Christian Right candidates within a specific context (and, later, studying school board governance by conservative Christians), the case studies suggest new insights into how and why conservative Christians run for school board, as well as new explanations as to how religious people govern at the local level. In particular, both cases reveal certain characteristics that can enhance the influence of prophetic politics and diminish the effectiveness of priestly politics. Although the two cases are geographically close, they are not meant to be representative of most school boards nationwide. Instead, the two cases offer appealing contrasts in terms of the majority and minority status of conservative Christians on the school boards, their socioeconomic status and diversity, and the role of political parties in school board elections (where they played a major role in Fairfax County, but not Garrett County).

In Garrett County, a majority of conservative Christians was elected to the school board for the first time in 1994. (They retained their majority status after the 1996 elections, when several were up for reelection.) A minority of Christian Right activists was elected to the school board in Fairfax County in 1995. (One activist was not reelected in 1999, and another currently remains on the board.) Fairfax County, unlike Garrett County, is an affluent suburb of Washington, D.C., with a highly educated population. By contrast, Garrett County is an isolated, rural county in the mountains of western Maryland, with economic and education measures far below those of Fairfax County.

In these two counties, anonymous interviews were conducted with eleven Christian Right candidates and twenty of their non–Christian Right opponents.[4] Appendix C contains a list of interview questions that were asked of all school board candidates in both counties as well as a brief questionnaire that candidates were asked to complete. Other data from the cases come from school board minutes; newspaper accounts; participant-observation at board meetings[5]; and informal interviews with parents, education activists (some of whom were conservative Christians), and local reporters who cover education issues in the two counties.

The Christian Right: Who's a Member of the Movement?

Christian Right classification provokes a heated debate among many religion and politics scholars. Some early studies of the Christian Right that relied on survey research typically used three criteria to classify those individuals most likely to identify with the political attitudes of the Christian Right: religious tradition or denominational affiliation, biblical interpretation, and "born-again" experience. Religious identities and denominational affiliation can be powerful predictors of political attitudes (Green and Guth 1993). A broad distinction is often made between Jews, Catholics, Protestants, and others. Early studies of the Christian Right often put members of evangelical Protestant denominations into a Christian Right classification. The two other components most often associated with Christian Right identity in early studies involved biblical interpretation and born-again experience (Leege and Kellstedt 1993). Among three choices, conservative Christians are most likely to believe that the Bible is the literal word of God as opposed to the "inspired" word of God or a book written by men. Being born again, a basic tenet of evangelicalism, is an experience conservative Christians have that results in a deep, personal commitment to follow Jesus Christ as savior. As a result, early studies of the Christian Right often labeled those individuals who believed that the Bible should be literally interpreted and those who were born-again Christians as members of the Christian Right.

There are, however, problems associated with using some of these measures as criteria for classifying whether an individual is part of the Christian Right. The use of strict religious traditions is difficult because the Christian Right as a political movement often draws members from across denominational lines, including some Catholics, black Protestants, and conservative Orthodox Jews. Also, some general titles shared by denominations can have different meanings. For example, whereas Southern Baptists generally take conservative social and political positions, American Baptists are more moderate on many of the same issues (such as the ordination of women). The important point here is that if someone identified him- or herself as a "Baptist," it would be impossible to determine whether he or she belonged to a conservative or moderate sect. Even a more specific identification does not guarantee that an individual shares the same political and social views as the denominational leadership. Former President Bill Clinton identifies himself as a Southern Baptist, yet he is certainly not a spokesman for the Christian Right.

There are also problems with lumping all born-again Christians into the Christian Right category. Although born-again, or evangelical, Christians are the target constituency of the Christian Right (or the group of citizens most likely to identify with the Christian Right's beliefs), not all evangelical and born-again Christians hold conservative political views (Wilcox 1992, 60; Wallis 1995). Some born-again Christians such as former president Jimmy Carter and evangelical organizations such as Sojourners tend to stress the importance of social justice issues such as poverty and political equality rather than issues of personal morality.

A different problem arises with using biblical interpretation as a classification criterion for Christian Right membership. Although it is true that those individuals who take a literal interpretation of the Bible do tend to closely mirror the views and attitudes of the Christian Right movement (Kellstedt and Smidt 1993), studies have shown that some people who take less than a fundamentalist position on the Bible also share Christian Right attitudes. For example, Wilcox's (1992) study of Pat Robertson's campaign contributors shows that the vast majority of them believe that Christians can disagree about what the Bible means. Further, groups such as the Christian Coalition have made efforts in recent years to recruit Catholics and conservative Jews to their organization, two groups that do not believe in a fundamentalist interpretation of the Bible. As a result, classifying only literal interpreters of the Bible as being part of the Christian Right leaves out some individuals who might otherwise be a good fit.

Other early studies of the Christian Right instead relied on issue positions to identify individuals as part of the movement. In one well-known study, John H. Simpson (1983) examined attitudes among General Social Survey respondents with respect to four issues about which early Christian Right groups such as the Moral Majority regularly expressed opinion: a traditional view of women's roles in society (i.e., it's better that men be achievers outside of the home than women); opposition to abortion; opposition to homosexuality; and support for school prayer. By combining those respondents who supported or strongly supported all four issues, Simpson found that "the views of 30 percent of the respondents coincide with those of the Moral Majority" (1983, 190). This method, however, also came under criticism. As Sigelman and Presser (1988) noted, there is a difference between support for the Christian Right's social and moral principles as opposed to its policy positions. They demonstrated that, if Simpson had instead looked at support for more specific *public policy* platforms within the General Social Survey data—for example, substituting support for the Equal Rights Amendment as opposed to support for the notion that society would be better off having women stay at home—then support for the Moral Majority agenda would have shrunk dramatically. Sigelman and Presser's larger point is that identifying individuals as supporters of the movement is perilous business and that it is difficult to estimate fairly by a single number or indicator (1988).

Although the present study uses support for issue positions to help identify survey respondents as part of the Christian Right, it also relies on other indicators for a more complete and complex coding process. Those other indicators, however, do *not* include religious variables, in light of the various measurement error problems such usage could bring as identified above. Instead, identification with various Christian Right organizations is given paramount importance in this study's coding scheme. Those individuals in the survey who are members of Christian Right organizations are automatically considered part of the movement. In addition, the study also considers "general support" for these organizations, combined with support for the education issue agenda of the movement, as criteria for classifying survey respondents as part of the Christian Right. What follows is a more complete discussion of these two broad criteria. In contrast to the survey data, case study participants were identified as part of the movement on the basis of their interviews, interviews with their opponents, and their stands on various education issues.

Christian Right Status: Group Members, Group Supporters, and Supporters of Christian Right Issue Agendas

The survey asked candidates whether they were members of any of more than thirty different organizations (see appendix B for a copy of the survey), including the following Christian Right organizations: Citizens for Excellence in Education, Christian Coalition, Eagle Forum, Focus on the Family, Concerned Women for America, and the National Association of Christian Educators. With the recognition that survey respondents could also be part of local or state Christian Right organizations, they were given the option to check "other profamily organization," a term the movement often uses to describe itself. In addition, several candidates listed membership in two other Christian Right groups in an open "other" group category: the American Center for Law and Justice (Pat Robertson's legal organization) and the American Family Association. In total, forty-six survey respondents, or 7 percent, were members of one or more of these Christian Right organizations.

Survey respondents who are not members of these groups, however, are not precluded from Christian Right identification, per se. Respondents were also asked whether they "supported" these organizations, as opposed to being members. Two hundred six survey respondents checked that they generally support the views of one of the seven Christian Right organizations (or "other profamily" groups) listed—31 percent—but were not members of such organizations. (Many of the Christian Right group members also support various other Christian Right groups.) In total, 252 survey respondents—38 percent— are members of or generally support Christian Right organizations.

Survey respondents were asked whether they strongly supported, supported, opposed, strongly opposed, or were neutral or undecided about fourteen different education issues. Prominent Christian Right organizations have taken vocal positions on eleven of the issues listed in the survey, including charter schools, vouchers, multicultural programs, school prayer, sex education, homosexuality, school-to-work programs, parental rights, creationism, phonics, and outcomes-based education. Table 2.1 shows not only the wording of those eleven questions, but also a breakdown of survey respondents' support or opposition to such policies.

Twenty-five percent (165/671) of respondents hold a majority of Christian Right positions on such issues. All but seventy of these respondents are members or supporters of Christian Right organizations, meaning that 10 percent of survey respondents support a Christian Right agenda but do not belong to or identify with such groups.

Depending on what criteria one uses, then, the number of potential Christian Right school board candidates in the survey ranges from 7 percent to 38 percent. As indicated before, Christian Right candidates are identified in two ways. First, survey respondents who are members of the Christian Right organizations are automatically coded as part of the movement. Second, others are identified using a "double-hurdle" classification scheme that combines group identification and issue agenda support. If respondents support Christian Right groups and hold a majority (at least six of eleven) of the same positions as do the Christian Right on education issues, they are coded as part of the movement. There are 127 survey respondents (19 percent) who fit these two criteria. Although this classification scheme is somewhat conservative, generally supporting a Christian Right organization does not necessarily constitute identification with the movement. Therefore, the inclusion of issue agenda support is used as a check for those individuals who may be supportive of a Christian Right organization. Nonetheless, the differences between Christian Right group members, supporters, and issue agenda supporters are also analyzed in future chapters to allow for a more nuanced comparison among such groups, permitting a fuller exploration of the data. Table 2.2 contains a breakdown of these various categories.

Table 2.1
Support for Christian Right Issues

Christian Right Issue	Strongly Support or Support (%)	Neutral/ Undecided (%)	Strongly Oppose or Oppose (%)
Creating charter schools	30	42	25
Voucher systems (including tuition tax credits) to pay tuition at private schools	25	18	54
Multicultural programs that stress the history and culture of minority students	44	31	22
Opening class with a prayer	37	28	33
Abstinence-based sex education courses	69	20	9
Opposing the mention of homosexuality in sex education or other courses	30	28	38
Spending more on vocational-technical or "school-to-work" programs	75	17	6
Granting parents greater rights through parental rights legislation	48	38	12
Creationism being taught as an alternative theory to evolution in science courses	39	31	28
Phonics used to teach reading in elementary schools	79	15	3
Outcomes-based education being used in your district	36	35	25

Note: N = 671. Rows do not total 100 percent because of missing values that range from 2.1% to 3.7% for each of the questions. Percentages indicate the number of responses to the following question on the National School Board Survey: "Several issues and programs currently debated among public school administrators, boards of education, and teachers are listed below. Please indicate whether you strongly support, support, oppose, strongly oppose, or are neutral/undecided about these issues or programs by checking (√) the appropriate response below."

Table 2.2
Classifications of Christian Right Candidates

Type of Classification	No. (%)
Member of Christian Right group	46 (7)
Supporter of Christian Right group (not member)	206 (31)
Supporter of Christian Right issue agenda (neither member nor supporter of Christian Right group)	70 (10)
Combination variable:	
Christian Right candidate in survey (either member of Christian Right group or supporter of Christian Right group and supporter of issue agenda)	127 (19)
Non–Christian Right candidate	544 (81)

Note: N = 671.

School Board Candidates: A Religious Profile

Although this study does not rely on specific religious criteria to determine whether candidates are part of the Christian Right, religion is nonetheless of vital importance to the study at hand. How, then, do school board candidates shape up in terms of religious belief? Survey respondents and case study interviewees were asked which, if any, of the following religious terms reflected their religious beliefs: fundamentalist Christian, Pentecostal or Charismatic Christian, evangelical Christian, born-again Christian, mainline Christian, liberal Christian, Conservative/Reform Jew,[6] traditional Catholic, progressive Catholic, ethical or secular humanist, agnostic, and religious non-Christian. Among Judeo-Christian terms, each can be roughly categorized as either conservative or liberal; the last three categories (ethical or secular humanist, agnostic, and religious non-Christian) are considered separately. Table 2.3 contains a breakdown of all survey respondents who identified with the various terms. Roughly 10 percent of all survey candidates (*N* = 64) indicated that they identified with none of these terms; an additional 4 percent left this question blank. Among thirty-four case study candidates, 27 percent (*N* = 9) did not answer the question, whereas an additional 15 percent indicated that they identified with none of these terms.

Conservative Protestant religious categories include fundamentalist Christian, Pentecostal/Charismatic Christian, evangelical Christian, and born-again Christian. In essence, born-again and evangelical Christian are similar categories. I included both terms as options out of a concern that some individuals

Table 2.3
Religious Identities of School Board Candidates (Survey)

Religious Identity	School Board Candidates (%)
Conservative fundamentalist Christian	13
Pentecostal/Charismatic Christian	3
Evangelical Christian	13
Born-again Christian	14
Traditional Catholic	15
Mainline Christian	21
Liberal Christian	10
Conservative/Reform Jew	3
Progressive Catholic	11
Other ethical or secular humanist	2
Agnostic	4
Religious non-Christian	1
None of these terms	10
Not answering	4

Note: N = 671. Column does not total 100 percent because individuals could select more than one category to describe their religious beliefs.

from this category might not be as familiar with the term "evangelical" as they are with "born again." Thirteen percent of survey respondents identified with the term fundamentalist Christian, 3 percent with Pentecostal/Charismatic Christian, 13 percent with evangelical Christian, and 14 percent with born-again Christian. Among case study participants there were fewer: 9 percent identified with fundamentalist Christian, 6 percent identified with evangelical Christian, and none identified with Pentecostal/Charismatic Christian. All of the conservative religious identities share several core evangelical religious beliefs: a belief in the divinity of Jesus Christ, established through a salvation/conversion experience (being born again); acceptance of the inerrancy of the Bible; and a commitment to bearing public witness about one's faith (Shibley 1998). Fundamentalists are unique from other evangelicals in that they believe that the Bible is not just inerrant, but literally true. Historically, fundamentalists have also typically rejected modernism in theology and culture, a posture that has meant a more "separatist" identity from other evangelicals (Smith 1998). Politically, it has meant that, although both fundamentalists and non-fundamentalist evangelicals tend to embrace personally conservative positions on moral and social issues, fundamentalists are sometimes more likely to translate personal values into demands for legal action, though they tend to be similar in terms of partisanship and voting behavior (Jelen 1987). Though related to evangelicals, Pentecostals and Charismatics are unique in that they emphasize the power one receives through the "baptism of the Holy Spirit" (Smidt 1989, 54), which they believe empowers them to engage in supernatural acts such as speaking in tongues and faith healing.[7] Like evangelicals and fundamentalists, Pentecostals and Charismatics have more conservative views on political and social issues than the electorate at large, although they are less inclined to be mobilized politically than are other evangelicals (Smidt 1989).

The liberal religious categories include mainline Protestants, liberal Protestants, and Conservative or Reform Jews. The most frequent religious term that survey respondents checked was mainline Christian (21 percent). Ten percent of survey respondents indicated identification with the term liberal Christian, and 3 percent were Conservative or Reform Jews. The case study findings parallel the survey findings in that the most popular category was mainline Christian (21 percent); only one case study candidate identified him- or herself as a liberal Christian, whereas two indicated that they were either Conservative or Reform Jewish. Jews form their own distinctive religious communities set apart from the other Christian traditions; however, Jews share with mainline and liberal Protestants more moderate positions on homosexuality, abortion, and the role of women in society and the church. Historically, mainline and liberal Protestants have been more willing than evangelicals (and particularly fundamentalists) to accommodate cultural changes and modernism, such as an acceptance of evolution theory as being compatible with their religious faiths (McKinney 1998; Smith 1998). This acceptance of science, for example, stems from mainliners' belief that the Bible is more open to interpretation, with an emphasis on symbolism. Recall from chapter 1 that this split among Protestant traditions was revealed during the first debates over evolution theory in the 1920s in the United States. Mainliners also accept different sources of religious truth aside from the Bible, and, rather than emphasize a need for evangelism, emphasize a "social gospel" of helping those individuals in need, following Christ's example in the Bible (Warner 1988).

In many ways, the Catholic Church incorporates elements from and shares similar social beliefs as evangelical and mainline Protestants. For instance, although the Catholic Church tends to be conservative on abortion and homosexuality, it typically takes more liberal stands on social justice issues such as the death penalty or poverty. At the risk of oversimplification, this "split personality" manifests itself in a division among practicing Catholics into those who are more "traditional" and those who are more "progessive." As the labels imply, traditional Catholics—such as Pat Buchanan—are generally more conservative in their politics, while progressive Catholics—Senator

Ted Kennedy is an example—are more liberal. In that respect, conservative Catholics are grouped in the "conservative" religious identities in table 2.3, while progressive Catholics fall under the "liberal" identities. Slightly more survey respondents indicated that they are traditional Catholics (15 percent) than progressives (11 percent). Two case study respondents identified themselves as conservative Catholics, and three said they were progressive Catholics.

Finally, respondents were also given the opportunity to check ethical or secular humanist, agnostic, or religious non-Christian as alternatives to the Judeo-Christian groups. As table 2.3 demonstrates, very few survey respondents identify with such groups: 2 percent checked the term ethical or secular humanist, 4 percent checked agnostic, and 1 percent checked religious non-Christian. Secular humanism, as noted by Christian fundamentalists Mel and Norma Gabler (1985), is rooted in the idea that values and virtues are human made rather than ordained by a higher being. Secular humanism, then, is distinguished by placing moral action in the "welfare of humanity rather than in fulfilling the will of God" (Honderich 1995). To be an agnostic, however, is not to reject a higher power, per se, but rather to admit an uncertainty about the existence of God (Honderich 1995). The religious non-Christian category is meant to capture those individuals who have a religion set apart from Christianity and Judaism.

As Kenneth Wald notes, despite the rapid modernization of the United States over the last two centuries, Americans remain a religious people. He finds that 82 percent of the American public identifies with a religious tradition or identity (1997, 12). School board candidates enjoy similar high rates of identification with religious identities—only 10 percent of survey respondents indicated that they did not identify with any of eleven religious terms (an additional 4 percent chose not to answer the question). Although case study participants have lower rates of religious identification, those results should be interpreted with caution because of the very small sample size in the case study and the large percentage (27 percent) that did not complete the questionnaire. At any rate, at a national level, at least 85 percent of survey respondents identified with one or more religious identities, which is comparable to national survey data of the general public. Although identification also appears to be split somewhat evenly among conservative and liberal categories, according to table 2.3, if "multiple" responses are removed, the numbers favor the more liberal groups: a total of 43 percent of respondents identified with one or more liberal identities compared with 38 percent of conservative religious identifiers (data not shown). Only 6 percent of respondents described their religious beliefs as humanist, agnostic, or religious non-Christian. Among conservative groups, roughly one quarter (24 percent) of survey respondents identified with one or more of those groups

that are most likely to be the target constituency of the Christian Right: fundamentalist, evangelical, and Pentecostal/Charismatic Christians (data not
shown).

Religious Beliefs and Support for Education Issues

With this understanding of the religious beliefs of school board candidates,
how do such beliefs impact their attitudes about education policies? Religious
ideas are potentially powerful sources of political motivation, as the various
waves of Christian Right activity depicted in chapter 1 demonstrate. With
respect to attitudes about public schools, more generally, research shows that
religiously conservative individuals are most likely to think that public schools
are hostile to their moral and spiritual values (Sikkink 1999). Religion's ability
to influence opinions about social and political issues (see, for example, Jelen
1989; Jelen, Smidt, and Wilcox 1993; Green et al. 1996; Wilcox 2000), combined with the salience of education in American politics today, merits an
examination of how religion impacts public opinion with respect to education
policies that most concern the Christian Right. Is support for such issues
determined mainly by religious variables or by other factors?

In table 2.1, survey respondents were asked whether they supported a variety of issues about which the Christian Right has taken public stands. In only
in a few cases do the majority of school board candidates share the same issue
positions as Christian Right leaders. Further, only a few of the issues advocated
by the Christian Right appear to elicit high levels of support among survey candidates more broadly, such as phonics and abstinence-based sex education,
whereas others, such as vouchers and vocational-technical or school-to-work
programs (in this case, spending less on such programs) do not.

Yet the question remains whether support for or opposition to such issues
is linked to religion. If Christian Right leaders are correct, individuals who profess a conservative religious background should have higher levels of support
for issues that motivate the movement, while those coming from a more liberal
or moderate background should have lower levels of support. The lowest level
of support might be likely to come from individuals with a nontraditional religious background or no religious background. Table 2.4 provides a breakdown
of the education attitudes of survey respondents who identified with each of
the three religious groupings: religious conservatives, religious liberals, and
those who make up a separate "other" religious category (ethical or secular
humanists, religious non-Christians, agnostics, or those professing no religion).

Table 2.4
Mean Level of Support by Religious Identities

Issue	Religious Conservatives	Religious Liberals	Religious Other
Charter schools	3.08	3.09	3.17
Vouchers	2.84***	2.22***	2.32
Multicultural programs	3.05***	3.42***	3.67**
School prayer	3.46***	2.78***	1.48***
Abstinence-based sex education	4.19***	3.75***	3.12***
Opposing mention of homosexuality	3.28***	2.77**	1.71***
Vocational-technical or school-to-work spending	3.98	3.96	3.88
Parental rights legislation	3.68***	3.35***	3.18*
Creationism	3.69***	2.89***	1.88***
Phonics	4.35***	4.04***	3.85*
Outcomes-based education	2.82***	3.29***	3.73***

Note: Mean scores are shown, on a scale where 1 = strongly oppose, 5 = strongly support. Difference of means tests were run to test significant differences between individuals from each religious identity versus individuals who do not share the same religious identity.
*$p < .05$.
**$p < .01$.
***$p < .001$.

Instead of reporting percentages, I report mean levels of support (1 = strongly oppose; 5 = strongly support).

There are statistically significant differences among the group members in ways that are largely expected. Religious conservatives report clear and distinct differences of opinions about nine education issues from those survey respondents who do not identify themselves as religious conservatives. (I report only the scores for religious conservatives.) The only two categories in which differences do not emerge are charter schools and vocational-technical/school-to-work spending, although such group identifiers have higher mean levels of support for vouchers and lower levels of support for school-to-work spending than survey respondents who are not religious conservatives (data not shown). Similar findings emerge among the other two group comparisons. The one exception is that those from the religious other category do not have significantly different levels of support for vouchers than do survey respondents who are not from the religious other category. At the same time, it is clear that the views of religious liberals and the views of those in the religious other category are, for the most part, markedly different from the views of religious conservatives. The differences among the three groups concerning issues that have a clear religious or moral dimension are particularly striking. For example, religious conservatives report a mean level of support for school prayer at 3.46—on a five-point scale—compared with 2.78 for religious liberals and just 1.48 for religious others. Support for creationism yields similar differences among the groups, with conservatives reporting a mean score of 3.69, liberals a score of 2.89, and others a score of 1.88.

Although conservative religious identifiers have different levels of support for various issues from liberal or nontraditional religious identifiers, how much of the difference can be explained by religious belief and how much by other factors? Though not reported here, I employ multiple regression to take into account the impact of religious identities on three issues in which their were large differences among religious identifiers: vouchers, school prayer, and creationism.[8] With respect to these three controversial, even polarizing, issues, independent relationships between religion and education attitudes continue to be maintained while controlling for political views, race, gender, and regional and community differences. It is not surprising that differences fell largely between the conservative and liberal religious camps. Identification with conservative religious beliefs was significantly related to support for all three controversial policies in the initial models. Church attendance is positively related to support for creationism but is not related to support for either school prayer or vouchers. The major factor related to support for all three issues is political ideology—the more conservative the candidate, the more likely he or she is to support creationism, school prayer, and vouchers.[9]

Religion can have a powerful, direct effect on attitudes about various education policies. Candidates who are religious conservatives have a distinct approach to education policy, which is an important finding in light of the fact that there is a correlation between professing conservative religious views and being a member of the Christian Right, as the next section will show. Demonstrating such a link between religion and education attitudes among school board candidates becomes especially important when one considers that many of these candidates will have a hand in shaping education policies on local school boards.

The Religious Beliefs and Behavior of Christian Right Candidates

Membership in a Christian Right organization or support for such an organization is correlated with religious identity. For example, 70 percent of Christian

Right group members identify with the various conservative religious groups identified in table 2.3, which is significantly higher than individuals who are not members of Christian Right groups, only 40 percent of whom are religious conservatives. Supporters of Christian Right groups are also significantly more likely to be religious conservatives than are nonsupporters (table 2.5). At the same time, respondents who identified with the liberal religious identities in the survey are less likely to be a member of or a supporter of such groups, although this difference is only statistically significant in the latter case. Although there is clearly a relationship between religious identity and membership in Christian Right organizations, it is noteworthy that a substantial minority of Christian Right group members and supporters did *not* identify with conservative religious groups, which indicates that using religious belief as a criterion of Christian Right status might yield misleading results.

Continuing with the theme of religion in more detail, the survey asked respondents several questions about their religious behavior (table 2.6). A substantial majority of candidates consider themselves to be church members; however, Christian Right candidates are significantly more likely to be church members (94 percent) than are non–Christian Right candidates (73 percent), as reported in the first two columns of table 2.6.[10] Combined, the categories in the first two columns of the table represent all of the respondents in the survey. This religious measure is just one of several that differentiate the two types of candidates. Of those candidates who are church members, Christian Right candidates are significantly more likely to be active within their churches and more often report that political issues are very frequently or somewhat fre-

Table 2.5
Religious Identities of Christian Right Members and Supporters

Religious Identity	Member of Christian Right Group (%)	Supporter of Christian Right Group (%)
Religious conservative	70***	58***
Religious liberal	33	35**
Religious other: secular humanist, religious non-Christian, agnostic, or no religion	7	2

Note: $N = 671$. χ^2 tests were not run on the "Religious other" category, because of the small sample size.
*$p < .05$.
**$p < .01$.
***$p < .001$.

Table 2.6
Religious Behavior of School Board Candidates

Religious Behavior	Christian Right Candidate (%)	Non–Christian Right Candidate (%)	Christian Right Group Member (%)	Christian Right Group Supporter (%)	Christian Right Issue Agenda Supporter (%)
Church member	94***	73	94	88	82
Active in church[a]	80***	61	79	74	61
Frequency political issues discussed at church:[a]					
Very frequently	8**	5	10	6	4
Somewhat frequenty	39	29	46	32	23
Hardly ever	52	66	44	62	72
Church attendance:					
Weekly	79***	42	72	64	50
Monthly	11	17	17	12	17
Several times a year	6	18	7	12	19
Rarely, if ever	4	24	4	11	14
Type of church attended:[b]					
Evangelical	50***	23	52	37	36
Mainline	18	34	22	23	33
Catholic	24	28	17	28	21
Jewish	1	3	—	2	—
Other	6	6	9	4	6
Secular	2	8	—	4	4

Note: $N = 671$. Statistical tests performed between variables in first two columns only. Difference of proportions is used for church member, active in church, and type of church attended, whereas difference of means is used for political issues discussed in church and church attendance.
[a]Percentages reflect only those individuals who indicated that they were church members.
[b]Type of church attended is recoded into evangelical and nonevangelical for purpose of statistical testing.
*$p < .05$.
**$p < .01$.
***$p < .001$.

quently discussed in their churches (again, focusing on the first two columns). Most telling, perhaps, are the statistically significant differences in rates of church attendance: 79 percent of Christian Right candidates attend church one or more times a week, compared with 42 percent of non–Christian Right candidates.

   Studies that examine the church in terms of social context have typically found that theologically conservative churches are more likely to shape the political views of church members than other types of churches (Wald, Owen, and Hill 1990). Table 2.6 also lists the breakdown of the types of churches to which candidates in the survey belong. Christian Right candidates are most likely to attend conservative churches. More than half of all Christian Right candidates attend evangelical Protestant churches (50 percent), whereas only 18 percent attend mainline Protestant churches, which are more theologically liberal. A relatively large number of Christian Right candidates (24 percent) are Catholics; however, when asked to describe themselves as either "progressive/ liberal" or "traditional/conservative" Catholics, 88 percent of these Christian Right candidates place themselves in the traditional category.[11] When candidates were asked if they attended evangelical or nonevangelical churches, Christian Right candidates were significantly more likely to attend such churches than were non–Christian Right candidates, an important finding in light of the fact that evangelical churches are the types of churches most often targeted by Christian Right organizations.
   Turning to the last three columns, some interesting differences emerge among the three groups. Christian Right Group members have the highest rates of church membership, church activity, and church attendance and are the most likely to attend evangelical churches. At the other end of the table, supporters of the Christian Right issue agenda (those who neither belong to nor support Christian Right organizations) more closely resemble the non–Christian Right candidates in the second column than do the other two groups, which demonstrates that support for a Christian Right political agenda alone does not necessarily come as the result of religious convictions.
   Research from the case studies also suggests that school board candidates, regardless of Christian Right status, are active religiously. Of the thirty-four candidates who returned questionnaires ($N = 24$), 80 percent ($N = 19$) report being church members and half of respondents ($N = 12$) are active in their churches. During interviews with school board candidates in both Fairfax and Garrett Counties, many mentioned that they were active in their churches or parishes, which included service as deacons, eucharistic ministers, and, in one case, a pastor of his small church. Because almost one-third of the case study respondents did not return the questionnaire that asked questions about their religious behavior (among other things), it is difficult to generalize about the behavior of all Christian Right and non–Christian Right candidates who participated in the case studies. The initial data, however, suggest patterns that are similar to the national survey. For example, of seven Christian Right candidates who completed the survey, six report attending church once a week or

more (86 percent), compared with 39 percent ($N = 7$) of the seventeen non–Christian Right candidates who completed the survey. Further, 71 percent (five of seven) of Christian Right candidates report being active in their churches, compared with 41 percent of non–Christian Right candidates.

Socioeconomic Status: A Comparison

Although there are important (and not unexpected) differences between Christian Right and non–Christian Right candidates with respect to religious behavior, when it comes to socioeconomic status, there are many remarkable similarities between the two types of candidates. Many scholars contend that the extent to which citizens participate in politics and the ways in which they do so are structured by their social circumstances. For example, studies routinely demonstrate that those citizens who are most likely to participate in politics are older, have high education and income levels, and tend to reside in their communities for long periods of time (see, for example, Verba and Nie 1972; Wolfinger and Rosenstone 1980; Conway 1991). Another way to conceptualize this theory is to think in terms of resources—individuals possessing higher socioeconomic status are more likely to have the time, money, and knowledge that help make participating in politics easier (Verba, Schlozman, and Brady 1995).

Although few studies focus on the socioeconomic characteristics of school board candidates, several political scientists have examined the socioeconomic background of citizens who participate in their local schools, either by attending PTA (parent-teacher association) or school board meetings. It is not surprising that Rosenstone and Hansen (1993) find a positive relationship between income and education levels and attendance at local political meetings (including school board meetings). Greater income often provides individuals with more time to do things, whereas individuals with higher levels of education are likely to have greater knowledge about local government. In turn, these individuals are more politically efficacious, meaning that they feel a sense of "personal competence" in terms of figuring out what is going on in local politics, a quality that Rosenstone and Hansen find makes people significantly more likely to go to local meetings (1993, 72–73). Salisbury (1980) conducted a study of citizen participation in local schools and found results similar to those of Rosenstone and Hansen. Again, citizens who participated in the local schools were predominately middle-class, long-term community residents. Most important, more than 99 percent of these participants were parents.

Salisbury's study took into account different leadership positions among citizen participants with the highest level being school board candidates who made up 12 percent of the participants. Salisbury found that the more "prestigious" the leadership role, the higher the average income and education levels (1980, 144). Finally, the *American School Board Journal* conducted a survey of school board members, polling members on their demographic information as well as their attitudes on various education policies (Upperman et al. 1996). Their 1996 survey found that the vast majority of school board members are parents who typically reside in the suburbs or small towns and own their own homes. Board members are well educated, with nearly 40 percent holding advanced degrees, and they tend to have high levels of income, with 50 percent earning family incomes of between $40,000 and $79,000 annually. Another 37 percent earn more than $80,000 per year.

These studies on citizens who participate in the local schools as well as past research on socioeconomic status and political participation would lead one to predict that recent school board candidates are likely to score high on socioeconomic measures. The results from the school board survey typically support such findings. Table 2.7 provides a glimpse of some general characteristics of school board candidates from the survey.

The first two columns of data of table 2.7 report socioeconomic status characteristics of Christian Right candidates (as defined by the combination variable) and their non–Christian Right counterparts. Tests that measure differences of proportions and means were performed on the data to determine whether the differences between the two groups are statistically significant. The remaining columns report the statistics for candidates who are members of Christian Right organizations, supporters (but not members) of such groups, and those individuals who support the issue agenda but do not identify with Christian Right groups in any way.

Focusing on the first two columns initially, Christian Right candidates appear to be statistically distinct from their non–Christian Right counterparts in some ways but similar in others. All candidates running for school board have levels of income and education well above the national average.[12] School board candidates are also far more likely to be married than the average citizen.[13] Although not reported in the table, Christian Right and non–Christian Right candidates are of similar ages: the median ages for Christian Right candidates and non–Christian Right candidates is 46 and 47 years, respectively. Virtually every candidate is a parent (less than 1 percent report having no children). The median number of children for Christian Right candidates is 3.1, whereas the median number of children for non–Christian Right candidates is 2.6 children (data not shown). With the exception of median number

Table 2.7
Socioeconomic Status Characteristics of School Board Candidates

Characteristics	Christian Right Candidate (%)	Non–Christian Right Candidate (%)	Christian Right Group Member (%)	Christian Right Group Supporter (%)	Christian Right Issue Agenda Supporter (%)
Female	26**	41	30	33	33
Annual income:					
<$25,000	7	8	9	6	11
$25,000–$49,999	29	23	24	25	36
$50,000–$74,999	32	26	33	27	28
$75,000–$99,999	16	22	7	21	19
>$100,000	17	22	26	20	6
Education:					
High school diploma	11	10	9	11	16
Some college	33	25	33	30	34
College degree	33	34	35	34	34
Graduate degree	23	31	24	25	16
Married	96*	89	98	93	91
Community type:					
Rural	72***	64	69	70	69
Suburban	18	29	15	24	24
Urban	11	7	15	5	7
Occupation:					
Self-employed	28	21	28	24	29
Executive/manager	13	18	17	17	11
Professional	15	17	13	16	13
Education	9	17	13	14	11
Clerical	3	4	4	3	10
Part time	1	2	—	2	1
Not employed	5	6	2	6	4
Other	26	15	22	18	20

Note: $N = 671$. Statistical tests performed between variables in first two columns only. Difference of proportions is used for gender and married, difference of means is used for income and education, and χ^2 is used for community type; no statistical tests were run for occupation.
*$p < .05$.
**$p < .01$.
***$p < .001$.

of children, none of these differences between the two groups reaches statistical significance.

In other ways, however, Christian Right and non–Christian Right candidates are statistically different, including gender. Christian Right candidates are less likely to be female (26 percent) than non–Christian Right candidates (41 percent). This finding is not surprising, in view of the fact that members of conservative Christian denominations are less likely to be supportive of gender equality than are other religious traditions, such as mainline Protestants and Jews (Wald 1997, 185–86). Also, Christian Right candidates are more likely to be married, although both types of candidates report being married at much higher levels than the national average, which in 1998 was 56 percent of all American adults (United States Census Bureau 1999). Differences are also apparent in terms of occupation. Christian Right candidates report being self-employed at higher levels than non–Christian Right candidates, and the former are less likely to come from a career in education. Finally, Christian Right candidates are significantly more likely to come from rural *or* urban, as opposed to suburban communities, as are non–Christian Right candidates.

Turning to the last three columns of table 2.7, we see that a comparison among the three groups shows few differences when it comes to socioeconomic characteristics. Worth mentioning is the finding that 98 percent of Christian Right group members are married, which is higher than any other category, particularly those individuals who simply support a Christian Right agenda but in no way identify with the movement's organizations. Also interesting is the fact that, of the three groups, members of the Christian Right appear to be the most highly educated. This finding is not surprising if one considers that members of any interest groups tend to be more highly educated than nonmembers (Walker 1991). Generally speaking, however, there appear to be few differences among the different categories in these columns.

A similar picture emerges when we turn to the candidates who ran for school board in the two counties featured in the case studies. All but two candidates for school board in the 1995 Fairfax County elections had at the minimum a bachelor's degree, while more than half had postgraduate degrees. Many of the candidates for school board had extensive backgrounds in education as teachers, administrators, or professional tutors. Careers in government and law were also common among the candidates in Fairfax County. Only two candidates, stay-at-home mothers, indicated that they were not employed at the time of the elections, although both had extensive volunteer experience in the Fairfax County public schools. All in all, the majority of the successful candidates— both Christian Right and non–Christian Right—were a highly educated group with high-status, white-collar occupations. In general terms, the candidates in Garrett County had lower education levels and fewer had professional or education-related occupations. This finding, however, speaks to the larger socioeconomic differences found in the two counties. Fairfax County, a suburb of Washington, D.C., has the highest median family income level ($65,201) in the entire country and has the nation's sixth highest percentage of adults holding bachelor's degrees (49 percent). Garrett County, which is relatively isolated in the mountains of western Maryland, has the lowest per-capita income level in the state ($26,365), with only 9.5 percent of the adult population holding bachelor's degrees (*County and City Databook* 1994). Among the four Christian Right candidates in Garrett County, none had a bachelor's degree, but two attended college. Another conservative Christian candidate completed a one-year course of study with the Moody Bible Institute, an evangelical seminary. He also had served in the military. All four of the non–Christian Right candidates attended college, with three completing a bachelor's degree (the fourth finished an associate's degree). One of these candidates had a master's degree in education. Similar to the school board candidates in the survey, both Christian Right and non–Christian Right candidates in Fairfax and Garrett Counties generally fit the "profile" of politically active individuals: most have college degrees, and many have professional careers. Further, a substantial number of the candidates (fifteen) have careers in education, a fact that echoes the findings of previous research on school board members.

Conclusion

Like most Americans, the vast majority of school board candidates—both Christian Right and non–Christian Right—identify with a religion. And such religious identities help to delineate issue positions among survey respondents more generally. When it comes to religious behavior, however, there are important differences between the two groups. Christian Right candidates are more likely to be members of churches, be active in those churches, and to attend them more frequently than their non–Christian Right counterparts—all behaviors that will have important ramifications for their campaigns for school board as later chapters reveal. Yet at the same time, Christian Right candidates share with non–Christian Right candidates many of the same high socioeconomic characteristics that are often affiliated with individuals who run for political office. In the next few chapters, I look closely at other similarities and differences between these candidates with respect to their motivation for running, the way they campaign, and the likelihood of winning their races.

Chapter Three

Why Conservative Christians Run for School Board

Perhaps no other type of political activity requires more time, money, or energy than running for political office. Considering the demands potential candidates face, why do people decide to run for office? When one Christian Right candidate in this study was asked why he decided to run for school board, he did not hesitate to offer this reply: "We as Christians need to be involved. I guess the bottom line is . . . if you do a little study in the Bible, it encourages, it demands that a Christian not be separated from the rest of government but be involved in government. I guess that is the bottom line. We are instructed to be involved. We are instructed to play a part." For this candidate, and numerous other Christian Right school board candidates, religion is a powerful motivator that helps to overcome the potential hardships that individuals encounter as political candidates.

Numerous studies have been devoted to the analysis of the political recruitment of candidates, although most are geared toward figuring out why certain individuals decide to run for Congress and state legislatures (see, for example, Kazee 1994). Such studies find that eligibility for public office often depends on considerations such as occupation, education, and social standing (Verba and Nie 1972; Conway 1991; Verba, Schlozman, and Brady 1995). Further, many of these studies maintain that office seekers exhibit a certain type of "political personality"—that is, they are psychologically invested in running for office, whether for the purpose of pursuing power more generally or for championing a specific ideological cause (Wilson 1973; Verba, Schlozman, and Brady 1995). Other political recruitment studies concentrate on outside, contextual factors that influence an individual's decision to run for office, such as the decision of an incumbent to not seek reelection (Jacobson 1992) or the availability of support from a political party or interest group (Herrnson 1995).

While identifying many important factors that relate to an individual's decision to seek political office, political recruitment studies typically downplay the role of religion as a source of political motivation (but see Leege, Lieske, and Wald 1991). As chapter 1 revealed, religion has proven to be a powerful source of inspiration for political movements historically. Despite such periods in American political history and the current wave of Christian Right political activism, religion—particularly the salience of religious beliefs to individuals—largely continues to be neglected in studies that focus on political recruitment (and political participation more generally). The push by Christian Right organizations in recent years to recruit candidates to run for political office, including school boards, highlights a need to examine more closely the role that religion plays in motivating citizens to become political candidates.

This chapter explores why conservative Christians decide to run for school boards. What role does religion play in motivating them to become school board candidates? What other types of factors contribute to their decisions to run for this local office? Further, how do their decisions to run differ from the decisions of school board candidates who are not part of the Christian Right? Is religion also a significant factor in the decisions of non–Christian Right candidates to run for school board?

I undertook two general approaches analyzing why conservative Christians run for school board. First, candidates were asked specifically why they decided to run for office. As both the survey and case study findings will reveal, candidates run for a variety of reasons, including religions ones. Yet the decision to run for office is not made in a vacuum. For that reason, candidates were also asked who encouraged them to run, with the recognition that interest groups and parties (among others) often play an important role in mobilizing individuals to become involved in the political process. Such an approach is important in light of the attempts by Christian Right organizations such as the Christian Coalition in the past decade to recruit individuals to run for school board and other local offices. Are Christian Right candidates being mobilized to run by such groups? Or are their decisions to run for office more individually motivated?

Reasons They Run

In both the survey and case studies, candidates were asked why they decided to run for school board. Whereas the case study interviews gave candidates the opportunity to express in great detail the reasons behind their decisions to become school board candidates, survey research did not offer that luxury. Instead, survey respondents were asked to check off whether a series of reasons were not very important (coded 1), somewhat important (coded 2), or very important in their decision to run for office (coded 3). Table 3.1 lists the mean scores (ranging from 1 to 3) for each of the categories, with a difference of means test performed between Christian Right candidates and non–Christian Right candidates in the first two columns to see whether there are significant differences between them with respect to the candidates' reasons for running for school board.

Each of the reasons for running listed in table 3.1 can be separated into three categories loosely based on James Q. Wilson's *Political Organizations* (1973). Adapting Mancur Olson's (1965) rational choice theory, used to explain the circumstances under which individuals can be expected to work collectively toward a common political goal, Wilson maintains that individuals will participate in politics when the benefits of such participation outweigh the costs. Wilson argues that there are three categories of reasons or benefits that propel individuals to take political action: material, solidary, and purposive. Material benefits involve economic or other self-interest. For example, a person might decide to run for office to increase his or her name recognition or visibility, which, in turn, could help promote his or her career. The other benefits offer less tangible rewards. Solidary benefits include the social enjoyment citizens receive from participating in politics. Purposive benefits, meanwhile, include those reasons that are driven by policy or community. In other words, citizens participate in politics out of some sense of duty, whether that duty derives from strong policy and ideological beliefs, which could include religion, or from a more general sense of obligation to make the community a better place to live.

Two reasons in table 3.1 tap into so-called material benefits. Candidates were asked whether their decision to run for school board stemmed from a desire to "further their job goals" or "gain political experience" in hopes of running for a higher political office in the future. As Verba, Schlozman, and Brady (1995) note, however, some caution must be taken with regard to interpreting respondents' reports about their motivations for getting involved in politics. Candidates might be reluctant to admit motivations that might be construed as selfish. As expected, neither Christian Right nor non–Christian

Table 3.1
Reasons for Running for School Board

Reason for Running	Christian Right Candidate	Non–Christian Right Candidate	Christian Right Group Member	Christian Right Group Supporter	Christian Right Issue Agenda Supporter
Material:					
Further job goals	1.21 (.500)	1.28 (.560)	1.19 (.450)	1.26 (.538)	1.25 (.526)
Political experience	1.23 (.511)	1.16 (.448)	1.21 (.470)	1.23 (.515)	1.16 (.441)
Solidary:					
Found it exciting	1.59 (.720)	1.59 (.695)	1.52 (.762)	1.63 (.695)	1.54 (.674)
Work with people who share my ideals	2.14 (.786)	2.20 (.754)	2.27 (.780)	2.20 (.750)	2.28 (.784)
Be with people I enjoy	1.45 (.632)	1.48 (.657)	1.51 (.637)	1.48 (.662)	1.43 (.675)
Purposive:					
Influence policy	2.52 (.704)*	2.35 (.739)	2.43 (.728)	2.41 (.726)	2.53 (.717)
Learn about politics	1.69 (.759)	1.69 (.751)	1.84 (.754)	1.65 (.729)	1.78 (.802)
Make community better place	2.94 (.275)	2.91 (.310)	3.00 (.000)	2.92 (.301)	2.91 (.329)
Apply religious/ moral beliefs	2.12 (.782)***	1.39 (.653)	2.02 (.886)	1.84 (.806)	1.70 (.773)
Return schools to traditional values	2.67 (.819)***	2.14 (.839)	2.61 (.618)	2.52 (.655)	2.67 (.675)

Note: $N = 671$. Mean scores are given, with standard deviation in parentheses. Difference of means tests performed between variables in first two columns only.
*$p < .05$.
**$p < .01$.
***$p < .001$.

Right candidates were likely to say that either of these reasons was of great importance to their decision to run for office.

Whereas such selfish reasons seem to matter little to school board candidates, more support is found for solidary, or social, benefits. The survey included three responses that tap into solidary reasons for participating in school board elections. The first reason—"I ran to be with people I enjoy"—results in the lowest mean scores for both groups in the first two columns. The mean scores are slightly higher for the next response—"I ran because I found it exciting." The final reason—"I ran because I wanted to work with people who share my ideals"—yields the highest mean scores for both Christian Right candidates (2.14) and non–Christian Right candidates (2.20). Christian Right candidates, however, are not significantly more or less likely than non–Christian Right candidates to list these reasons as being important to their decision to run for school board.

The most important types of reasons that relate to a candidate's decision to run for school board clearly are purposive, or ideological. Of the five purposive reasons listed for candidates, by far the most popular reason for running for office is the desire to "make the community a better place to live." This response, which relates to the importance of civic service, generates extremely high mean scores for both Christian Right (2.94) and non–Christian Right candidates (2.91) alike. A less popular purposive reason for running for office is "learning about the political system," the responses for which are virtually identical for both types of candidates. A more inspirational source of motivation for all candidates seeking school board positions was the potential opportunity to influence school board policy. The mean score here for Christian Right candidates is 2.52, compared with 2.35 for non–Christian Right candidates—a difference that reaches statistical significance.

The two remaining reasons elicit strong, statistical differences between the two types of candidates. With a mean score of 2.67, Christian Right candidates are significantly more likely than non–Christian Right candidates (mean score, 2.14) to indicate that returning schools to traditional values is an important reason they decided to run for office. Christian Right candidates were far more likely than non–Christian Right candidates to indicate that applying their religious or moral convictions was important to their decision to run for school board, resulting in mean scores of 2.12 and 1.39, respectively. Expressed as a percentage, 75 percent of Christian Right candidates believe that applying their religious or moral beliefs to education policy was very or somewhat important to their decision to run for school board, compared with 29 percent of non–Christian Right candidates (data not shown). As this statistic indicates, religion is important in distinguishing differences in motivation between these two types of candidates.

These two significant differences merit further examination. Do the differences concerning the application of religious and moral beliefs to school policy and restoring traditional values to school hold once additional controls are added? Table 3.2 lists the results of two separate regression analyses (ordinary least squares [OLS]) using the combined Christian Right variable as the main independent variable, while controlling for education (1 = high school; 4 = graduate school), income (1 = less than $25,000 per year; 5 = more than

Table 3.2
Ordinary Least Squares Regression: Analyzing Importance of Applying
Religious/Moral Beliefs to Education Policy and Returning Schools
to Traditional Values in Running for Office (Standardized
Coefficients Reported)

Independent Variable	Model 1 Dependent Variable: Applying Religious/ Moral Beliefs	Model 2 Dependent Variable: Returning Schools to Traditional Values
Christian Right Status	.282***	.051
Church Attendance	.132***	.110**
Education	−.079[a]	−.173***
Income	−.095*	−.120**
Gender	−.0.0	−.044
Race	−.015	−.172***
Ideology	.123**	.330***
Democrat	−.087	−.062
Republican	−.091	−.008
Independent	−.026	−.026
South	.062	.032
West	.078	.004
Midwest	.052	−.025
Rural	−.060	−.006
Suburban	−.050	−.034

Note: $N = 671$. Interaction effects for Christian Right status by education, gender, race, and church attendance added to model 1 and model 2 were not significant.
[a]Significance level $p = .051$.
*$p < .05$.
**$p < .01$.
***$p < .001$.

$100,000), region (Northeast as the reference variable), race (1 = white; 0 = nonwhite), party ("other" party as the reference variable), ideology (1 = very liberal; 7 = very conservative), community type (urban as the reference variable), gender (1 = female; 0 = male), and church attendance (1 = rarely attends church; 4 = attends once or more per week). Standardized coefficients (beta weights) are reported. The results in the first column, which examine the importance of applying religious and moral beliefs to education policy in terms of running for office, reveal that Christian Right status maintains its significance when additional controls are applied. In addition, the results indicate that education and income levels are negatively related to this reason for running for office, whereas political conservatism is positively related.

Finally, the more individuals attend church, the more likely they are to list religious and moral reasons as important to their decision to become a school board candidate.

The regression results in the second column tell a different story. Christian Right status is no longer significantly related to the reason for running that involves returning traditional values to the public schools. Instead, the beta weights reveal that political ideology is the most strongly linked to wanting to return traditional values to schools—the more conservative a candidate, the more likely he or she is to indicate that this reason was important to his or her decision to run for school board. Also positively related to such a reason is church attendance. Nonwhites are more likely than whites to list this reason as important, while both education and income are negatively related to the desire to return schools to traditional values.

Why does Christian Right status significantly relate only to applying religious and moral beliefs to public schools and not with a desire to return the schools to traditional values? Part of the reason might be that "traditional values" is a term that is more open to interpretation, one that lacks an obvious religious connotation. Whereas we see that returning schools to traditional values is still a highly valued reason for running for school board among Christian Right candidates, other candidates who do not affiliate themselves with the movement are also likely to think this reason is important, which is supported by analyzing the mean scores in table 3.1 for Christian Right group members, Christian Right group supporters, and Christian Right issue agenda supporters. The highest mean score for this variable (2.67) is found among those candidates who support the Christian Right's agenda but do not belong to or support any Christian Right organizations. This same group is also much less likely than Christian Right group members, for example, to say that applying religious and moral beliefs to schools was important to their decision to run for office (1.70 mean score, compared to 2.02). This finding suggests that a candidate can share some of the educational policy goals of the Christian Right without necessarily sharing its religious values.

When the results are taken as a whole, both Christian Right and non–Christian Right candidates do not appear to consider material and solidary reasons as very important to their decision for running for office. A glance at the final three columns in table 3.1 also reveals few differences among Christian Right group members, group supporters, and agenda supporters with respect to such reasons for running for school board.

Instead, purposive and ideological reasons dominate the respondents' answers. Making the community a better place was the most popular reason all candidates gave for running for office (indeed, all forty-seven Christian Right group members ranked this reason as very important to their decision). It would be highly unlikely, however, that candidates would not check off this box, in light of the normative implications that are associated with it. Who would not want to help make their community a better place to live if given the opportunity? That reason aside, most of the high mean scores among Christian Right candidates concerning their reasons for running involved implementing their policy goals, usually of a traditionally moral or religious bent. Influencing policy is also important to non–Christian Right candidates (although not as important as it is to their Christian Right counterparts), but relatively few wish to apply their moral or religious convictions to these policies.

More telling are the responses given by the candidates in the case studies during extensive interviews. Many of the responses echo those found in the survey. For example, most candidates in both counties indicated that their decision to run for school board stemmed in part from a desire to "give something back" to their communities. Along similar lines, several candidates believed that they "could make a difference for kids." Most of the thirty-one candidates first became active within the schools by being involved with their own children, sparking an initial interest in later pursuing school board office. Some parents also attributed their active involvement with local and county parent–teacher associations (PTAs) with helping to inspire them to run for school board.

Recall from chapter 2 that a large number of candidates in Fairfax County had experience in education, either as tutors, teachers, or administrators. Nearly every candidate with teaching or education experience had a desire to put this background to use as a school board member. One candidate, a retired elementary school principal and former teacher said, "I ran because I was a child advocate. . . . I felt that the school board needed on board, especially since it was the first school board to be elected, an educator." Another candidate in Fairfax County echoed this thought. As a former teacher, she believed she better understood the needs of children, and she hoped to "represent a teacher's standpoint" on the board. A third retired teacher cited her "life-long passion over education issues" as vital to her decision to become a candidate. The three candidates cited were not conservative Christians, although two were moderate Republicans.

One candidate in Garrett County ran because of a school-busing situation. Another, in Fairfax County, ran hoping to represent more effectively the needs of homeschooling families. Although a few of the candidates were concerned about these types of single-policy issues, most candidates mentioned broad policy concerns as important to their decision to run. Among those with wider concerns, a conservative Christian candidate in Garrett County ran because he was "interested in maintaining the excellence of . . . [the] school system." Most of the moderate to liberal candidates in Fairfax County ran on a similar pledge, expressing their desire to maintain the basic structure of the schools, a stand that was particularly distinct from the more conservative candidates in the county. Most Christian Right candidates in Fairfax County (and several moderate Republicans as well) expressed a desire to make substantial changes to curriculum and administrative policies (including a pledge to replace the man who, at the time, was school superintendent). Alternatively, one Democratic candidate decided to run because he believed that the Christian Right candidates in the county were "painting a horrible picture of one of the best school systems in the state."

Among changes advocated by Republican candidates in Fairfax County, many involved opening lines of communication between parents and the school administration. According to one moderate Republican candidate, "One concern I had about the ways schools were run is that decisions were not being made at the school level; parents had very little say in their local schools." Another moderate Republican decided to run because she believed that the school system was too intimidating and that having parents involved with curriculum or more substantive issues challenged school administrators. She remarked, "I figured someone had to speak up against this system and try to make the system more accountable to parents." One social conservative in Fairfax County ran because she believed that running for a seat on the school board would be "the only way" her voice would be heard by the school administration.

Christian Right candidates in both counties (with the exception of the Garrett County candidate quoted above) had a tendency to promote changes for the school system that corresponded to their own conservative and sometimes moral philosophies. Virtually all Christian Right candidates (and several of the moderate Republicans) ran on a "back-to-basics" platform, as evidenced by a candidate in Fairfax County who decided to run because she felt that the public schools were "operating beneath a very poor, left-wing philosophy. We need to get a handle on schools as academics. We need to get a basic grip on core subjects." Another Fairfax County social conservative ran because he believed that "there is not a desire on the part of the [school] administration to teach academics."

Several conservative Christians became candidates because they hoped to instill in children a better sense of the difference between "right and wrong," which would begin, according to one Fairfax County conservative Christian, by having "people running the schools who understand the difference between right and wrong." Other candidates gave specific examples of policy areas where this type of moral code could be applied, including a conservative Christian in Garrett County who said, "My feeling is that we should promote chastity, that we should send a clear message and not a mixed message to our students. . . . That is the way I would like to see us go, as opposed to anything goes, whatever you decide to do is okay." Another Christian Right candidate in Fairfax County believed that "schools should teach 'universal' virtues, such as obedience and respect for parents, teachers, and authority figures" rather than the current system, in which "students are taught to examine information, consider viewpoints, and alternatives," a philosophy that is inconsistent with her view that schools should stress absolute values.

Some conservative Christian candidates specifically linked their moral visions for the schools to their religious philosophies. Said one in Garrett County, "I believe that Judeo-Christian values make for prosperity and success in every endeavor, and they should be applied to education in this country." Another social conservative candidate in Fairfax County was more blunt about why he ran. As he recalled, "Schools are doing a tremendous amount of harm. They are undermining religious values and they are not preparing [students], with the exception of the motivated and bright children who will work even when the schools do not require it. Except for those [students], the school system really doesn't want to teach children much. So children emerge unprepared to function economically. They are bored, which actually makes them more susceptible to drugs and alcohol. [T]here is this pervasive atheism that the schools teach that undermines the values that children need to keep happy and make them productive."

Every Christian Right candidate, when asked specifically in the interview, indicated that their religious or moral convictions inspired them to run for office, including a candidate in Garrett County who indicated that people of faith have a duty to organize politically and "to remember their values and concerns and to follow that path once they are in office." One socially conservative candidate in Fairfax County ran because of a concern with the moral direction of the schools and the nation at large. He said, "I think it was a concern for where we are heading. Hitler hit me right between the eyes when he said, 'Let me control the school books and I'll control the country.' I don't want this country to become a socialist state, and you find yourself on a slippery slope when you've lost your moral compass."

For other conservative Christian candidates, the lines between politics, religion, and secular life are impossible to separate. According to a socially conservative candidate in Garrett County, society "shouldn't look at religion and the secular, political life separately. . . . [F]or me, there is no way to separate my religious life from the rest of me—it is who I am; it is what I do."

Similar views were expressed by Christian Right candidates in Fairfax County, including one social conservative who asked, "How does a person separate their beliefs, what they base their life on, what they base their principles that they live [by], from the decisions that they make? I'm not willing to say I do that. I don't think anybody does that." The fact that morality or religion was instrumental or even paramount to the decisions of conservative Christians to run for office comes as little surprise, considering the salience of religion to most Christian Right political activists.

More surprising, however, was that several of the non–Christian Right candidates were willing to link part of their decision to run for school board back to their religious heritage. For example, some candidates indicated that their decision to run for school board was one way to demonstrate good Christian stewardship. Said one, an Episcopalian, the Christian expression "feed my sheep" also means "teach my sheep." Another candidate acknowledged that one reason she was involved with the school system was that her Roman Catholic religious background "includes service to others," a belief shared by a Jewish candidate in Fairfax County who had a long career in education. He linked his decision to run for school board to his Jewish faith, which stresses responsibility to serve. As he put it, "I feel that with my background and understanding, it is my responsibility to serve the community." Finally, another candidate, a moderate Republican, said, "I prayed hard about running and saw it [the decision to run] as a sign from God." Her decision to run came only after much spiritual reflection.

A few moderate candidates indicated that their decision to run was linked to their religious beliefs in a different way. These individuals became candidates, in part, to express a moral or religious philosophy rooted in tolerance. Said one Garrett County candidate, "I think my moral convictions include inclusion and compromise. I don't like intolerance. I think we need to be framing our education with those values in mind." At least one moderate candidate hoped that her decision to run would demonstrate that not all Christians shared a conservative philosophy. She remarked, "I would say my decision to run was probably based on my religious beliefs. As a Christian, I wanted to demonstrate that there has to be a separate view and a separate voice out there; that not all Christians feel the way they [the Christian Right] do." She ended by saying that she hoped to demonstrate that not all Christians are "this narrow-minded."

Finally, religion was linked to another reason many of the more liberal candidates gave for why they ran for school board. Twelve of the non–Christian Right candidates in both counties indicated that their decision to run was linked to a desire *not* to have the Christian Right win a majority of school board seats. Typical of many of their responses was this one by a liberal candidate in Fairfax County who ran against a Christian Right candidate in his district: "My feeling was that if people like me weren't willing to do jobs like this, then we would be getting people who were outside the mainstream with some sort of hidden agenda." Another in Garrett County had similar thoughts. He said:

> A lot of people I consider members of the Christian Right [in Garrett County], I like personally. . . . And I think that they really feel that what they are doing is correct, and they are coming from a basis of what they view is important, and I don't have any animosity toward them personally. On the flip side, my basic belief is that a lot of those people who were running with that purpose do not support public education, do not support a clear separation of church and state. [They] are more inclined to want to privatize a lot of the education, and put a lot of emphasis on specific values. When a lot of these people got elected [in 1994], I helped form a group of people . . . and one of the missions of that group was to identify people to run for the next time. And so when it came to run for the next time [in 1996], I contacted three or four people and I said, "Hey, would you run?" and they all turned me down. And it got to the point where I felt we needed a candidate from [my] area, just looking at the districts, and that I anticipated that the [Christian] Coalition would be nominating a candidate from [my] area. And when I couldn't find anyone else to do it, I volunteered myself.

Moderate to liberal candidates who faced Christian Right opponents in their districts typically expressed their concern that conservative Christian candidates who won might try to use the school board as a means to spread their religious views, a potential factor that motivated many of them to become candidates. The mere presence of Christian Right candidates in both counties resulted in the mobilization of more moderate to liberal candidates.

In summary, both the survey and case study results point to the overriding importance of purposive or ideological reasons to the candidates' decision to run for school board. Especially important to school board candidates, Christian Right and non–Christian Right alike, was a desire to do what they think is best for the children of the community. Further, most candidates seemed genuinely interested in affecting education policy within their school districts, although their ideological points of view differed. Part of these differences revolved around the issue of values. Christian Right candidates were more likely to believe that restoring "traditional values" to the classroom was a very important goal, as indicated by the survey and case study research. The case study interviews also tapped into another important difference between the two types of candidates that concerns values. Christian Right candidates often remarked that schools fail to transmit to students a clear picture of the differences between "right and wrong," a view not shared by any of the non–Christian Right candidates. In fact, non–Christian Right candidates said in several interviews that values such as tolerance and diversity should instead be emphasized in the schools. The candidacies of Christian Right candidates resulted in a countermobilization on the part of some non–Christian Right candidates, affecting the very nature of their motivation for running for school board.

Political Mobilization: Who Encouraged Their Candidacies

Although school board candidates clearly indicated a variety of personal reasons that led them to run for office, their decisions were also likely shaped by other actors. As James Rosenau (1974) describes it, politics is typically "interactive." Rosenau states, "For most active citizens, there is an activator—another citizen, an organization, or public official who evokes the behavior that we call participation through an appeal for support" (1974, xxix). Indeed, for most school board candidates, their decision to become politically engaged—in this case, by running for a local political office—was encouraged by a host of different activators, usually friends, family, or individuals active within the schools and, in some cases, political parties and interest groups.

Political scientists have long recognized that a person's political behavior is often linked to his or her day-to-day environment, which includes home, work, community, and church. Individuals who are very active within their communities, especially, are among those most likely to participate in politics, often because such participation exposes them to information about politics. In the words of Robert Huckfeldt and John Sprague, "A variety of organizational forms serve intentionally or accidentally as vehicles of political mobilization, and thus they become important to the diffusion of political information. . . . [E]ven though the choice [to belong to a group] is seldom predicated on an explicitly political basis, it may generate important political consequences" (1995, 285). Hence, *why* individuals participate in politics might be affected by whom they see on a regular basis.

Of particular importance in this dynamic, according to some political scientists, are political actors. One theory of political participation—the mobilization model—holds that political leaders such as party officials, public officeholders, or interest group leaders play an important role in motivating or "mobilizing" people to participate in politics. In other words, people do not necessarily go to politics; sometimes politics comes to them. For example, Steven Rosenstone and John Hansen (1993) argue that the presence and mobilizing efforts of interest groups, political parties, and candidates can reduce the costs of gathering political information and make political participation more appealing to citizens. When it comes to running for political office, in particular, studies find that contact by political parties and other political figures results in potential candidates being more likely to run than potential candidates who have generally not been asked to run (Maisel, Stone, and Maestas 2001).

School board candidates in this study were asked about who encouraged them to run for school board as a way to gauge how their environment shaped their decision to become a candidate. These "sources" of encouragement can be divided into four broad categories: friends, family, and neighborhood connections; people within the education community; political figures; and fellow church members or ministers. Survey respondents were given a list containing these specific types of individuals who might have encouraged them to run for office. (For exact question wording, see appendix B.) The findings in table 3.3 demonstrate the importance of encouragement in a candidate's decision to run for office. As the first two columns detail, only 13 percent of Christian Right candidates and 18 percent of non–Christian Right candidates replied that "no one encouraged them" to run for office. Among all five categories of candidates listed in table 3.3, the highest percentage of candidates to report that no one asked them to run were Christian Right issue agenda supporters.

Family, Friends, and Community

Turning first to the most intimate acquaintances, candidates were most likely to indicate that their friends and family encouraged them to run for office. It is difficult to imagine that a person would run for political office without the support of his or her family or friends. Moreover, 43 percent of Christian Right candidates and 39 percent of non–Christian Right candidates indicated that various "community leaders" (broadly defined) encouraged their decision to run, suggesting that candidates tend to be active within their communities and that this activity reinforces their desire to serve on school boards. Christian Right group members, group supporters, and issue agenda supporters report similar findings in the final three columns. Recall that many of the candidates said that "giving something back to their community" was an important factor in their decision to run for office.

Table 3.3
Individuals Who Encouraged Candidates to Run for School Board

Source of Encouragement	Christian Right Candidate (%)	Non–Christian Right Candidate (%)	Christian Right Group Member (%)	Christian Right Group Supporter (%)	Christian Right Issue Agenda Supporter (%)
Current board member	58	50	61	61	39
Retired board member	21	27	30	32	30
Friend, family member	67	64	61	68	63
Community leader	43	39	48	45	41
Representative of voluntary organization	9	10	9	14	9
Political party leader	12	12	9	17	13
Fellow church member	27***	13	24	24	16
Minister	7*	3	9	5	7
No one asked me to run	13	18	17	12	26

Note: $N = 671$. Difference of proportions test performed between variables in first two columns only.
*$p < .05$.
**$p < .01$.
***$p < .001$.

The day-to-day environment or "context" of school board candidates in Garrett and Fairfax Counties appears to be similar to the survey respondents in several ways. For example, most candidates in the two counties—both Christian Right and non–Christian Right—were likely to say that someone encouraged them to run for office. Among those candidates who were encouraged to run in the two counties, most were likely to say that friends and family influenced their decisions to become school board candidates. Candidates often noted that other parents with children in the schools were likely to encourage them to run, including one moderate Republican candidate in Fairfax County who said that she was encouraged by "parents who were also frustrated with the school board." Another candidate in Fairfax County, a conservative Christian, said that he was encouraged to run by other parents who met monthly in a local coffee shop to discuss education issues in the county.

Education Community

Members of the education community also appear to mobilize individuals to run for school board. As table 3.3 reveals, current school board members were likely to encourage both Christian Right (58 percent) and non–Christian Right candidates (50 percent) to run. Twenty-one percent of Christian Right candidates and 27 percent of non–Christian Right candidates indicated that retired board members also encouraged them to run. The encouragement provided by both current and retired school board members to potential school board candidates suggests that most candidates are somehow involved in local education matters or at least closely follow the activities of the school board. This finding is supported by earlier research on the governance of school boards, which found that most board members were initially encouraged by past and present board members to consider running for office (Ziegler and Jennings 1974; Cistone 1975). In some sense, then, it appears that potential candidates often find themselves living within an "education context," similar to the type of social environment provided by a neighborhood, workplace, church, or wherever else they might spend a significant amount of time. One notable exception among candidates, however, might be Christian Right issue agenda supporters, of whom only 39 percent report being tapped by current board members to run for office. This finding suggests that these individuals might somehow be less involved with the schools than other types of candidates.

Candidates in Fairfax County were very likely to find encouragement from various people within the education establishment, including teachers, current or previous board members, administrators, and other individuals they knew from their experiences working within the schools. This finding in Fairfax County is expected, in view of the fact that close to half of the candidates had careers that were related to education, including teaching, tutoring, or working within educational administration. In addition, virtually all interviewed candidates in Fairfax County were involved to some extent with their local PTAs or had been asked to serve on special committees under the supervision of the previously appointed school board, experiences that later led directly to their decision to run for school board. For one conservative Christian candidate, her decision to run stemmed in part from her experience serving on the controversial family life education committee, which covers sex education. She recalls, "When the time came around for the elected school board, at that point, parents who agreed with me on the [family life education] committee . . . and [other] people were coming up to me and saying, 'Why don't you run? You've been there, you know what kinds of things need to be done.' I had not thought about it. It was not a burning passion of mine." This candidate's experiences on the family life education committee were not unique. Several of the more liberal candidates also decided to run because of their prior service to this committee, including one Democratic candidate who "got encouragement through [her] work with FLE and by speaking out at school board meetings."

By contrast, candidates in Garrett County typically had less experience with the public schools, although at least half of them did volunteer on behalf of their children. Of the eight candidates interviewed for this study, only one, a teacher, had career experience in education. Five of the candidates had children in the school system at the time they first decided to run for school board, including two Christian Right and three non–Christian Right candidates. Another non–Christian Right candidate had grandchildren attending the schools but was not as actively volunteering in the schools as she had been when her own children were school age. Two of the Christian Right candidates did not have children in the Garrett County public schools when they decided to run for school board. One of these candidates was not a parent at the time he ran for school board, and the other taught his children at home. Less involvement with the schools, either by working within education circles or participating within local PTAs, meant that fewer candidates in Garrett County were encouraged to run by individuals who were part of the education establishment. Just two of the Garrett County candidates said they were encouraged to run for office by individuals affiliated with education, both of whom were Christian Right candidates. The first candidate said she was asked to run for school board by "fellow parents" who had served on the county council of PTAs with her, while the second indicated that he had been "in contact" with two board members (one current, one past) about his decision to become a school board candidate.

Political Parties and Organizations

Turning to political elites, the encouragement of party leaders and representatives from voluntary organizations is less important to the decision of candidates to run for school board compared with the encouragement of school board members. Only 12 percent of both Christian Right and non–Christian

Right candidates indicated that a political party leader encouraged their decision to run for school board. Christian Right group members, supporters, and issues agenda supporters also report low levels of encouragement from party leaders. These figures might be low because most school board elections are nonpartisan—in fact, 92 percent of survey respondents report running in nonpartisan races (data not shown). Political parties have little to gain in local school board elections and, as a result, probably spend more time recruiting like-minded citizens to run for other partisan offices.

Political party also appeared to be a nonfactor in terms of political motivation in Garrett County. Only one candidate there—a conservative Christian—said that it was "at the request of a county commissioner" that he considered running for school board. By contrast, local party officials in Fairfax County were active in recruiting candidates to school board, despite the nonpartisan nature of the contest. Nine of the twenty-four candidates interviewed in Fairfax County stated that the political parties were very encouraging in the initial stages of their decision to run for school board. Moreover, at least fifteen candidates indicated that they were active in local party politics, which suggests that the parties could have played a more indirect part in their decision to become involved in the elections. For instance, some Fairfax school board candidates attended Virginia's nominating conventions (which are held in lieu of primaries), served as precinct captains during other elections, or held local offices within the party. Of these fifteen candidates, five were conservative Christians (all of whom were Republicans). In addition, despite the nonpartisan nature of the elections, both parties endorsed a slate of twelve candidates each, which meant that at some point in the process candidates (or potential candidates) had to become familiar with local party mechanisms. (Chapter 4 discusses in greater detail the involvement of the parties in the campaigns of the candidates.) Of course, the direction of causality here could be an issue—some candidates might have already had an interest in pursuing school board office and decided to become active in the parties to ensure an endorsement or to use the party's political resources. Nonetheless, it is possible that, for some candidates who were not directly encouraged by party leaders to run for school board, their activism within the local parties played an indirect role in their decision to seek school board office.

Because so few races are partisan at the national level, it is not surprising that party officials did not encourage many school board candidacies. More puzzling, however, is the fact that just 9 percent of Christian Right candidates and 10 percent of non–Christian Right candidates indicated that a representative from a voluntary organizations offered encouragement for their candidacies—a finding echoed among the three other types of candidates listed in table 3.3. Political analysts have long known that there is a positive relationship between political participation and membership in voluntary organizations and interest groups (see, for example, Lane 1959 and Verba and Nie 1972). As Rosenstone and Hansen (1994) demonstrate in their study on political partici-pation, membership in an organization causes people to be more frequently targeted by political leaders for mobilization. The survey data demonstrate that school board candidates are indeed joiners. Three of four indicate that they are members of education or political interest groups, while more than half (51 percent) belong to two or more organizations (data not shown).

Why is there so little encouragement offered from representatives of vol-untary organizations when so many candidates belong to these groups? If an interest group representative or member who encourages a candidate is a close friend or acquaintance of that candidate, this number might be understated. A candidate might be encouraged by such an individual but view him or her only as a friend and not in another capacity (i.e., a member of the Christian Coalition). Alternatively, there might be reluctance on the part of candidates to admit that they were encouraged or recruited to run for office by interest groups, despite being a member of such groups. Further, it is impossible to know the extent to which these candidates are involved in the organizations. Some might be active members, even in leadership roles within the groups, whereas the involvement of other members might be limited to paying annual dues. Moreover, the type of organization to which survey respondents belong might restrict their access to encouragement. The American Association of Retired Persons, or AARP, serves as a useful example. Education issues are not the main concern of AARP or of several of the other voluntary organizations to which the survey respondents belong.

Nonetheless, many of the groups to which these survey respondents belong are interested in education and political issues. For example, candidates were most likely to belong to two education organizations: the National School Board Association (33 percent) and PTAs (29 percent). Although only 9–10 percent of candidates report that representatives from interest groups directly encouraged them to run, groups such as the PTA or the NSBA could have influ-enced the decisions of respondents to become candidates in other ways. For instance, interest groups are a good source of information about political and educational issues, issues that could have sparked an interest or desire among potential candidates to think about serving on their local school boards. Further, some of these organizations not only encourage their members to get involved in local politics, but also provide "nuts-and-bolts" information in their literature on the basics of local political activism. The Christian Coalition and Citizens for Excellence in Education, two Christian Right organizations, offer its members access to manuals that explain how to campaign at the precinct level, target voters in certain areas, and hone their campaign messages.

Interest groups (as well as local political parties and public officeholders) potentially influence the decisions of individuals to become school board candidates through indirect mobilization as well, most specifically by working through "social networks." As Rosenstone and Hansen explain: "For politicians, parties, interest groups, and activists, access to social networks reduces the costs of making contact. Leaders need not communicate with every person directly. Instead, leaders contact their associates, associates contact their colleagues, and colleagues contact their friends, family, and co-workers. Through social networks, leaders get the word out, and citizens get the word. Social networks multiply the effect of mobilization: Direct mobilization reverberates through indirect mobilization" (1994, 27–28).

The direct and indirect influence of these groups is a bit speculative. There is no way to link a candidate's decision to run for office specifically to either his or her membership in these groups or his or her contact with other members of these groups (at least regarding the survey data). The direction of causality again might also work in an opposite way. For instance, these individuals might have already made up their minds about becoming candidates and decided to join specific education or political groups to get information that might prove valuable to their campaigns.

Although no Christian Right candidates in Garrett County reported that interest group members encouraged their candidacies, one interest group in particular might have had an indirect hand in their mobilization. All four of the conservative Christians interviewed for this study were at some point involved with the Garrett County chapter of the Christian Coalition, though their level of involvement varied.[1] One of the candidates was largely responsible for founding the Garrett County chapter and served as its first chairman (a seat he resigned after deciding to become a school board candidate in 1994). Though none of these four candidates indicated that fellow members of the Christian Coalition, per se, encouraged him or her to run for office, it is probable that involvement in the organization provided an encouraging atmosphere, because a major goal of the Christian Coalition is to elect like-minded citizens to political offices such as school boards. Attendance at chapter meetings certainly exposed these individuals to this goal. Further, the Christian Coalition's monthly publications and websites often focus on problems within the public schools, perhaps giving their members further impetus to run for school board. For example, one of these candidates said that he ran for school board because he "began to hear more and more from the Christian community about problems in the school system." Involvement in the Christian

Coalition was likely more vital to the decision of two of the conservative Christian candidates, both of whom did not have children in the public schools. The other two candidates had been active in the schools through their children and through the more "traditional" route of PTAs.

Religious Community

Finally, vital parts of any community are religious organizations such as churches, parishes, and synagogues. Like the schools and neighborhoods in which people live and volunteer, churches provide an important social context that shapes the lives of many citizens. Recent studies have found that church life has important ramifications for political life. Gilbert (1993), for example, has demonstrated that an individual's regular discussion of politics with fellow church members—whom Gilbert refers to as "discussion partners"—reinforces and shapes that individual's political behaviors and attitudes. On a more practical level, Verba, Brady, and Schlozman's (1995) work on political participation finds that, for many citizens, being active in their churches (such as through organizing a food collection for the needy) often provides them with the resources necessary to promote civic volunteerism and political activism.

The findings regarding religion in chapter 2 suggest that church life plays a more important role in the social lives of Christian Right candidates, an unremarkable discovery in light of the salience of religion to those individuals who identify with the Christian Right. These significant differences regarding the religious lives of respondents initially carry over into their decision to run for school board in two important ways, as detailed in table 3.3. First, Christian Right candidates are twice as likely to be encouraged by fellow church members to run for school board (27 percent) than are their non–Christian Right counterparts (13 percent), a difference that is statistically significant. More Christian Right group members and supporters also report that fellow church members encouraged their candidacies, compared with Christian Right issue agenda supporters. Second, although far fewer ministers encourage candidates to run for school board than do fellow church members, ministers are still significantly more likely to encourage Christian Right candidates to run for office (7 percent) than non–Christian Right candidates (3 percent).

Multivariate analysis, however, reveals different findings. Table 3.4 shows two logistic regressions. The first model examines the likelihood of fellow church members encouraging candidates to run; the other examines the likelihood of ministers encouraging candidates to run for school board. Both

Table 3.4
Logistic Regressions: Impact of Christian Right Status on Whether Fellow Church Members, Minister Encouraged Decision to Become Candidate

Independent Variables	Model 1 Dependent Variable: Fellow Church Member Encouraged Candidacy		Model 2 Dependent Variable: Minister Encouraged Candidacy	
	Coefficient B (standard error)	Maximum Likelihood Estimate	Coefficient B (standard error)	Maximum Likelihood Estimate
Christian Right Status	.3554 (.2922)	1.427	.3478 (.5526)	1.4159
Church attendance	.8751 (.1624)***	2.399	.8211 (.3324)*	2.2729
Education	.3199 (.1419)*	1.377	.0019 (.2716)	1.0019
Income	−.0248 (.1082)	.9755	−.0170 (.2092)	.9831
Gender	.2906 (.2531)	1.3373	.8876 (.4849)	2.4292
Race	.2827 (.4451)	1.3267	−.5512 (.7061)	.5763
Ideology	.0936 (.0977)	1.0981	.1820 (.1927)	1.1996
First time running	−.2927 (.2397)	.7463	−.1422 (.4647)	.8675
Geographic region:				
South	.5651 (.4313)	1.7597	−3834 (.7229)	.6815
West	.3547 (.4054)	1.4257	−3026 (.6570)	.7389
Midwest	.3292 (.3658)	1.3899	−.9940 (.6532)	.3701
Rural	−.2814 (.4243)	.7547	−.9751 (.6700)	.3772
Suburban	−.4833 (.4707)	.6168	−.8331 (.7599)	.4347

Note: N = 632 (thirty-nine missing cases). Interaction effects for Christian Right status by education, gender, race, and church attendance added to both models were not significant. Model 1: 84.87 percent categorized correctly; −2XLLR = 462; model χ^2, 73; 13 degrees of freedom; $p < .000$; model 2: 96.7 percent categorized correctly; −2XLLR = 161; model χ^2, 23; 13 degrees of freedom; $p < .0382$.
*$p < .05$.
**$p < .01$.
***$p < .001$.

regressions control for some of the same variables found in the previous OLS regressions: education, income, gender, political views, race, church attendance, community type, and region. In addition, a variable that controls for whether it is an individual's first time running for office (1 = yes; 0 = no) is also added, because candidates running for the first time might rely more heavily on outside encouragement than those who are experienced candidates. In both cases, Christian Right status is no longer statistically significant once controls are introduced. Instead, church attendance stands out as the most important factor. The reason is largely self-evident: the more individuals attend church, the better their chances of being asked by a fellow church member or minister.

There is an important difference concerning the role of churches among survey and case study candidates. No candidate in the two counties indicated that a fellow church member or pastor encouraged his or her decision to run for school board, with the exception of one Christian Right candidate in Fairfax County, who said that "a couple of friends from church" said that he "ought to run for school board."[2] This finding is somewhat surprising, in view of the fact that a sizable portion of school board candidates in these elections were conservative Christians, all of whom were members of churches. In addition, at least 75 percent of non–Christian Right candidates in the two counties also belong to churches or synagogues. This finding does not mean, however, that churches played an insignificant role in the decision of these individuals to become candidates. A pastor or a church member may have had a more indirect effect on the decision of some candidates to run for office. For example, one Christian Right candidate noted that he decided to run for school board because he "had begun to hear more and more from the Christian community about problems in the school system." This candidate, a very active participant in his church, also indicated that political events are often discussed in his church. Both his rationale for running for school board and his active level of participation within the church suggest that the church might have provided for him a context in which political participation more generally was encouraged. For some candidates, then, their church life might facilitate an environment that both raises awareness about local issues and offers support for those members who wish to address these issues in the political arena.

Summary

At times it is difficult to determine how an individual's social environment directly affects his or her political behavior. In this study, the survey and case study interviews asked candidates specifically who encouraged them to run for school board, one attempt at measuring how the decision of individuals to become candidates might have been influenced by people with whom they interact socially on a regular basis; however, some evidence from the interviews with school board candidates suggests that political mobilization by friends, neighbors, or colleagues at church might be more indirect. The social settings in which these candidates place themselves—for example, as active church members or as busy volunteers with PTAs—probably provided an atmosphere that facilitated, if not directly encouraged, political participation.[3]

Important differences exist between the candidates in terms of who encouraged them to run for school board. One difference concerns the role of education "elites." The survey results demonstrate that many candidates were encouraged to run for office by either current or retired school board members, which was not the case in Garrett County, where candidates were typically not as active in the schools prior to becoming school board candidates. Candidates in Fairfax County, however, seemed more comfortable and active within the local schools. Many candidates mentioned that teachers or administrators, as well as parents with whom they were active on school committees and within PTAs, asked them to run for office. Returning to the survey data, one notable exception with respect to the importance of the mobilizing efforts of the education establishment can be found among supporters of the Christian Right issue agenda, fewer of whom reported being encouraged by current board members to run for school board, which is less than any other group in table 3.3. In addition, recall that 26 percent of these issue agenda supporters claimed that no one asked them to run, which is higher than any other group. These differences might suggest that Christian Right issue agenda supporters, compared with group members or supporters, are somehow less connected to their local communities. This finding might be related to resources: recall in chapter 2 that Christian Right agenda supporters had relatively lower levels of education and income than individual school board candidates in other classifications. As a significant amount of political science research indicates, participation at all levels of government is positively related to resources such as education.

Turning to political elites, local political party officials significantly influenced the decisions of school board candidates in Fairfax County only. Relatively few candidates in the survey indicated that local party leaders encouraged their decision to run for office (less than 12 percent), and no candidates in Garrett County said that party officials asked them to run for school board. Close to half of all candidates in Fairfax County, however, both Christian Right and non–Christian Right, were encouraged by local party leaders to run for school board. Relatively few candidates in either the surveys or case studies report that local representatives from political or voluntary organizations encouraged their candidacies. As the case in Garrett County details, though, such organizations might have had an indirect hand in encouraging such candidacies. Finally, although fellow church members and ministers appear to encourage the candidacies of school board candidates on a limited level, they do so among individuals who attend church frequently, despite Christian Right status.

Other Factors

There are other factors individuals might consider when deciding to run for office. For example, they might decide to become candidates if they suddenly have more resources, such as additional free time and money, at their disposal. The survey asked respondents about these two specific issues, which, it turns out, are relatively unimportant in their initial decision to become candidates. Just 13 percent of both Christian Right and non–Christian Right candidates said that having more free time influenced their decision to run for school board; similar percentages result for Christian Right members, supporters, and issue agenda supporters (data not shown). Far fewer said that more money or resources mattered. Just 2 percent of both Christian Right and non–Christian Right candidates said it factored into their decision to run for school board. Although a few candidates in both counties were retired, giving them more free time for community-related activities, most worked full time. No candidate in either county mentioned that greater access to resources was an important factor in their decision to run for school board.

More important to the decision of most survey respondents, however, was the availability of open seats (seats in which incumbents declined to seek reelection). The majority of both Christian Right and non–Christian Right candidates said that an opening on the board was important in their initial decision to run for office (71 percent and 69 percent, respectively). Candidates in Fairfax County were faced with a unique situation: every seat on the school board was open, because the elections in 1995 represented the first school board elections held in that county in more than forty years. The election resulted in the filing of 37 candidates for 12 open seats.[4] Many individuals in the county decided to run because they believed that an open election could represent their first real opportunity to serve on the school board. In Garrett County, the availability of open seats was not an issue. Christian Right and non–Christian Right candidates ran for seats that were filled (or ran for reelection in one case) during the 1994 and 1996 elections.

Conclusion

This chapter has explored why people choose to run for school board. More specifically, it has asked whether Christian Right candidates are motivated to run for school board for different reasons than candidates who do not identify with the Christian Right. In many ways, the two types of candidates have common sources of motivation in their quest for school board office. Candidates decide to run because they have children in the public schools and serving on the school board is a good way to give something back to the community. Very few candidates, however, indicated that their decision to run was completely self-motivated. Most were encouraged to run by friends, family members, community leaders, or, perhaps most important, current or past school board members. Finally, relatively few candidates, Christian Right or non–Christian Right, indicated that they were actively encouraged or mobilized to run for school board by political elites, such as interest group representatives or party leaders. A noted exception is the role of party leaders in the Fairfax County elections, which will be discussed in detail in the chapter that follows.

Nonetheless, one major difference in motivation sets Christian Right candidates apart from other candidates. Christian Right candidates are significantly more likely than non–Christian Right candidates to say that applying their "religious or moral beliefs" to school policy was important to their decision to run for office, even after controlling for other factors. Christian Right candidates interviewed in the case studies believed that their decision to run was linked to a specific calling demanded of them by their religious or moral beliefs, as illustrated by the remarks of one conservative Christian, who said Christians "are instructed to be involved."

Religion matters to the decisions of conservative Christians to become school board candidates and helps to differentiate Christian Right candidates from the other candidates. But some effects of religion are not isolated to Christian Right candidates. As the case study interviews reveal, several non–Christian Right candidates also linked their decision to run to their own deeply held religious convictions. These candidates linked their desire to serve on school board with what they considered as a sacred duty and responsibility to serve others, consistent with the social gospel that is often espoused by mainline Protestant and Roman Catholic religious doctrine. In addition, this study finds that regular church attendance—regardless of Christian Right status—is significantly related to whether candidates are encouraged by church members or ministers to run for school board.

Religion alone, however, does not completely explain why most conservative Christians (and certainly non–Christian Right candidates) ran for school board. A decision to participate in politics is multifaceted. Nonetheless, ignoring religion as a motivating factor, as many political scientists do, means missing out on a vital resource that explains the participation of certain individuals.

The next chapter addresses the question of how school board candidates run for school board office, by focusing on which issues candidates stressed in their campaigns, where they campaigned, and how much money they spent. It also takes a closer look at the role that parties and interest groups played in endorsing, consulting, and contributing financially to the campaigns of candidates. The chapter also studies how (or even if) the campaigns of conservative Christians significantly differ from the campaigns of non–Christian Right candidates.

The Campaign Strategies of Christian Right Candidates

There is much speculation, largely brought on by the media and liberal interest groups opposing the Christian Right's political agenda, that Christian Right candidates are running "stealth campaigns" in school board races. This term became popular after a 1992 *Los Angeles Times* interview with Ralph Reed, who at the time was executive director of the Christian Coalition, the largest and most visible Christian Right organization in the country in the 1990s. In the interview, Reed described the type of campaign strategy his group advised Christian Right candidates in local races to follow: "It's like guerrilla warfare. If you reveal your location, all it does is allow your opponent to improve his artillery bearings. It's better to move quietly, with stealth, undercover of night. You've got two choices: You can wear [camouflage uniforms] and shimmy along on your belly, or you can put on a red coat and stand up for everyone to see. It comes down to whether you want to be the British army in the Revolutionary War or the Viet Cong. History tells us which tactic was more effective" (Horstman 1992, A1).[1]

After the article appeared, critics of the Christian Right began to accuse conservative Christian candidates with ties to Christian Right groups of having been coached to hide or downplay such connections to the general public while campaigning on more moderate platforms (Jones 1993; Galst 1994; Zingarelli 1994; Reich 1995; Sinclair 1996; Detwiler 1999). Moreover, critics claimed that these stealth candidates quietly organized sympathetic voters in conservative churches. Local elections such as school board elections are often marked by low voter turnout, particularly when they do not coincide with federal or state elections (Townley, Sweeney, and Schnieder 1994). Therefore, carefully targeted campaigning in churches can lead to success in such races.

Reed's stealth strategy seemed to describe several school board elections that took place in the early 1990s in states as diverse as California, Texas, Florida, and New Hampshire (Arocha 1993; Brooks 1995; Wald 1995; Ammis 1996). In Vista, California, conservative Christian candidates were elected to the local school board after they gave little indication of their conservative religious views while campaigning. Once elected as a majority in 1992, they voted to include discussions of creationism (and scientific evidence that disputes the theory of evolution) in history and language arts classes (Granberry 1996). The board majority also turned down $650,000 in government funds for a school breakfast program and school-based social services because they believed that such services interfered with business that should be handled by the family. Further, the board voted to replace the school district's sex education curriculum with an abstinence-only sex education curriculum, a move that was repeated by the Christian Right school board majorities in Merrimack, New Hampshire; Plano, Texas; and Lake County, Florida, among several others.

The controversial elections that resulted in these conservative Christian majority school boards have led anti–Christian Right organizations to label virtually all school board campaigns run by conservative Christians as stealth. Further, the efforts of liberal interest groups to publicize this "phenomenon" has been aided, in part, by the news media's desire to write about controversial and noteworthy issues. Although a focus on stealth campaigns might help sell newspapers, how accurately does it describe how most conservative Christians run for school board? Are stealth campaigns widespread among Christian Right candidates, or is this description of the campaign style of conservative Christian candidates misleading? If stealth campaign strategies are widespread among conservative Christians, the integrity of the election process is compromised.

To determine how Christian Right candidates campaign, and whether they use stealth campaign techniques, this chapter addresses different aspects of their campaigns and compares them with the campaigns of their non–Christian Right counterparts. First, this chapter explores the types of issues that conservative Christians emphasize in their campaigns. Are Christian Right candidates likely to campaign on those issues that are near and dear to the heart of the Christian Right movement, speaking in a prophetic voice calling for radical change, or are they more likely to stress the same issues as non–Christian Right school board candidates? Second, this chapter explores the mechanics behind the campaign: finance, volunteers, and campaign sites. How much do Christian Right candidates spend on their campaigns, and from whom do they receive campaign donations? How many volunteers do Christian Right candidates recruit, and from where do they recruit them? Where do Christian Right candidates campaign? Are they likely to campaign in churches and other religious sites, as the stealth theory would predict, or do they campaign in the same sorts of places that non–Christian Right school board candidates do? Finally, the chapter examines the role of Christian Right interest groups and political parties in the campaigns of conservative Christians by asking candidates whether they received campaign donations, endorsements, or advice from such groups.

Before turning to the data, a caveat is in order. A surprisingly large percentage of candidates who ran unopposed—27 percent ($N = 180$)—returned surveys for this study. In chapter 3, all candidates ($N = 671$), regardless of whether they faced opposition, were included in the data analysis. Although analyzing the motivations for running for school board—even in uncontested seats—is appropriate, examining the campaign strategies of unopposed candidates makes little sense if they likely did not have to wage any sort of campaign. Therefore, in the analysis that follows, I focus on only those individuals ($N = 491$) who faced competition in their bids to be elected to school board.

Issue Positions

Exploring the types of issues that Christian Right school board candidates stress in their campaigns is important for two reasons. First, doing so can help shed light on whether they use stealth strategies during their elections. On the one hand, if most conservative Christians indicate a willingness to openly campaign on issues that matter most to the Christian Right movement—such as sex education, vouchers, or outcomes-based education—these candidates are not hiding their ideological philosophy in a stealth manner while campaigning. On the other hand, if Christian Right candidates choose not to stress such controversial issues in their campaigns for school board, the possibility exists that they are using stealth techniques. It is important to stress that such a finding would only indicate a *possibility* of stealth campaigning. Christian Right candidates might be running on less controversial issues because they sincerely believe that such issues are the most important ones facing their school districts.

The second reason it is important to look at the issues that Christian Right candidates stress in their school board campaigns is to determine whether their choice of such issues somehow depends on the suggestions or guidance of interest groups or political parties. Although the survey data enable the study to get at this aspect only indirectly, the case studies better demonstrate the linkages between parties, interest groups, and issue positions.

Table 4.1 shows the percentage of candidates from the survey who stress each of eleven different issues in their campaigns. These issues include major concerns of Christian Right organizations, such as sex education, vouchers, outcomes-based education, academic standards, and discipline issues. As in chapter 3, the data are broken down into five categories. Statistical analyses were run comparing the data in the first two columns—Christian Right and non–Christian Right candidates. Recall that Christian Right candidates here

Table 4.1
Issues Stressed in Campaigns

Issue	Christian Right Candidate (%)	Non–Christian Right Candidate (%)	Christian Right Group Member (%)	Christian Right Group Supporter (%)	Christian Right Issue Agenda Supporter (%)
Tax/revenue	50	41	55	46	42
Technology	33**	50	36	51	40
Test scores/ academics	68*	56	70	66	72
Sex education	13*	7	15	10	13
Crime, drugs, violence	21	21	27	23	22
School construction, repair	29*	41	46	33	40
Vouchers	8	5	0	8	7
Privatization	4	3	0	4	3
Outcomes-based education	14	9	12	15	7
Discipline	38*	30	36	33	42
Character education	29*	18	33	21	28

Note: $N = 491$. Difference of proportions tests performed between variables in first two columns only.
*$p < .05$.
**$p < .01$.
***$p < .001$.

refer to members of Christian Right organizations as well as supporters of the movement who also share a majority of the movement's education issue positions. In addition, data are reported for Christian Right group members alone, Christian Right group supporters alone, and individuals who are neither members nor supporters of Christian Right organizations but who share a majority of the same issue positions as the movement.

The data show that conservative Christians run on more conservative campaign issues than do non–Christian Right candidates. Most, however, do not stress the issues that are most controversial, what some might call prophetic, in that they require a fundamental policy change. Although Christian Right organizations such as the Christian Coalition or the Family Research Council routinely emphasize sex education, for example, relatively few Christian Right candidates (13 percent) stress sex education issues in their campaigns, although they are significantly more likely to do so than non–Christian Right candidates (7 percent). Even fewer Christian Right candidates (8 percent) are likely to run on a platform that emphasizes vouchers, compared with just 5 percent of non–Christian Right candidates (a difference that is not significant). Christian Right candidates are more likely than non–Christian Right candidates to bring up outcomes-based education when they campaign (14 percent to 9 percent), although the difference is not significant.

Instead, Christian Right candidates are more likely to emphasize in their campaigns generally conservative issues that are less controversial and have a broader appeal to groups other than the Christian Right. For example, tax and revenue issues are popular with both types of school board candidates: 50 percent and 41 percent of Christian Right and non–Christian Right candidates stress tax issues in their campaign platforms (a difference that just barely misses statistical significance: $p < .067$). Also fairly popular between both types of candidates are discipline issues, followed by character education; however, the most popular campaign issue for both candidates involves academics such as concerns about raising test scores. The survey finds significant differences regarding these broader conservative issues. Christian Right school board candidates (68 percent) are significantly more likely than non–Christian Right candidates (56 percent) to run on academic issues, as well as discipline and character education. Meanwhile, non–Christian Right candidates are significantly more likely than conservative Christian candidates to campaign on both technology issues and school construction and repair—issues that can be construed as more "liberal" than other issues if one assumes that they involve increased spending. Very few candidates are likely to mention privatizing food, bus, and other services as important to their campaign platform.

Turning to the results in the last three columns, there is relatively little to distinguish Christian Right group members, Christian Right group supporters, and Christian Right issue agenda supporters from either themselves or the Christian Right candidates coded in the first column. For example, although Christian Right group members are the most likely of any of the groups in table 4.1 to stress sex education as an issue in the campaign—a conservative issue—they are also the most likely to stress school construction and repair—one of the more liberal issues listed. Overall, the candidates in these last three columns share more similarities with the Christian Right candidates in column one than the non–Christian Right candidates when it comes to issues that they stress in their campaigns.

Though the survey demonstrates that, generally speaking, Christian Right candidates run on more conservative issue positions than do non–Christian Right candidates, these conservative Christian candidates shy away from the more controversial subjects identified with the Christian Right movement. The implications of these findings in terms of the stealth hypothesis, however, are unclear. There is no way to determine the exact motivations behind why these candidates choose to stress the issues that they do. Taken at face value, however, Christian Right candidates illustrate their conservative nature by stressing more conservative issues than do non–Christian Right candidates—but not those controversial issues that perhaps have a limited appeal to the general public.

One alternative way to examine how or if the stealth hypothesis is at work here is to consider candidates from the survey who are members of Christian Right organizations such as the Christian Coalition but who do not claim to support a majority of issue positions that the movement does. Suppose that these individuals—fifteen in all—were true stealth candidates according to the criteria laid out by critics of the movement. In other words, let us assume that they decided to run on a more moderate platform and to indicate to potential voters that they did not share a majority of issue positions with the movement. One could also assume that, on receiving this study's survey in the mail, these candidates decided to maintain their moderate issues positions with respect to the battery of survey questions that asked about their attitudes on vouchers, sex education, and so forth, even though they might not actually hold such issue positions. Although it is impossible to determine the exact motives of survey respondents in any survey, comparing these *potential* stealth candidates with other Christian Right candidates might reveal some interesting findings. Table 4.2 compares how these stealth candidates match up to the regular Christian Right candidates with respect to the issues they stress in the campaigns. (Bear in

Table 4.2
Stealth Candidates on Issues Stressed in Campaigns

Issue	Christian Right Candidates (%)	Stealth Candidates (%)
Tax/revenue	50	60
Technology	33	40
Test scores/academics	68	73
Sex education	13	13
Crime, drugs, violence	21	20
School construction, repair	29	47
Vouchers	8	—[a]
Privatization	4	—[a]
Outcomes-based education	14	13
Discipline	38	33
Character education	29	33

Note: Christian Right candidates, $N = 127$; stealth candidates, $N = 15$.
[a]No response.

mind that these fifteen individuals have been coded to be part of the movement in the original category.) With respect to the stealth hypotheses and this data, however, the findings are mixed. On the one hand, the stealth candidates here are more likely than Christian Right candidates to stress noncontroversial conservative issues (as the theory would predict): tax/revenue, test scores, and character education, with the exception of discipline. On the other hand, roughly the same percentage of stealth candidates emphasize the more controversial issues such as sex education and outcomes-based education as do Christian Right candidates, though they do not even touch on vouchers. Remember that the data here are speculative, based on both a small number of respondents ($N = 15$) and the assumption that these so-called potential stealth candidates were willing to mislead the study by indicating false issue preferences—perhaps a weak assumption at best. Also, it might be the case that these individuals decide to stress these issues because they truly support them and are simply more moderate than candidates who support the movement's agenda.

Similar to the survey results, the case studies reveal that Christian Right candidates offered voters conservative campaign platforms regarding a variety of education issues. The differences between conservative Christian candidates and their more liberal opponents in both counties, however, are far more pronounced than are differences between Christian Right and non–Christian Right candidates in the survey. Christian Right candidates, particularly in

Garrett County, showed a greater willingness to include religious themes in their campaign platforms.

There are several reasons to speculate why different findings emerge from the two methods. First, part of the reason for the differences might have to do with the nature of case study research compared with survey research. Interview subjects in both counties were given the chance to describe in detail their campaign platforms, whereas survey respondents were limited to close-ended questions (although they were given a brief amount of space to write in other issues, an option that few candidates chose). This fuller description might have revealed more information about their campaign platforms, allowing for nuances and subject areas to be revealed and explored. Second, the differences regarding the findings might also reflect the unique characteristics of the counties in which the case study school board candidates campaigned. For example, a campaign with religious themes might have played well in Garrett County because of the conservative nature of the area. Finally, as will be discussed shortly, the political parties played an important role in the school board campaigns in Fairfax County, and Christian Right and non–Christian candidates who were backed by the Republicans or the Democrats used unified campaign platforms that were specifically designed to differentiate the party-endorsed candidates from one another.

Christian Right candidates in Garrett County had campaign platforms that reflected their conservative and religious beliefs. For instance, one conservative Christian candidate in Garrett County described his campaign message as "maintaining Christian representation, socially, as well as fiscally"—a theme that was echoed in his campaign literature and advertisements, which touted him as a "conservative voice for fiscal responsibilities and family values." The phrase "family values," long popular with the Christian Right, was used by most conservative Christian candidates in Garrett County during their campaigns. Another popular campaign issue among Christian Right candidates was the "back-to-basics" theme, as illustrated by this conservative Christian candidate, who described his stump speech in the following way: "I think we need to go back to basics in education. We need to protect our community schools. I'm opposed to consolidation. Traditional family values should be reinforced in the public schools." This candidate indicated that these types of phrases were those that he regularly used while he campaigned.

Three conservative Christian candidates running in the 1994 Garrett County elections (all of whom were elected to the school board) joined forces by running a series of campaign ads in the county's weekly paper, the *Republican*. Several of the ads were paid for by other groups of citizens, including one that contained the endorsement of more than ninety Garrett County citizens, including eleven clergy. This ad urged citizens to vote for the three candidates and linked its endorsement to religious themes. It read:

> Our children are our most precious resource. But much more, they are a gift from God to be nurtured into the future. Deciding on leaders to entrust them to for their education is a decision that calls for prayer, wisdom, and discernment. Experience is not always the most important factor to consider. Rather, do the candidates' lives reflect the values, integrity, faith, and character that are needed to make wise decisions regarding your children and as your elected representative [sic]? Letters of endorsement come cheap. We believe that the best endorsement comes from families who want to see the best for the future of our children.

The advertisement ended with a Bible verse from the book of Proverbs: "Know that wisdom is thus for your soul; if you find it, then there will be a future, and your hope will not be cut off."[2]

Non–Christian Right candidates in Garrett County did not use religious themes in their campaign platforms. In 1996, one of these candidates made a controversial busing issue, involving the transport of Garrett County children living near the edge of the county to public schools in the next county, the major theme of her campaign. She and most of the other non–Christian Right candidates (in both the 1994 and 1996 elections) routinely stressed the importance of maintaining the current excellence of the county's schools. Implicit in their platforms was the idea that high academic standards would be easier to maintain if fewer Christian Right candidates were elected to the board. For instance, one candidate who ran in 1996 had "watched with dismay" for two years the effects of having a conservative Christian majority run the school board. She routinely emphasized her displeasure with the management style of the board during her campaign and asked voters to question the commitment of one of these members, a conservative Christian whose children were taught at home. As she recalled, "[I stressed] that we have a good school system. We don't need micromanagement like some of the [current] school board members. Also, board members who homeschool? Don't these members have any faith or value in the system they are overseeing? Support the teachers—they are professionals. There is nothing wrong with the school system." This statement illustrates that the job performance of Christian Right candidates elected to the board in 1994 directly influenced the types of issues that some non–Christian Right candidates chose to highlight in their campaigns for school board in 1996.

Other non–Christian Right candidates tried to counter the Christian Right's "family values" platform by offering their own definition of "values" in their campaigns, including this candidate who ran in Garrett County in 1996 and said,

"We hit on the issues of values—hard work, responsibility, initiative—and things like that which I truly believe in. . . . I tried to frame the argument of values in my own terms as opposed to homosexuality or some of the other buzz words that I didn't really think applied to education." This newer take on values, however, was not successful for this candidate or most of the other non–Christian Right candidates who ran in 1994 and 1996. Conservative Christian candidates won four of the five seats on the school board during elections that were held in those two years.

In Fairfax County, clear differences emerged early among the candidates running for school board in 1995, in large part because of the county Republican and Democratic Parties, which chose to endorse candidates despite the nonpartisan nature of the elections. The Republican-backed candidates, more than half of whom were conservative Christians, chose to run on a united back-to-basics theme, stressing common issues of academic achievement, phonics-based reading instruction, strict discipline in the classroom, and "responsible" budgeting. As one conservative Christian noted, "Basics, fundamental, core curriculum . . . that was where we needed to place focus. I wanted to see high academic achievement. The other issue that was of great concern to me was law and order in the classroom. I felt very strongly that we need to have safe schools and classrooms . . . so, it was achievement, safety, and accountability. In the area of finances, I felt that too many times we start programs that were never evaluated, programs that weren't producing, and they still continued on. In Fairfax County, a program never dies. It just continues on!" This candidate's statement accurately describes the three "B's" discussed by other candidates backed by the Republicans: the basics of education, the budget, and behavior of students.

The endorsement of the Republican Party largely dictated the choice that many Christian Right candidates had with regard to the types of issues they could stress in their campaign platforms. Hence, conservative Christians who were backed by the GOP towed the party line by focusing mainly on broad conservative themes rather than more controversial elements such as sex education or vouchers. Despite this major focus on back-to-basics issues, several Republican-endorsed, Christian Right candidates campaigned on other issues that more deeply resonate with the Christian Right, to mixed success. One successful Christian Right candidate told voters in her campaign flyers that she "has watched the school system usurp our parental rights" in a way that "affect[s] the health and moral well-being of our students." Another successful conservative Christian candidate passed out a campaign piece that spoke against the National Education Association, which he believed "sold pretty well" in his district. The title ran "Stop the Union Drive to Dominate Your School Board!" Other Christian Right candidates backed by the Republican Party, however, found less success when their campaigns strayed from the party line, including this candidate who tried to talk to voters about outcomes-based education and said, "We have a big [school] system in Fairfax County. There are a lot of different things happening. There are outcomes-based education principles being used in some schools here in Fairfax County. It is too ridiculous! . . . There was an article in the *Washington Post* recently about how some teachers want to teach math. There are four birds in a tree, and three fly away, so how do you feel about that? That is the outcomes-based realm, where the interest isn't so much the math as it is the attitudes." This candidate, who lost his race, acknowledged that the outcomes-based education issue "didn't catch on" as he would have liked.

Those Christian Right candidates who were not endorsed by the Republicans were free to run on the platforms of their own choosing. Two Christian Right candidates, one of whom was nonaligned, the other a Libertarian, ran on more extreme platforms that challenged the current existence of public schools. One candidate chose to make vouchers the highlight of her campaign. The other candidate, who was brought into the race because of his concern about home-schoolers, routinely asked voters, "Do we really need the government to do this? I would apply this question to all sorts of issues, like broad ones (do we need a public school system?) to smaller ones (political classes in the classrooms that make students "volunteer" to work on election day). For example, one for-profit corporation, Landmark Education, does a good job of educating people. I just think that there are other alternatives people should look at before paying taxpayer's money." Christian Right candidates without official Republican Party support had the freedom to make issues that deeply resonate with the Christian Right, such as vouchers or homeschooling, the major focus of their campaigns. The only conservative Christians to be elected to school board, however, were those whose platform choices were largely dictated by the endorsement of the Republican Party in Fairfax County.

Like the Republican-backed candidates, the Democratic-endorsed candidates also ran on a unified platform described by one successful candidate as "fighting for the future." Designed to counter the back-to-basics theme used by the Republicans, Democratic candidates decided to impart to voters the idea that radical changes in Fairfax County were not necessary. One Democratic candidate described the platform this way: "It was really a voice of reason—maintaining the integrity of the school system, building on what we had, what we do have. I went after it from the perspective that Fairfax County is one of the best school systems in the country. There are issues that need to be addressed but without a doubt it is one of the best, and you build on that. That it is not a matter of tearing down what we have but building up what we have." This candidate indicated that he also stressed the need for greater technology in the school system, a theme that was also promoted by several other Democratic Party–endorsed candidates.

Most candidates endorsed by the Democratic Party chose to make the involvement of the Christian Right in the Fairfax school board elections a major part of their platforms by portraying their opponents as extreme with close ties to the national movement. Perhaps the most effective strategy used by Democratic-endorsed candidates was to share with the press the results of a candidate survey distributed by the Fairfax chapter of the American Family Association. As one successful Democratic candidate recalled:

> We were getting questionnaires from far right groups. We knew that Fairfax County was a major target and money was coming into the county. I kept a thick file of things that turned on a red light, and obviously, we were a major target. . . . [W]hen we finally got the American Family Association's questionnaire, which, for better or worse, the local AFA people were not as slick as the [local] Christian Coalition (their questionnaire was good). As soon as we were able to get the results of it, we [the Democrats] felt that we had to let the public know that these were not just a group of fiscally conservative Republicans. These people were further to the right than Ralph Reed!

The *Washington Post* was the first newspaper to break the story about the American Family Association questionnaire results three weeks before the elections. The focus of the article, which made the front page of the paper, was on creationism, drawn from a question from the survey that asked school board candidates if they would "support the teaching of both the creation and evolution theories of origin."

The *Post* article and subsequent pieces in the local Fairfax papers had an immediate impact on the school board race by affecting the primary issues that Democratic school board candidates chose to stress in their campaigns. Democratic-backed candidates rushed to mail pieces to voters that illustrated the issue differences between them and their conservative Christian opponents. One candidate mailed a flyer that urged voters in his district to "find the moderate" by comparing his stands on issues such as creationism and sex education with those of his Christian Right opponent. Another Democrat distributed a campaign piece containing a dramatic photograph of several parents with their hands tied and tape over their mouths with the message "Don't lose your voice when it comes to your child's education." Inside the flyer, she described her opponent as a "radical, right-wing conservative with a purely political agenda and no educational experience" and pointed out differences that the candidates had with regard to issues such as sex education, Goals 2000, and the proper role of guidance counselors in the public schools.

About two weeks prior to the election, the Fairfax County Democratic Party decided to mail its own campaign flyer to further illustrate what it considered to be radical issue positions held by Republican candidates on creationism, sex education, academic standards, and support for vouchers. The campaign piece charged that these candidates were "supported by the ultra-conservative Christian Coalition, American Family Association, and Concerned Women for America" and that they were running "stealth campaigns." This piece, according to one Democratic candidate, was targeted at Republican women in Fairfax County, "the soccer Moms," whom Democrats believed were the swing voters in the county.

Both the Democratic Party's emphasis on Christian Right issues and the media's coverage of these issues (particularly creationism) largely had the effect of distinguishing the candidates in a crowded field of thirty-five individuals running for school board. In the words of one successful Democratic candidate, the creationism issue became a "litmus test," and if "you were against it, you were somehow a good candidate." Not all Democratic candidates chose to play up creationism or the "Christian Right angle." Some placed greater emphasis on other education issues such as the county's English as a second language program and similar multicultural issues. Nevertheless, most Democratic candidates believed that their focus on the role of the Christian Right ultimately helped to elect eight Democrats to the twelve-member board.

Christian Right candidates in both counties ran for school board using more conservative platforms than their non–Christian Right opponents. Their choice of platforms was largely dictated by environmental factors. In Garrett County, conservative Christian candidates' emphasis on both broad conservative issues and "profamily" issues that were geared toward the Christian Right community resonated with many voters in this conservative county—a fact that prompted one conservative Christian candidate to indicate in an interview for this study, "There are no stealth candidates in Garrett County!" Meanwhile, in Fairfax County the involvement of the political parties shaped the political platforms of most conservative Christian candidates. Despite their emphasis on broader conservative issues such as academic excellence, school safety, and discipline, the views of Christian Right candidates on controversial issues such as creationism became a major issue in the elections, in large part because of the efforts of the Democrats. The Democrat-endorsed candidates and the Democratic Party chose to make these controversial elements a major focus of their campaigns in the weeks leading up to the election. Fairly or not, Democratic candidates in Fairfax chose to portray conservative Christian candidates as running stealth campaigns who attempted to downplay their attitudes about creationism.

Christian Right candidates in the survey more closely resemble the conservative Christian candidates in Fairfax County than in Garrett County. The conservative Christians in the survey tend to stress more mainstream conservative issues in their campaigns that have broader appeal, such as academic reform. In addition, these Christian Right candidates are less likely than non–Christian Right candidates to stress issues involving greater amounts of spending such as more technology in the classroom or school construction and repair.

Mechanics of the Campaign: Finance, Volunteers, and Locations

This study finds that Christian Right candidates are significantly more likely than non–Christian Right candidates to stress conservative issues in their campaigns. What about other aspects of the school board campaign? This section examines the "mechanics" behind school board campaigns and the differences between the two types of candidates regarding these measures. More specifically, this section explores the amount of money candidates spend on their campaigns as well its sources. It also looks at the number of volunteers candidates recruit as well as where they tend to recruit them. Finally, it examines where candidates choose to campaign.

Campaign Finance

How much do school board candidates spend on their campaigns? Table 4.3 gives financial information about candidates' school board campaigns nationwide, which shows that spending on school board campaigns is very low: 77 percent of Christian Right candidates and 81 percent of non–Christian Right candidates spend less than $1,000 on their races. Most of this spending comes from either the candidates themselves or from family members. Relatively few candidates receive contributions from either political groups or community organizations. Church groups typically do not make contributions to school board campaigns—only 2 percent of Christian Right candidates reported receiving a contribution from a church group or religiously affiliated organization.[3] Examining the other three categories of Christian Right status shows similar findings—no group stands out in terms of how much they spend or where they draw their money. Similar to the first two categories, these individuals spend little on their campaigns and typically finance the campaign themselves or through family donations.

Table 4.3
Cost of Race, Source of Funding

Financial Information	Christian Right Candidate (%)	Non–Christian Right Candidate (%)	Christian Right Group Member (%)	Christian Right Group Supporter (%)	Christian Right Issue Agenda Supporter (%)
Cost:					
<$1,000	77	81	76	82	88
$1,000–$5000	21	17	17	12	10
$5,001–$10,000	2	2	—[a]	2	—[a]
$10,000–$20,000	—[a]	1	—[a]	—[a]	—[a]
Financial sources:					
Family, self	71	72	67	74	73
Supporters	40	37	39	38	37
Advocacy, political group	7	10	9	8	3
Community, voluntary group	6	5	12	3	2
Church group	2	1	1	2	2

Note: N = 491. Differences between Christian Right and non–Christian Right candidates are not significant regarding campaign spending and source of campaign funds.
[a]No response.

In Garrett County, candidate spending on school board races closely resembles the survey findings. Most candidates in the 1994 and 1996 elections spent less than $1,000 on their races. One, a successful candidate in 1996 who was not part of the Christian Right, was an exception: he spent close to $8,000 on his campaign. By and large, these candidates financed their campaigns through their own means or from donations from friends. Few reported receiving donations from political interest groups, though one moderate candidate did receive financial assistance from a teachers union. Christian Right candidates did not report receiving funds from church groups or Christian Right organizations, which resembles the findings from the survey.[4] Again, this finding is not surprising in light of the fact that many such groups are not eligible to contribute money to candidates, because of their tax-exempt status as 501(c)(3) organizations.[5]

Campaign finance in Fairfax County was a different story, as thirty-five school board candidates competed for the attention of voters in a county with more than 800,000 residents. Spending on school board races ranged from $105 to more than $45,000 (Clevenger 1995). The lowest amount that a successful candidate spent on his or her campaign, however, was $8,500. On average, Christian Right candidates spent $16,000, the same amount as non–Christian Right candidates (data not shown).

The source of campaign revenue for both Christian Right and non–Christian Right candidates in Fairfax County differed little. None of the candidates reported receiving financial contributions from church groups, and all but two got money from their families. All reported receiving donations from their friends, whereas the majority of candidates held fundraisers such as coffees or ice cream socials. Some candidates sent mailings targeted to sympathetic groups of voters to appeal for funds, including one Christian Right candidate who used the mailing list of the Fairfax County chapter of the American Family Association. Unlike survey respondents or candidates in Garrett County, most candidates in Fairfax County received campaign funds from interest groups, particularly groups that were connected to education, such as the Fairfax Education Association, which gave funds to several Democratic-endorsed candidates.[6]

Volunteers

Most campaigns rely on the services of volunteers to assist them. The number of individuals who served as volunteers for school board candidates in the survey ranges from one to more than a hundred. The mean number of volunteers for Christian Right candidates was 7.9, which was slightly (but not significantly) higher than the mean number of volunteers for non–Christian Right candidates, which was 7.1 (data not shown). Table 4.4 shows where candidates were likely to recruit these volunteers.

Most volunteers were family members or friends of the candidates. Both Christian Right and non–Christian Right candidates (32 percent and 25 percent, respectively) indicated that, rather than recruiting all of their volunteers, individuals sometimes contacted them to work on their behalf.

The only significant difference between Christian Right and non–Christian Right candidates regarding volunteer recruitment concerns recruiting at church: Christian Right candidates were twice as likely as non–Christian Right candidates to recruit volunteers from their churches. Such a finding could lend some support to the stealth hypothesis—it is one case in which Christian Right candidates rely more heavily on their church contacts than do non–Christian Right candidates. Relatively speaking, however, few Christian Right candidates (14 percent) used churches as recruitment sites for campaign

Table 4.4
Source of Volunteers

Source	Christian Right Candidate (%)	Non–Christian Right Candidate (%)	Christian Right Group Member (%)	Christian Right Group Supporter (%)	Christian Right Issue Agenda Supporter (%)
Family, friends	45	51	49	53	47
Business	13	14	12	17	17
Community	26	19	30	25	7
Church	15***	7	18	15	5
Contacted me	32	25	30	32	20

Note: $N = 491$. Difference of proportions tests performed between variables in first two columns only.
*$p < .05$.
**$p < .01$.
***$p < .001$.

volunteers. One reason for such a low percentage might be that their friends or family members could also be fellow church members, but instead of recognizing them as such, these candidates put them in the category of friends and family. The differences among the three other categories in the table offer some interesting findings, particularly with respect to the church category. Whereas close to one in five Christian Right group members recruited campaign volunteers from their churches, only 5 percent of Christian Right issue agenda supporters did so. Of all five categories, Christian Right group members were the most likely to recruit volunteers from the community, which could indicate that their involvement in an interest group might lead them to more opportunities for recruitment more generally.

Similar to the survey findings, the most popular source of campaign volunteers in Garrett County were family and friends. Wives or husbands of candidates often served as campaign treasurers or managers. In addition, parents with children in the schools (such as fellow PTA members) were often tapped to be a part of these campaigns. A similar situation existed in Fairfax County, but on a larger scale. Some candidates had dozens of volunteers working for them beyond members of their own families. Most were acquaintances or friends made through service to the public schools, such as an at-large Christian Right candidate who first made a name for herself by serving on a sex education (or "family life education") committee in the Fairfax County public schools. She recalled, "Most [volunteers] were friends I had come to know

through the Family Life Education committee. I had a core group of people, I
kept their names and addresses, and I let them know what they could do. I
found that they were very active campaigners. It was just moms and dads and
teenagers who would come together and do literature drops." This candidate
indicated that Republican Party members also helped with her campaign,
although somewhat later in the process. Her experience was not unique in
Fairfax County. Most of the candidates who were endorsed by the parties used
the parties as a source of volunteers. In addition, several candidates in Fairfax
County asked party activists (or their spouses, in some cases) to take leadership
positions in their campaigns such as campaign managers or treasurers; however, few candidates in Fairfax County, Christian Right or non–Christian
Right, recruited volunteers from their churches or synagogues.

Campaign Sites

Turning to campaign locations, table 4.5 lists places where school board candidates in the survey were likely to campaign. There are no significant differences
between the two types of candidates regarding where they chose to campaign
for school board. Campaigning door-to-door was the most popular site for
Christian Right candidates (46 percent), followed by attending candidate rallies (40 percent). Door-to-door campaigning was also important to the cam-

Table 4.5
Campaign Sites

Campaign Site	Christian Right Candidate (%)	Non–Christian Right Candidate (%)	Christian Right Group Member (%)	Christian Right Group Supporter (%)	Christian Right Issue Agenda Supporter (%)
Shopping malls	12	7	6	11	7
Rallies	40	51	36	47	48
Churches	10	7	12	9	7
Door-to-door	46	48	27	58	53
Community meetings	35	30	42	34	25
Coffees	17	20	24	20	17
Mailings	36	31	33	33	23

Note: N = 491. Differences between Christian Right and non–Christian Right candidates are not significant regarding choice of campaign sites, although campaigning at rallies comes close ($p < .051$).

paigns of non–Christian Right candidates (48 percent); a similar amount of non–Christian Right candidates were also likely to campaign at campaign rallies (51 percent). Christian Right candidates, in fact, were significantly less likely than non–Christian Right candidates to campaign in rallies ($p < .051$). More telling, perhaps, is that Christian Right group members—of all five groups in table 4.5—were the least likely to campaign in public rallies. Recall that one aspect of the stealth theory is that Christian Right candidates avoid mainstream political forums and instead focus their campaigning in churches and more sympathetic outlets. This finding with respect to candidate rallies, however, is offset by the fact that Christian Right group members were the most likely of the five groups to campaign in "community meetings," which implies a willingness to campaign in public and out in the open.

Few Christian Right candidates—only 10 percent—campaigned in church settings. Only 7 percent of non–Christian Right candidates campaigned in churches, a statistically insignificant difference. This finding runs counter to the stealth hypothesis, which predicts that conservative Christian candidates primarily use churches to gain support among sympathetic voters. Christian Right issue agenda supporters and Christian Right group supporters were also very unlikely to campaign in churches (7 percent and 9 percent, respectively), although Christian Right group members report campaigning in churches at a higher percent—12 percent—than any other group in table 4.5.

Returning to the stealth category of Christian Right candidates discussed earlier in this chapter, an interesting finding emerges with respect to campaigning in church as reported in table 4.6. Potential stealth candidates—those in the survey who are members of Christian Right groups but do not admit to sharing a majority of issue agenda positions—were much more likely to

Table 4.6
Campaign Sites for Stealth Candidates

Campaign Site	Christian Right Candidate (%)	Stealth Candidate (%)
Shopping malls	12	13
Rallies	40	47
Churches	10	27
Door-to-door	46	33
Community meetings	35	67
Coffees	17	33
Mailings	36	47

Note: Christian Right candidates, $N = 127$; stealth candidate, $N = 15$.

campaign in churches (27 percent) than Christian Right candidates (10 percent). In light of the fact that 20 percent of Christian Right candidates include these stealth candidates, the 10 percent figure is even more inflated. In other words—based on a weak assumption—we find that these potential stealth candidates were far more likely to campaign in churches than other conservative Christian candidates; however, the vast majority of so-called potential stealth candidates—73 percent, or eleven individuals—report that they did not campaign in churches, which does not give the stealth hypothesis much more support. But again, these data are merely speculative and based on the assumption that these fifteen candidates were intent on disguising their true issue positions in their survey responses (but not their campaign locations).

Where and how Christian Right and non–Christian Right candidates campaigned in Garrett County bear many similarities to candidates in the survey. The most popular form of campaigning for candidates in Garrett County was going door to door and handing out campaign literature. Several candidates in Garrett County, Christian Right and non–Christian Right, also relied on radio and print ads in the local newspaper. All of the candidates campaigned at the county fair and attended community and voter forums when they were held (which, according to the candidates, was not very often). One non–Christian Right candidate called registered voters from a list provided to him by the county's teacher's union to "introduce himself."

One point of divergence between Christian Right candidates in the survey and Christian Right candidates in Garrett County, however, concerned the role of churches. More than half (three of five) of the Christian Right candidates in Garrett County reported campaigning to some extent at sympathetic churches as part of their campaign strategy, which highlights an important connection between these conservative Christians and the conservative Christian churches that dot the landscape of the rural county. One Christian Right candidate, however, does not believe his use of churches as a campaign site constituted a "stealth candidacy" because he went to a "different church just about every Sunday, just to let them know [he] was running."

At least one non–Christian Right candidate decided to meet with a local organization of conservative ministers to express his point of view. He recalled, "I did go to a group or council of church leaders [the Mountain Top Assembly Ministerial Association]. I introduced myself and gave a little presentation. Some of the conservative ministers were clearly not happy to see me. They asked me questions like, "Would you support prayer in school?" And I said no, and they were surprised that I was saying that in front of them. So, I attended that [religious] forum, but I did not go [campaign] in individual churches. I did not, to my knowledge, send out my pamphlet to churches." This candidate also said that many of these same ministers, at least according to some acquaintances of his who attended their churches, specifically told their members not to vote for him or other candidates who did not fit a "profamily" profile. In both the 1994 and 1996 elections, several candidates remarked that conservative Christian ministers played an active role in the school board campaigns and, at least in the minds of some candidates, helped elect a majority of conservative Christians to the school board in 1994.

The campaigns of many school board candidates in Fairfax County more closely resembled campaigns for Congress than did those of school board candidates in Garrett County or the survey. The typical candidate in Fairfax County, both Christian Right and non–Christian Right, attended at least one (sometimes two) events a night during the fall before the November elections. The pace of the campaign was even faster for at-large candidates, who regularly attended events in each of the nine magisterial districts in the county. Popular with many candidates was attendance at "back to school" nights, held early in each school year, to bring together parents, teachers, PTA members, and union leaders.

Most candidates in Fairfax County campaigned door to door. One candidate reported knocking on more than 2,200 doors in his district. Handing out campaign literature at supermarkets, farmers' markets, and subway stations was also a popular campaign strategy. Unlike candidates in Garrett County, most candidates in Fairfax held several fundraisers, such as candidate coffees or ice cream socials. Another important difference between candidates in the two counties was that Fairfax school board candidates—at least the 24 candidates that were endorsed by the Democratic or Republican Parties—often campaigned with candidates running for higher office or appeared together at partisan events. Once again, the role of parties in the school board campaigns in Fairfax County stands out compared with the candidates from Garrett County or the survey.

Election forums and debates were also popular with candidates in Fairfax County. The League of Women Voters, a nonpartisan voter education organization, sponsored debates in each district and one that was held specifically for at-large candidates. These forums were the most frequently attended type of forum by school board candidates. Interest groups that were more ideological in nature sponsored some candidate forums, and attendance at these events became politically charged. Some candidates, depending on their ideological bent, refused to attend them, including one Democratic candidate who skipped what she described as "very far right" forums because "she did not want to get trapped in a conversation." Other candidates took a different path. As one Christian Right candidate recalled, "During the campaign, it was constant work—every Saturday and Sunday, doing literature drops, knocking on doors, having coffees. . . . Then there were more organized events sponsored by the liberal groups, which were designed to embarrass us, and I went to every one of them! I also answered all of their questionnaires, went to all the debates, and stressed the fact that I will always tell you what I believe, and I will not budge."

More typical was for Democrats and Republicans to avoid attending events sponsored by conservative or liberal groups, respectively. Most party-endorsed candidates avoided such events on the recommendation of the parties themselves and in order to avoid, in the words of some candidates, being "set up."

Churches and synagogues were popular sites for candidate events, which hosted both "neutral" events (such as the League of Women Voters forums) and more ideological debates. For instance, some churches sponsored their own forums to inform their parishioners or other voters in their districts, including several fundamentalist churches. One Christian Right candidate claims that conservative church forums were held to counter forums held by more liberal groups:

> There was an organization among church-going-type folks, not necessarily an organization, but [they] got together and said, "Hey, let's sponsor some forums that make sure that at least we're on our ground, so that we can bias our questions, we can bias them our way, recognizing that other groups did the same thing." And that's why some Bible churches held forums in this particular area. Although these forums may not have had a big impact, at least they were an encouragement to conservative candidates, that we could walk in a room and feel a little more comfortable and little more supported. Even if it was just for that, it was probably worthwhile.

Several other Christian Right candidates also believed that these forums were a source of encouragement, if not much help to the outcome of their races. Non–Christian Right candidates, not surprisingly, did not find these events welcoming. Although most of these candidates decided to skip these events, one non–Christian Right candidate (a moderate Baptist) recalls attending an event at a conservative Baptist church and feeling "dirty and unwelcome."

Several conservative Catholic churches also sponsored candidate events for at-large candidates and candidates within their districts, which sparked some controversy. Democratic-endorsed candidates claimed that they were not invited to these events, such as one candidate who did find out about one forum until it was too late. She recalled, "I was not invited to one Catholic church forum, to which [her Republican opponent] had been invited. I didn't find out about it until after it was done. It was as though the church had already selected who they wanted to win. It was outrageous." In one case, a Catholic church refused to allow several Democratic candidates to participate in their forum even after they were informed about the event. This "block-out" of more moderate candidates (several of whom were Roman Catholics) occurred after the Arlington *Herald*, which is the Catholic newspaper that covers northern Virginia, ran a full-page story about the campaign of one conservative Christian who was also a Catholic. At least one Democratic Catholic candidate believes that the paper decided to run the story to show its support of this candidate, who supported vouchers. It was only after several Democratic candidates protested that the paper agreed to run similar stories about other Catholics running for school board, although instead of being featured in a full-page article, they were given brief paragraphs.[7]

Though churches and synagogues in Fairfax County hosted candidate debates (both ideological and nonideological in nature), most clergy were not as actively involved in the school board campaigns as was the case in Garrett County. There were exceptions. One group of liberal clergy held a press conference a week before the elections to express its concern about the involvement of Christian Right organizations and stealth candidates in the school board races. Despite these stealth charges, there was no indication that Christian Right candidates in Fairfax County campaigned exclusively or even regularly in conservative churches (besides attendance at forums), which is similar to findings from the survey. Most Christian Right candidates in Garrett County, however, did campaign extensively in conservative churches throughout the county, but they were not secretive about this strategy.

Despite some important differences in terms of where and how Christian Right and non–Christian Right candidates campaigned in Fairfax and Garrett Counties, generally speaking, the study finds little differences between the two types of candidates. Both types of candidates spend little on their campaigns, and the money they do spend comes from the same sources. Further, Christian Right and non–Christian Right candidates from the survey have relatively few volunteers to assist them and tend to recruit them from the same places. Although the survey finds that Christian Right candidates are significantly more likely to recruit volunteers from their churches, few Christian Right candidates (14 percent) report doing so. Finally, Christian Right and non–Christian Right candidates campaign in the same types of places, the most popular site for both being "door to door." Christian Right candidates are not much more likely than non–Christian Right candidates to campaign in churches, according to the survey, and in Fairfax County—with one exception. The so-called potential stealth Christian Right candidates discussed earlier are more likely to campaign in churches (27 percent) than are Christian Right candidates (10 percent), but these findings are very speculative at best. Less speculative are the findings in Garrett County, where churches played a more important role in the campaigns of most conservative Christian candidates.

One important finding that emerges in Fairfax County concerns the important role that parties played in the school board campaigns. Parties provided school board candidates in Fairfax County with volunteers and helped to determine where they campaigned by sponsoring events that drew candidates together on one platform (often with candidates who ran for higher offices in the state and county). The next section focuses more extensively on the role that political parties and interest groups played in the campaigns of school board candidates from the survey and the case studies.

Role of Interest Groups and Parties in the Campaigns

Political interest groups and political parties often participate in elections by endorsing candidates, making campaign contributions, and, in some cases, consulting or training individuals who want to run for office. In recent years, Christian Right organizations, particularly the Christian Coalition and Citizens for Excellence in Education, have sponsored candidate training specifically targeted for school board elections. The sponsorship of such training prompted critics of the movement to claim that such groups were grooming conservative Christians to run stealth campaigns. What impact do these two groups as well as other political and educational groups have on the campaigns of school board candidates? Which types of groups endorse, make campaign contributions, or train Christian Right and non–Christian Right candidates?

Table 4.7 shows the percentages of Christian Right and non–Christian Right candidates from the survey that received endorsements, campaign contributions, and candidate training. Table 4.8 gives details about the specific groups that endorse, contribute to, or train these school board candidates. Perhaps the most remarkable finding is the sheer lack of participation by political and education groups in school board races. Few candidates indicate that interest groups endorsed their candidacies, contributed to their campaigns, or offered consultation or training services. This finding is in stark contrast to the involvement of interest groups and parties in races for higher office, such as Congress, who actively make endorsements and donations and routinely consult with or train candidates.

Table 4.7 shows that just 18 percent of Christian Right candidates and 23 percent of non–Christian Right candidates receive endorsements from

Table 4.7

Candidates Receiving Endorsements, Contributions, and Training

Campaign Help	Christian Right Candidate (%)	Non– Christian Right Candidate (%)	Christian Right Group Member (%)	Christian Right Group Supporter (%)	Christian Right Issue Agenda Supporter (%)
Received endorsement(s)	18	23	30	14	17
Received contribution(s)	8	11	12	7	5
Received training	11	10	12	13	10

Note: N = 491. Differences between Christian Right and non–Christian Right candidates are not significant regarding type of campaign assistance received.

political parties and interest groups (a difference that is not statistically significant). Among Christian Right group members alone, however, 30 percent of candidates received an endorsement, which could indicate that perhaps their member groups endorsed them in some capacity. Or it could indicate that these individuals are inclined to be group joiners, more generally, and perhaps such affiliations might lead to more endorsements as candidates.

As table 4.8 reports, political parties are more likely than other groups to endorse school board candidates, both Christian Right and non–Christian Right alike. Among ninety-seven Christian Right school board candidates, 2 percent say that they received an endorsement from the Democratic Party, whereas the Republican Party endorsed 8 percent. The political parties endorsed 10 percent of non–Christian Right candidates, with Democrats endorsing 6 percent and the Republicans endorsing 4 percent.

Christian Right and non–Christian Right candidates list state or local education groups as the next most frequent type of organization to endorse their candidacies. The involvement of these groups is limited: only 4 percent of Christian Right candidates and 8 percent of non–Christian Right candidates report receiving endorsements from state or local education organizations. Non–Christian Right candidates are likely to list next state or local political groups, followed by local newspapers and the National Education Association and the American Federation of Teachers—both professional teacher organizations—as groups that endorse their campaigns. Just 1 percent of Christian Right candidates received endorsements from political groups, and none received newspaper endorsements. The data show that the Christian Coalition

Table 4.8
Interest Group and Party Involvement in Campaigns of
School Board Candidates, by Group

Group	Endorsements		Contributions		Training	
	Christian Right Candidate (%)	Non–Christian Right Candidate (%)	Christian Right Candidate (%)	Non–Christian Right Candidate (%)	Christian Right Candidate (%)	Non–Christian Right Candidate (%)
Democratic Party	2 (2)	6 (22)	1 (1)	3 (12)	1 (1)	3 (11)
Republican Party	8 (8)	4 (17)	3 (3)	2 (9)	3 (3)	3 (10)
National Education Association	—[a]	2 (7)	—[a]	<1 (2)	—[a]	<1 (1)
American Federation of Teachers	—[a]	2 (8)	—[a]	1 (3)	—[a]	<1 (2)
Women's group	—[a]	1 (4)	—[a]	1 (4)	—[a]	<1 (2)
Citizens for Excellence in Education	3 (3)	1 (4)	2 (2)	<1 (2)	1 (1)	<1 (2)
Christian Coalition	—[a]	—[a]	—[a]	—[a]	1 (1)	<1 (1)
State/local political group	1 (1)	3 (11)	1 (2)	1 (5)	3 (3)	1 (5)
State/local education group	4 (4)	8 (31)	1 (1)	3 (13)	1 (1)	2 (9)
Newspaper	—[a]	2 (8)	—[a]	—[a]	—[a]	—[a]
AFL-CIO	1 (1)	—[a]	1 (1)	<1 (1)	—[a]	—[a]
Business group	3 (3)	2 (8)	—[a]	<1 (1)	—[a]	—[a]
Other	—[a]	6 (21)	—[a]	2 (8)	1 (1)	2 (6)

Note: N = 491. Whole numbers in parentheses.
[a]No response.

did not endorse any school board candidates, although Citizens for Excellence in Education endorsed 3 percent.

Even fewer groups donate money to school board candidates than endorse them. Table 4.7 shows that only 8 percent of Christian Right candidates and 11 percent of non–Christian Right candidates receive campaign donations from interest groups or political parties, a difference that is not statistically significant. There are few differences among the three separate categories of Christian Right candidates as well. Once again, as table 4.8 details, political parties are the biggest contributors to school board candidates.

Finally, the survey data reveal that 11 percent of Christian Right candidates and 10 percent of non–Christian Right candidates receive some type of candidate training or consulting with regard to their school board campaigns. Here, one might expect the participation of Christian Right organizations, such as the Christian Coalition and Citizens for Excellence in Education, to be higher, in light of the efforts of these groups to mobilize and train candidates to run for school board and other local offices. Instead, only 1 percent ($N = 1$) of Christian Right candidates report attending a training or consultation with the Christian Coalition, and an additional 1 percent of Christian Right candidates was trained by Citizens for Excellence in Education. Once again, political parties emerge as the group that is most likely to participate in school board campaigns. Political parties played the greatest role in training both types of school board candidates, although only 4 percent of Christian Right and 6 percent of non–Christian Right candidates indicate that they attended such training sessions.[8]

What are the implications of these findings from the survey regarding the role that interest groups and parties play in the campaigns of school board candidates? First, there is little evidence to suggest that interest groups or parties play a prominent role in most school board campaigns. For whatever reason, school board elections are of such limited stature that they do not appear to merit the attention of these types of groups in most races. Of those groups that do participate, parties emerge as the most likely to endorse school board candidates, contribute money to their campaigns, and offer them training and consultation, which are functions of political parties in many types of elections. The reason why relatively few parties participate in school board elections nationally is because so few are partisan: just 8 percent of the elections in which candidates in this survey ran for office were partisan (data not shown). Second, these findings show that Christian Right and non–Christian Right candidates once again share similarities with regard to various aspects of their campaigns, similar to the earlier findings regarding campaign finance, volunteers, and locations. Here, the data indicate that there are no significant differences between

Christian Right and non–Christian Right candidates regarding the percentages that are endorsed or receive campaign contributions or consultation from interest groups and political parties. Finally, the survey data demonstrate that, on a nationwide basis at least, Christian Right organizations are not deeply involved in the campaigns of candidates running for school board, which runs contrary to much of the conventional wisdom about school board elections and the Christian Right. There simply is little evidence to suggest that Christian Right organizations are having a major impact on the school board candidacies of conservative Christians. Of course, there is always the possibility that Christian Right candidates might elect not to mention that these groups are involved in the ways suggested on the survey. Taken at face value, however, it appears that groups such as the Christian Coalition are not as involved in the elections of school board candidates as their liberal critics fear.

The two case studies reveal mixed findings regarding endorsements, contributions, and training received by school board candidates, with the school board candidates in Garrett County more closely resembling the candidates from the survey than the Fairfax County school board candidates. Few candidates in the 1994 or 1996 elections in Garrett County reported receiving endorsements or candidate contributions from political or education groups. Only two non–Christian Right candidates received endorsements, both from teachers' organizations. Two non–Christian Right candidates were also given campaign contributions from another teachers' association. Political groups endorsed no conservative Christian candidates in Garrett County, nor did they offer financial assistance to their campaigns. One Christian Right candidate attended a candidate-training seminar run by the Free Congress Foundation, a conservative organization led by Paul Weyrich.

None of the Christian Right candidates in Garrett County attended candidate seminars or received assistance from other prominent profamily organizations such as the Christian Coalition, Citizens for Excellence in Education, the Eagle Forum, or the American Family Association. This finding does not mean, however, that Christian Right groups were absent from the campaign or that their presence did not register in the county's local political scene.

In Garrett County, the Christian Coalition best represented Christian Right interests. The Garrett County chapter of the Coalition was started by one of the conservative Christian school board candidates running in 1994 (after becoming a candidate, he removed himself as chair of the chapter). Every Christian Right candidate running in the 1994 or 1996 Garrett County school board elections either belonged to the Christian Coalition or attended some of its meetings at one point in time. Although the involvement of the Christian Coalition was slight in terms of making campaign endorsements or contributions, the organization was involved through the distribution of voter guides. Voter guides are popular tools with all types of interest groups, although the Christian Coalition nationally has made their wording and distribution into something of a (controversial) art form. For example, in elections that took place in 1998, the Coalition claims to have distributed more than 45 million voter guides.[9]

In Garrett County, candidates reported receiving questionnaires from the Christian Coalition and two other organizations, the county chapter of the National Education Association and the League of Women Voters. The Christian Coalition voter guide in 1994 contained ten questions (a similar guide was distributed in 1996) that covered such policy areas as vouchers and outcomes-based education, although most questions dealt with sex education. Whereas conservative Christian candidates in Garrett County viewed the Christian Coalition questionnaire as helpful and informative to voters in the county, non–Christian Right candidates believed that the selection of questions and their wording were misleading. According to one non–Christian Right candidate, "The Christian Coalition really got into it. They sent out a survey. They tried to put them in all the churches, and [one] question on the survey was, 'Do you approve of handing out condoms to our high school students?' Well, we weren't doing that, but that implied that we were. And I argued that was misleading. [Another] one was about teaching abstinence in the schools. And it was worded like we don't do that, and we do, my Lord, that's the best way to go!"

The first question referred to by the non–Christian Right candidate was actually the third question on the survey, which asked candidates whether they "supported the distribution of birth control paraphernalia and information in the public schools." The second question, referring to abstinence-based sex education, was next on the survey and was worded as follows: "Knowing that abstinence is the most effective means of preventing HIV and teen pregnancy, do you support a health curriculum that stresses abstinence based, family oriented sex education as a top priority?" Several non–Christian Right candidates in Garrett County believed that these questions were deliberately worded to lead candidates to one "correct" answer. One non–Christian Right candidate said questions such as one that asked respondents whether they "believe that government should have the final authority over the education of our children" were akin to asking candidates if "they still beat their wives." This candidate and other non–Christian Right candidates refused to answer the survey because they believed that the purpose behind the survey was not to inform voters, but rather to persuade them.

The Christian Coalition voter guides were distributed to conservative churches throughout Garrett County, where many ministers took an active role in the campaign either through the Mountain Top Ministerial Association (which interviewed school board candidates about their views on education) or reportedly from preaching in the pulpits about the school board elections. Although it is impossible to measure the direct impact on the Garrett County school board elections of the ministers' or the Christian Coalition's involvement, conservative Christian candidates met with great success in both the 1994 and 1996 school board elections. In a county with so few voters, grassroots mobilization by the Christian Right appeared to make an important difference in the election results.

The findings regarding endorsements, campaign contributions, and candidate training are much different for candidates who ran for school board in Fairfax County. Virtually every candidate received some type of endorsement, and most also received campaign contributions and attended training seminars. Twelve candidates—more than half of whom were conservative Christians—were endorsed by the Republican Party. The Democrats backed another twelve candidates, many of whom were also endorsed by the Fairfax chapter of the National Education Association or the American Federation of Teachers. Though several moderate Republican candidates were endorsed by education groups, Christian Right candidates were solely endorsed by the party or partisan-related organizations (such as a local Republican Women's Club). Candidate contributions were also lopsided between the two types of candidates. Most non–Christian Right candidates received financial assistance from the parties as well as education-related groups. Just two conservative Christian candidates received campaign donations, and both of their donations came from partisan-related organizations, such as Virginians for a GOP Majority.

Almost every school board candidate in Fairfax County attended at least one candidate-training seminar to prepare them for their school board races, which is in stark contrast to candidates in the survey or in Garrett County. The local parties offered the most popular training seminars for school board candidates. Most Democratic candidates (and a few moderate Republicans) also participated in a one-day training seminar sponsored by the National Education Association's Fairfax chapter. Three Christian Right candidates received candidate training from at least two Christian Right organizations, including the Free Congress Foundation. One candidate attended campaign seminars at Morton Blackwell's Leadership Institute, a training ground for many conservative and Christian Right political activists and lobbyists, including Ralph Reed.

One of the most significant findings in this case study is the role of political parties in the Fairfax County elections, despite the nonpartisan nature of the elections. Parties emerge as the most important group to have endorsed, trained, and given campaign donations to both Christian Right and non–

Christian Right candidates running for school board. The two major parties have had an interesting history in the state of Virginia, one that had important ramifications for the tenor and outcome of the school board elections.

Until the mid-1960s, Virginia state politics was dominated by a Democratic Party machine that was headed by Harry F. Byrd, who served as governor of Virginia from 1926 to 1930 and as U.S. Senator from 1933 until his retirement in 1965 (Barone and Ujifusa 1993; Rozell and Wilcox 1996). Despite domination by the Democratic Party in state politics, Virginians routinely supported Republican presidential candidates in almost every election since 1944 (with the exception of Johnson in 1964). As the national party grew more liberal, many of the more conservative members of the Byrd machine turned to the Republican Party (Rozell and Wilcox 1996). In 1969, Republicans elected their first Republican governor. By the late 1970s, Republicans had elected two U.S. Senators and held nine of Virginia's ten U.S. House seats. State Democrats made something of a comeback, as they went on to capture three consecutive governorships starting with the election in 1981 of Chuck Robb. In 1993, however, control of the governor's mansion again shifted to the Republicans.

The emergence of the Republican Party as a competitive party in Virginia within the past thirty years has been aided in part by the mobilization of conservative Christian political activists in the state. Yet their assistance in making the party competitive has left many long-time, moderate Republicans resentful of their influence. According to Mark Rozell and Clyde Wilcox, "Moderates who spent decades working in the socially moderate Virginia Republican party of the 1950s and 1960s see the Christian Right influx as an invasion by extremists who would seize control of their party just as it is finally poised to triumph. Social conservatives see the moderates as hostile to the very voters who have finally made the party competitive in state elections" (1996, 32). Several contentious elections in the 1990s only exacerbated this hostility between the two factions in the party, including the failed candidacies of Oliver North for U.S. Senate in 1994 and Michael Farris for lieutenant governor in 1993—both men favorites of the conservative Christian community. The Virginia GOP regrouped in 1996 with the reelection of U.S. Senator John Warner, a moderate Republican. Nonetheless, tensions remain high between the two factions at the start of the twenty-first century.

The Fairfax County Republican Committee, which is the county's Republican chapter, parallels the state (and national) party in that both social conservatives and moderates have struggled in the past decade over who should lead the party.[10] This internal division in the party had important implications for the 1995 elections in Fairfax County, for elections concerning

both the school board and the county's board of supervisors (or county council). Several political observers speculated that the Republicans decided to
compromise on the endorsements for the two races. Where possible, Christian
Right activists in the party would concentrate on endorsing social conservatives for school board seats, while mainly moderates would be endorsed for the
board of supervisors.[11]

This "arrangement" was controversial. Each magisterial district in Fairfax
County had a local Republican precinct committee, which was responsible for
interviewing candidates for the elections and recommending to the County
Committee a candidate for them to endorse. In most cases, this process was a
rubber stamp, whereby the county committee would heed the advice of the
district's decision. This pattern was not the case in one district where four
Republicans were vying for the party's nomination. In this district, the local
magisterial committee nominated a social moderate (and former teacher) to
be endorsed by the county, a decision that was challenged by the chair of the
Fairfax County Republican Committee. The county chair, who was a Christian
Right sympathizer, openly supported an outspoken conservative Christian
who was also running in that magisterial district for school board.

When the county committee met to select which candidates it would
endorse for the school board two months before the elections, both the social
moderate and social conservative were invited to speak before members of the
Republican Committee, who would ultimately select which candidate to
endorse from the district. Other speakers spoke on behalf of the two nominees
as well. Speakers who backed the social conservative made an issue of the moderate candidate's former career as a teacher and repeatedly emphasized her
membership in the National Education Association, a tactic that the moderate
candidate believes was orchestrated by the county chair. Ultimately, the county
committee overrode the suggestion of the district's committee in this case and
endorsed the conservative Christian (who would later go on to win the seat).

Although the compromise about the GOP endorsements might have
appeased some members of the two factions in the county's Republican party,
it apparently had little pull with the county's voters. Republicans failed to capture a majority of seats on either the school board or the board of supervisors.
An analysis of the board of supervisors election is beyond the scope of this
study, but Democrats running for school board were able to distinguish themselves successfully from the Republican-backed school board candidates, in
part by painting many of their opponents as extremists who supported the
teaching of creationism in the public schools.

The case study findings demonstrate that the parties played a pivotal role
in the school board elections in Fairfax County, which was a unique situation

when compared with the school board elections in Garrett County or with school board elections nationwide. What about the involvement of Christian Right organizations in the Fairfax County school board elections? Were Christian Right groups as active—and effective—as the parties in influencing the school board elections in Fairfax?

Similar to Garrett County, the involvement of Christian Right interest groups in Fairfax County was slight in terms of making campaign endorsements or contributions. There were, however, other ways that Christian Right organizations were (in the words of one Christian Right candidate) "decisively engaged," particularly through their distribution of voter guides. Christian Right groups were not the only groups who distributed such guides during the election. The thirty-five candidates running for school board in Fairfax County received voter surveys from close to twenty interest groups and newspapers. Some of these surveys were used for endorsement purposes, whereas others, such as the Christian Coalition survey in Garrett County, were ostensibly used for voter education. Among the groups distributing candidate questionnaires were education organizations such as the National Education Association and the American Federation of Teachers. This school board election, however, drew questionnaires from groups with little or no direct involvement with the public schools, such as the National Rifle Association.

The Christian Coalition was one of four different Christian Right organizations to distribute surveys to school board candidates in Fairfax County. Other groups included the Eagle Forum, HOPE (a local organization—"Help Our Parents Educate"—that was disbanded after the 1995 elections), and the American Family Association. The American Family Association questionnaire, similar to the other three Christian Right surveys, contained the typical range of questions regarding education issues that most deeply concern the movement, such as sex education, Goals 2000 and outcomes-based education, phonics, the role of guidance counselors in public schools, homosexuality, and, in the case of the Eagle Forum's survey, questions regarding the federal government's "school-to-work" program.

The wording of questions in the Christian Right surveys, like the wording of the Christian Coalition's survey in Garrett County, disturbed many of the non–Christian Right candidates, most of whom refused to respond to them. Some did not want to give the Christian Right "fodder" to use against them while helping the campaigns of their conservative Christian opponents; others did not believe that their answers would be represented honestly, mainly because of how the questions were worded. As one Democratic candidate remembered, "I had received the questionnaire from the American Family Association and had decided that there was no way I could answer that questionnaire and be true to my faith, and be totally honest, and have them report it any other way than that I was 'completely godless, atheistic, and antagonistic toward parents and children, etc.'" This candidate joked that he expected the Christian Coalition to one day distribute a voter guide with the question "Which candidate eats their young?"

The American Family Association was among the most active of interest groups in the school board race, particularly after the results of its survey were released in the press. The organization issued almost daily press releases, defending its position on creationism and other issues. In one press release, in which it accused the news media of looking "for smoke where there is no fire," the American Family Association pointed out that "there is no constituency that we are aware of in Fairfax County that has as its main agenda the introduction of a unit on creation in the Fairfax County Public Schools. However, thirteen out of twenty respondents to our survey indicated that they would be supportive of such a unit in some way or another. This question was asked as an indicator, to separate those who would censor the curriculum by excluding creation, from those who would be more broad-minded in this subject area" (American Family Association 1995b).

Subsequent press releases tried to link Democratic-endorsed candidates, none of whom filled out the American Family Association questionnaire, to the National Education Association, whose Fairfax chapter endorsed most of them. The press releases made mention of the fact that the National Education Association "supports the teaching of homosexuality, which happens to be a Class 6 Felony in Virginia" (1995b). Several days before the election, the AFA issued a press release imploring the media to no longer ignore "the obvious connection between the homosexual community and the Democratic Party endorsed School Board candidates," a call that, for the most part, fell on deaf ears (American Family Association 1995a).

Despite such commitment by the American Family Association, many candidates believed that their ultimate impact on the elections was not significant, including one Christian Right candidate who said, "The AFA is a small group of people. . . . I think they were working all of the time. Did they have an impact? I don't know, but they surely didn't sway the election. I think what they did was keep people honest. What this group did was to basically keep your conservative people where they were. They stopped people from being swayed by these lies on the left."

Few Christian Right candidates admitted to having strong ties with the American Family Association or other Christian Right organizations that were active in the 1995 elections, including another candidate—who belonged to the Family Foundation, a Virginia Christian Right organization that did not participate in the elections—who recalled, "Some [Christian Right] groups were involved. The AFA sent out their survey. See, I didn't know about these groups necessarily until I began the process. I did know about the AFA ... and I had heard about the Christian Coalition, but I had never been involved with the Christian Coalition, and they came to me and said, 'Will you fill out this questionnaire?' And that they agreed with my viewpoints. I was not a member of the Christian Coalition, and I did not have them campaign for me." According to this candidate, groups such as the Christian Coalition and the American Family Association played a limited role in the individual campaigns of candidates, focusing instead on influencing voters through voter guides.

Many conservative Christian leaders and activists in the county (many of whom were affiliated with local groups) played an important role as campaign volunteers. So, although candidates did not receive direct help from Christian Right groups in most cases, they did get volunteer assistance from their group members. One candidate recalled, "In all of my campaign contributions, I got nothing from any of those [Christian Right] groups. Besides, they couldn't with their tax status. Now, did I have some volunteers who were part of Concerned Women for America and those groups? Probably. But they were doing it as individuals, and they also happened to be affiliated with [these groups]."

As a group, then, Christian Right organizations had limited involvement in individual campaigns, mainly because of their tax status. But there was no shortage of activists to assist the candidacies of conservative Christian school board candidates in other ways, either as campaign volunteers or by working through the local Republican Party to influence which school board candidates would be endorsed.

Little evidence in either case studies or the national survey suggests that the Christian Right was heavily involved in endorsing candidates, training them, or making financial contributions to the campaigns of conservative Christian school board candidates. Yet research from the two case studies demonstrates that the Christian Right can be effective in local elections in other ways. In both counties, Christian Right organizations conducted candidate surveys and distributed the results to their members and to conservative churches, which could have easily had a profound impact on the voting decisions of church members. In Fairfax County, Christian Right activists also served as campaign volunteers and strongly influenced which candidates the Republican Party chose to endorse. It is impossible to determine whether Christian Right organizations are also involved to the same extent nationally as they were in these two counties. The survey of school board candidates does not ask whether candidates received such questionnaires.

Although the case studies demonstrate that there are other ways in which conservative Christian groups (and the activists that make up their membership) can participate in school board elections, their involvement might lead to mixed results. In Garrett County, it is probable that the involvement by the Christian Coalition and conservative activists helped Christian Right candidates win in the 1994 and 1996 elections. In Fairfax County, by contrast, their impact was less positive in most cases—only two conservative Christians (out of nine Christian Right candidates) were elected to the twelve-member board.

Conclusion

This study examines the ways that interest groups and parties traditionally get involved with electoral politics, namely, by endorsing candidates, giving them campaign contributions, and training them to run for office. Of particular interest is the role that Christian Right organizations play in how conservative Christians run for school board. Much attention in recent years has been given to the Christian Right's efforts to train and recruit candidates to run for local offices such as school boards. This study finds, however, that few school board candidates, regardless of whether they are part of the Christian Right, receive direct assistance from interest groups or political parties, as both the survey and case study in Garrett County demonstrate.

The situation in Fairfax County, however, was different, in that most candidates did receive endorsements, contributions, or training of some kind during their campaigns. One important difference between the two counties was that political parties played a crucial role in the campaigns of both Christian Right and non–Christian Right candidates in Fairfax County. In Garrett County, one possible reason that parties were not a major factor might have been the relative lack of party competition—the county is overwhelmingly Republican; however, the intense involvement of the parties in Fairfax County might have been simply a unique situation, because the survey results demonstrate that few candidates received assistance from parties in their campaigns nationwide.

In the case of Christian Right candidates, it is somewhat surprising that so few candidates attended training seminars offered by the Christian Coalition, Citizens for Excellence in Education, or other Christian Right groups, in view of the fact that the Christian Right has spent enormous energy and resources to cultivate grassroots political activism. There is little evidence in this study to suggest that these groups played an important role in recruiting conservative

Christians to become school board candidates or that they offered much assistance in terms of guiding them on how to run their campaigns.

Nevertheless, the case studies demonstrate several additional ways that Christian Right groups, and the activists who make up their membership, can participate in school board campaigns aside from endorsing and training candidates or making campaign donations. In both Garrett and Fairfax Counties, the Christian Coalition surveyed candidates and distributed the results of the survey to their members and conservative churches throughout the counties. In Fairfax County, three additional Christian Right organizations also distributed voter guides (including, most notably, the American Family Association). These candidate questionnaires had an important indirect impact on the campaigns of conservative Christian school board candidates, sometimes for the better (such as in Garrett County) and sometimes for the worse (as was the case for most Christian Right candidates in Fairfax County).

In addition to the participation of several Christian Right interest groups, Christian Right activists in Fairfax County played an important part in the campaigns of conservative Christian school board candidates as volunteers and as organizers of several campaign forums. Why were Christian Right groups and activists more likely to be involved in Fairfax County than in Garrett County? Probably for the same reason that political parties and so many other groups became involved in the school board elections in Fairfax County. There are important structural differences between the two counties, both socioeconomically and politically, that likely fostered an increased level of political participation from Christian Right and more secular organizations alike. As much political science research finds, high levels of education and income are good predictors of political participation. Fairfax County enjoys some of the highest levels of these socioeconomic indicators in the country, which means that its citizens are likely to participate in politics. Also, its proximity to the nation's capital, combined with its competitive party system and its heterogeneity, affords Fairfax County a unique political infrastructure—one that "cultivates" the participation of many types of interest groups. Paradoxically, the same factors that produce high levels of political participation from Christian Right groups and activists all point to a less responsive environment for Christian Right candidates in Fairfax County than in Garrett County, where the Christian Right's message is more likely to find greater appeal.

Turning to campaign strategies, perhaps one of the more interesting findings of this study is the remarkable similarity between Christian Right and non–Christian Right candidates, at least in terms of how they run their campaigns. Unlike campaigns for higher political office, school board campaigns are low key. The typical candidate running for school board, regardless of whether he or she is part of the Christian Right, spends less than $1,000 on his or her race, a sum the candidate usually provides personally or with the donations of family members. School board candidates in the survey have, on average, about seven volunteers working with them and are most likely to campaign door to door. Fewer than half of the candidates attend any type of campaign rally or event; even fewer campaign in shopping malls, community meetings, or at candidate coffees.

Evidence is mixed regarding issue positions. The survey demonstrates that Christian Right candidates are not typically running on the more controversial education positions that the Christian Right routinely emphasizes, such as sex education, vouchers or outcomes-based education. Christian Right candidates, however, are significantly more likely than non–Christian Right candidates to run on more mainstream conservative issues also endorsed by the Christian Right, such as increasing test scores and enforcing more discipline in the schools. Similar findings emerge in both case studies, particularly in Fairfax County, where Christian Right candidates ran on a broad back-to-basics theme. Christian Right candidates in Garrett County were also likely to incorporate more religious themes in their campaigns, as illustrated by several of their campaign advertisements in the local newspaper, one of which quoted Biblical scripture, but there is little evidence to suggest that Christian Right candidates were likely to run on campaign issues that were more prophetic in nature, calling for drastic, religious-based changes to school board policy.

Both the survey and case study findings offer little evidence that Christian Right candidates are running stealth campaigns. Of course, the concept of stealth is difficult to prove. One indication of a stealth campaign run by a Christian Right candidate would be a campaign that was primarily rooted in conservative churches. In other words, if the stealth hypothesis were valid, one would expect to find that Christian Right candidates would campaign primarily in churches. Just 11 percent of Christian Right candidates in the survey, however, reported that they campaigned in churches, which is not significantly different than the level for non–Christian Right candidates. In several cases, this study looked at potential stealth candidates, based on fifteen individuals in the survey who are members of Christian Right groups but do not profess to holding a majority of issue positions with the movement. Although there is much reason to doubt the results of such a finding, in light of the assumption that these candidates are purposively misleading the researcher by not confessing their "true" stands on education issues, one interesting result is that twice as many of these individuals campaign in churches than do other Christian Right candidates. Yet again, these data are speculative, at best, and still result in a minority of potential stealth candidates campaigning in churches. Taken together, there is still little empirical data here to suggest that the stealth hypothesis is an accurate one.

Few Christian Right candidates in Fairfax County campaigned in churches, other than attendance at church-sponsored forums or debates, which non–Christian Right candidates also frequently attended. Despite this finding and the fact that conservative Christian candidates in Fairfax ran on a back-to-basics theme, as did more moderate Republicans, most Democratic-endorsed candidates in Fairfax County were convinced that Christian Right candidates were running stealth campaigns. The Democrats pointed to the American Family Association's survey results, which demonstrated support by Christian Right candidates for more controversial issues, such as reintroducing the theory of creationism into the classrooms. There is no way to know whether the conservative Christian candidates would have tried to make such changes to education policy had they been elected as a majority to the school board, and it might be the case that several of the conservative Christians who did attend candidate training with the Free Congress Foundation or the Leadership Institute were coached to downplay their religious values and their support for more controversial education issues such as creationism. There is, however, no indication that the strategies that these candidates used were far different from the strategies used by moderate Republican candidates or Democratic-endorsed candidates. All candidates knocked on doors, attended back-to-school nights, distributed campaign literature, and participated in non-ideological candidate forums. Christian Right candidates in Fairfax County were not in any way shielded from public view as the stealth theory would hypothesize.

In contrast to the survey results, conservative Christian candidates in Garrett County openly campaigned for school board in area churches. In fact, one candidate visited different churches each Sunday "just to let them know" he was running. Further, unlike school board candidates in Fairfax County or the national survey, these candidates openly used religious references in their campaign platforms, in both religious settings such as churches and in nonreligious settings such as the local paper. In the words of one Christian Right candidate, "There is no such thing as a stealth candidate in Garrett County." This comment reflects the fact that the values and ideas that these conservative Christians emphasized in their school board campaigns were values and ideas that were shared by many other citizens in the small, close-knit community. This is not to say that their ideas and values were shared by all citizens in the county (or that, once they were elected to the board, their actions were not without controversy, as chapter 6 will detail), but simply that their message appealed to a solid core of citizens in the county.

Though the campaign strategies examined in this chapter yield little empirical support for the stealth hypothesis, another way to approach it is to look at the election results. In other words, the stealth theory maintains that Christian conservatives are somehow advantaged in school board elections if they use underhanded campaign techniques. Although there is little evidence to support that notion in this chapter, chapter 5 takes a more thorough look at the success rates of Christian Right candidates and non–Christian Right candidates. If Christian Right candidates are more likely to win their races, controlling for a variety of other factors, then perhaps the stealth hypothesis could have some merit.

A Christian Right Takeover?

In an interview with the *Los Angeles Times,* Bob Simonds, president of Citizens for Excellence in Education, offered this advice to prospective Christian Right candidates: "There are two ways you can run. You can say 'I'm a Christian. I believe in traditional values. I believe in teaching both viewpoints, creationism and evolution.' The other way is [to run] as a conservative parent who says: 'I'm running because I love my children.' You don't have to say up front that you're a Christian."[1]

Simonds believes that candidates were helped by this advice in school districts such as Lake County, Florida, where in 1993 conservative Christians campaigned successfully by distributing voter guides to like-minded churches the Sunday before the election. The guides depicted the school board incumbents—all Republicans—as pro-choice on abortion and as being "opposed to giving parents a say in educational decision-making" (Shogren and Frantz 1993, A1). Incumbents claimed that their views were not only unsolicited, but misrepresented. As one defeated incumbent said, "It was just misinformation. They did a great job of slam campaigning" (Shogren and Frantz 1993, A1).

This chapter examines whether Christian Right candidates are more likely than other types of candidates to win school board elections. In one sense, it is a test of the oft-repeated claim by opponents of the movement that the Christian Right is "taking over" school boards nationwide. According to critics of the

Christian Right, conservative Christian candidates are advantaged in school board elections because they employ stealth campaign techniques. The case in Lake County is an example often touted by liberal groups such as the Institute for First Amendment Studies, whose director, Frederick Clarkson, writes that Christian Right candidates "have capitalized on the long-term decline in voter participation in America, and exert clout vastly disproportionate to their real numbers" (Clarkson 1998). On the one hand, candidates who use stealth campaign techniques, as the theory goes, would be given a "built-in" advantage in elections characteristically marked by low voter turnout such as school board. On the other hand, if Christian Right candidates do win at higher rates than non–Christian Right candidates, it could be that they simply possess greater resources or other advantages not enjoyed by non–Christian Right candidates.

Using the survey data of those candidates running in contested races, I examine the impact of Christian Right status on electoral success while also controlling for other factors that might help predict whether a candidate is likely to be elected to school board. Relatively little political science research is devoted to the outcomes of school board elections. One study of an isolated school board election found that incumbents have an advantage over nonincumbents in school board elections because of greater name recognition and ability to raise more money and recruit more campaign volunteers (Taebel 1977). Several other studies about school board elections focus on ethnicity, specifically how minorities fare in school board elections. Success for minority school board candidates is positively related to the percentage of minority voters within the districts they run (Garcia 1979; Stewart, Englund, and Meier 1988; Meier and Stewart 1991) as well as the electoral structure of the district. Studies show that minorities are disadvantaged in school board elections that use at-large, as opposed to single-member, districts (Robinson and Englund 1981).

By contrast, the political science literature that focuses on electoral success in other types of elections, particularly congressional elections, is abundant. These studies consistently demonstrate that incumbency, party, money, and the quality of candidates relates to whether candidates win elections. The most important variable related to electoral victory is incumbency (Jacobson 1992; McCurley and Mondauk 1995; and Box-Steffensmeier 1996). As David Mayhew (1974) first pointed out, congressional incumbents enjoy many advantages over their challengers, including greater name recognition, staff, franking privileges, and a committee system designed to ensure that members of Congress can best "bring home the bacon" to their districts. Further, Gary Jacobson (1992) notes that incumbents scare off potential "quality" challengers and instead usually face less-qualified opponents in their races. Studies about state legislative races also reveal that incumbents are more likely to win their races than are nonincumbents, for many of the same reasons as congressional incumbents (Owens and Olson 1977; Tucker and Weber 1987; Jewell and Breaux 1988; Cassie and Breaux 1998). It stands to reason that incumbents running for school boards are also advantaged in these local races, especially because of greater name recognition.

One factor that likely affects national, statewide, and local elections more evenly is money. The literature on races for offices higher than school board shows a positive relationship between candidate spending and vote share—particularly in state legislative races—although money tends to make more of a difference for challengers than for incumbents (Tucker and Weber 1987; Gierzynski and Breaux 1991; Jacobson 1992; Ansolabahere and Gerber 1994). School board elections are much less expensive than elections for Congress or the state house, but greater spending by candidates should give them an advantage in local races as well. Another resource to consider in school board races is number of volunteers. Because spending levels are relatively low in school board races, candidates might be more advantaged than their opponents if they have greater numbers of volunteers to assist their campaigns.

Political scientists also consider candidate quality as it relates to electoral chances, usually by analyzing an incumbent's voting record and ability to bring large amounts of federal spending to his or her home district, Mayhew's "bacon." For example, congressional incumbents whose "credit claiming" about federal spending in their districts is consistent with their votes on federal spending receive more votes in reelection bids than do incumbents who are less consistent (Sellers 1997). There is also a relationship between vote choice in congressional elections and the quality or integrity of incumbents by their ranking in the *Almanac of American Politics* (McCurley and Mondauk 1995). This approach to measuring candidate quality is less relevant in school board races, however, because voters in school board elections are probably less aware of an incumbent's voting record than they would be aware of the voting record of their congressional representatives. The number and type of endorsements a candidate receives, however, can be used as alternative measures of candidate quality at the school board level. Candidates who are endorsed by education groups might be more likely to win their elections than candidates who are not endorsed by such groups. Finally, candidates who receive training or consultation from political organizations such as parties or interest groups are likely better equipped to handle their campaigns than school board candidates who do not receive such advice. Chapter 4 reveals that very few conservative Christian candidates received assistance from Christian Right organizations such as the Christian Coalition and Citizens for Excellence in Education, but several did receive help from parties and other groups, as did non–Christian Right candidates. Such professional advice might help candidates win seats to school boards.

There are also structural and contextual factors to consider in any analysis of success in school board elections. For example, the type of election—partisan or nonpartisan, at-large or single-member district—might influence the results. Further, whether a candidate is running in an election for an open seat or facing an incumbent might also influence his or her odds of winning the race. In terms of contextual factors, one that might bode well for Christian Right candidates in particular is level of evangelicalism. Christian Right candidates might fare better in areas that are more highly populated with evangelicals—the target constituency of the Christian Right. In the same vein, Christian Right candidates may also benefit from a highly traditionalistic regional culture, such as the South or Midwest, regions in which evangelicals are more likely to live (Kosmin and Lachman 1993, chap. 3). Christian Right candidates running in these regions might have an advantage over those running in the Northeast or West.

Building the Model

Because the dependent variable—whether a candidate won or lost an election—is dichotomous, I use logistic regression to determine whether affiliation with the Christian Right gives those candidates an edge in school board elections. The main independent variable under study is Christian Right status, using the double-hurdle classification first introduced in chapter 2, which identifies candidates as being part of the Christian Right by using two criteria: identification with various Christian Right organizations and views on education issues. Survey respondents who are members of Christian Right organizations are automatically coded as Christian Right candidates. Respondents who both support Christian Right groups *and* share a majority of issue positions are also coded as part of the movement.

In addition to examining whether Christian Right status is linked to electoral success, my logistic regression model controls for incumbency, because the research cited above indicates that incumbents in any type of election are at an advantage over nonincumbents. The model also controls for resources in the forms of money (measured ordinally; see appendix B for exact question wording) and number of volunteers. Candidates who have more of each will likely be more successful in school board elections.

I also include several measures of candidate quality—endorsements and training experience—in the model. First, the model considers endorsements under the assumption that, the more endorsements a candidate receives, the better his or her chances of winning. The type of endorsements received by candidates might also matter. Candidates who are endorsed by education groups might be more advantaged than candidates who are not. Such an endorsement might signal to voters that the candidate is more "qualified" to serve on the school board than his or her opponent. Finally, the model considers whether candidates received any candidate training or consultation from political parties or other groups. Those candidates receiving such help might be more advantaged in the elections than those who did not receive such help.

Electoral structure has been shown to influence the outcomes for certain types of candidates running in school board races. The model includes a variable that measures whether the election takes place in an at-large or single-member district. Whereas electoral structure has an effect on election results for minority candidates, such as African Americans or Latinos (who appear to benefit from single-member districts), whether electoral structure matters to Christian Right candidates is unclear. Although individuals who would be classified as part of the Christian Right are a minority of the U.S. population,[2] they may not be a minority in specific school districts. If they are a minority in such districts, they may not necessarily be a "visible" minority in the same way as African American or Latino candidates, so electoral structure might not matter as much to Christian Right school board candidates as it does to minority candidates. Nonetheless, a control for whether an election takes place in an at-large or single-member district is included in the model.[3]

The model also controls for whether the election is partisan. Although the majority of school board elections are nonpartisan, a Christian Right candidate's chances of winning might be affected by partisan races. Research indicates that the Christian Right is very active in Republican Party politics in various states (Smith 1997; Green, Rozell, and Wilcox 2000) and thus might be able to influence which slate of candidates run for local offices such as school board, as it did in the Fairfax County school board case profiled in chapter 3. Furthermore, the mobilizing efforts of the political parties in partisan school board races could be an important factor in the outcomes of the election. The model also controls for whether the candidate is running in an open race (one that is free of incumbents) or a closed race.

In terms of contextual variables, the model considers regional influence by including candidate residency in the South, Midwest, and West as dummy variables, with the Northeast being the reference category. Two other dummies—rural and suburban—are included to control for type of community in which candidates reside (urban is the omitted reference group). The model also attempts to control for level of evangelicalism at a more local level. The Glenmary Research Center has collected data on churches and church membership in each county of the United States.[4] The model includes a control variable that measures the number of adherents of evangelical churches, expressed as a percentage of the total population (both churchgoers and nonchurchgoers alike) in each county in which the school district is located.[5] In some cases, such as Florida and Nevada, a school district is made up of an entire county. This, however, is the exception rather than the rule. Although including a county-level control variable for school district–level analysis runs the risk of committing an ecological fallacy,[6] it might be the best measure available of the specific religious context in which individual candidates find themselves. We would expect to find that Christian Right candidates would likely fare best in school districts located in religiously conservative counties. Finally, the model considers other personal characteristics of candidates, including gender and education, that might be related to whether he or she is elected to school board.

Results

A simple cross-tabulation of results for the 491 candidates who ran contested races shows that 46 percent of Christian Right candidates and 52 percent of non–Christian Right candidates won their races—a difference that is not statistically significant (see table 5.1).

Although not reported, the rates of success for Christian Right group members alone, Christian Right group supporters, and Christian Right group issue agenda supporters were virtually the same as the combined category of Christian Right candidate used in table 5.1.

Though the bivariate model demonstrates no significant findings, how does the inclusion of various controls that might affect a candidate's chances of

Table 5.1
Success of Christian Right Candidates Compared with
Non–Christian Right Candidates

Election Outcome	Christian Right Candidate %	Non–Christian Right Candidate %
Won	46 (45)	52 (203)
Lost	54 (52)	49 (191)

Note: N = 491. Differences between two candidates are not significant. Whole numbers in parentheses. Column totals do not total 100 percent, because of rounding error.

winning a school board election affect the electoral success rates of Christian Right candidates? Table 5.2 includes data from the multivariate, logistic regression model. (The number of selected cases drops from 491 to 417 because of missing data, although the model remains significant.) Again, we find that there is no significant relationship between success in school board races and

Table 5.2
Logistic Model Success in School Board Elections

Independent Variable	Coefficient B (Standard Error)	Estimated Odds Ratio/Maximum Likelihood Estimate
Christian Right Candidate	−.0781 (.278)	.9249
Incumbent	1.7956 (.275)***	6.0023
Resources:		
Money Spent on Race	.1663 (.238)	1.1810
Number of Volunteers	.0151 (.008)	1.0152
Number of Endorsements	.0897 (.210)	1.0939
Endorsed by Education Group	.3362 (.525)	1.3996
Received Candidate Training	.2367 (.396)	1.2671
Electoral Structure:		
At Large District	.0616 (.228)	1.0635
Partisan Election	.1990 (.406)	1.2202
Ran in Open-Seat Race	.3575 (.269)	1.4298
Contextual Factors:		
South	−.6234 (.516)	.5361
Midwest	.1051 (.348)	1.1108
West	−.1870 (.3729)	.8294
Rural	.8484 (.4163)*	2.3359
Suburban	.4862 (.440)	1.6261
Percent Evangelical	−.8126 (1.483)	.4437
Other Factors:		
Education Level	−.0495 (.123)	.9517
Gender	.2661 (.230)	1.3049
Constant	−.47310 (.699)	

Note: $N = 417$ (seventy-four missing values). Percent categorized correctly, 68.82%; −2XLLR = 501.766; model $\chi^2 = 76.201$, 18 degrees of freedom. $p < .0000$.
*$p < .05$.
**$p < .01$.
***$p < .001$.

Christian Right status. In other words, Christian Right candidates are not more likely to win school board elections than candidates who are not part of the Christian Right. Instead, the major predictor of success in school board races is incumbency, which is highly significant ($p < .0000$) and accounts for most of the variance.

Most of the other factors wash out in this statistical analysis, although the number of volunteers per candidate just misses the significance threshold ($p < .0587$)—the more volunteers a candidate has, the more likely he or she is to win election to school board. The other sources of resources one might expect to help in a race for school board—amount of money spent, number and type of endorsements—do not appear to play a part in a candidate's chances. In terms of contextual variables, only one stands out. The odds of victory for candidates from rural communities are higher than for candidates from urban communities, although it is hard to speculate why this is so. Region and percentage evangelicals in the county in which a candidate lives do not appear to influence the odds of electoral success for candidates more generally. The structure of school board elections, whether they are at-large or partisan, does not appear to factor into a candidate's overall chances of success. Whether a candidate runs in an open seat does not appear to be a significant factor either. Further, individual characteristics such as levels of education and gender are also nonsignificant in the model.

It could be the case that, although contextual and structural variables matter little to most candidates in the study, they could have a more specialized influence on Christian Right candidates. Table 5.3 lists the results for the original model as well as interaction terms for Christian Right status on eight different contextual and structural variables to determine whether such factors somehow enhance the electability of Christian Right candidates; however, none of these interactions is statistically significant. Of particular surprise is the fact that there appears to be no relationship between Christian Right status and percentage of evangelical church members in the counties in which they reside. Southern or Midwestern residency has no bearing on Christian Right candidates' odds of winning; nor does their rural or suburban status. Whether a Christian Right candidate runs at large or in a partisan race is also not a factor in his or her chances of winning.

Because incumbency is such a dominant explanatory variable in this model, it might be worthwhile to examine the success rates of incumbents and nonincumbents, and their impact on Christian Right status, independently. Of the 491 candidates running in contested elections, 349, or 71 percent, were not incumbents. Likewise, 142, or 29 percent, were incumbents. Examining nonincumbents first, table 5.4 demonstrates that 38 percent of Christian Right

Table 5.3
Logistic Model Success in School Board Elections with Interaction Terms

Independent Variable	Coefficient B (Standard Error)	Estimated Odds Ratio/Maximum Likelihood Estimate
Christian Right Candidate	.5299 (.994)	1.6987
Incumbent	1.7645 (.281)***	5.8388
Resources:		
Money Spent on Race	.1591 (.241)	1.1724
Number of Volunteers	.0145 (.008)	1.0146
Number of Endorsements	.0856 (.215)	1.0893
Endorsed by Education Group	.3971 (.537)	1.4875
Received Candidate Training	.2488 (.403)	1.2825
Electoral Structure:		
At-Large District	−.0595 (.263)	.9422
Partisan Election	.1185 (.459)	1.1258
Ran in Open-Seat Race	.1220 (.304)	1.1298
Contextual Factors:		
South	−.6732 (.573)	.5101
Midwest	.1566 (.374)	1.1695
West	−.1847 (.388)	.8231
Rural	.9782 (.510)	2.6597
Suburban	.7364 (.530)	2.0884
Percent Evangelical	.0503 (1.665)	1.0516
Other Factors:		
Education Level	−.0381 (.126)	.9626
Gender	.2341 (.233)	1.2638
CR × Percent Evangelical	− 3.4550 (4.146)	.0316
CR × Open Seat	.9751 (.677)	2.6514
CR × At Large District	.3354 (.576)	1.3984
CR × Partisan Election	.4298 (.999)	1.5368
CR × South	.1262 (1.127)	1.1346
CR × Midwest	−.2862 (.655)	.7511
CR × Rural	−.4733 (.918)	.6229
CR × Suburban	−.8716 (1.010)	.4183
Constant	−1.3997 (.723)	

Note: $N = 417$ (seventy-four missing values). Percent categorized correctly, 69.78%; −2XLLR = 496.272; model χ^2 81.695, 26 degrees of freedom; $p < .0000$.
*$p < .05$.
**$p < .01$.
***$p < .001$.

Table 5.4
Success of Christian Right Candidates Compared with Non–Christian
Right Candidates: Nonincumbents versus Incumbents

Election Outcome	Christian Right Candidate %	Non–Christian Right Candidate %
Nonincumbent[a]		
Won	38 (26)	41 (114)
Lost	62 (42)	60 (167)
Incumbent[b]		
Won	66 (19)	78 (89)
Lost	35 (10)	21 (24)

Note: Differences between candidates are not significant; whole numbers in parentheses.
[a]$N = 349$.
[b]$N = 142$.

candidates won their races compared with 41 percent of non–Christian Right candidates—a difference that is not significant. Although not reported, a scaled-down logistic regression model that controls for open seat status, number of volunteers, region, community type, and percentage of evangelical residents living in the same county as respondents does not alter this initial finding.[7]

The analysis of incumbents in table 5.4 also yields no significant findings. At a bivariate level, Christian Right incumbents (66 percent) are less likely than non–Christian Right incumbents (79 percent) to win their bids for reelection, but this difference is not statistically significant ($p = .136$). A multivariate analysis that again controls for open seat status, number of volunteers, region, community type, and percentage of evangelical residents living in the same county as respondents does not appear to alter the significance of this finding, although the variable for Christian Right status in this model does approach statistical significance ($p < .074$) (data not shown). These results are questionable, however, in light of the fact that the model was not significant ($p < .226$), a result (most likely) of the small sample size ($N = 133$), which excluded an additional nine cases because of missing data.

Discussion

Progressive opponents and media critics of the Christian Right have it wrong—the likelihood of a Christian Right takeover of local school boards does not seem imminent. This chapter finds that Christian Right candidates are no more likely to win school board elections than non–Christian Right candidates, a finding that corresponds nicely with the survey research from chapter 4. In the preceding chapter, little evidence suggested that Christian Right candidates use stealth campaign techniques to try and be elected to school boards. Instead, both Christian Right candidates and their non–Christian Right counterparts campaign in very similar ways. Perhaps such similarities explain why both Christian Right and non–Christian Right candidates, overall, are likely to win at the same rate. This finding again tends to cast doubt on the stealth approach as a viable weapon employed by Christian Right candidates across the country.

The major predictor of victory in school board elections is incumbency, similar to other types of elections in American politics. The number of resources a candidate possesses, the structure of the school board election, or the context in which candidates find themselves largely do not determine success in school board elections. As detailed in chapter 4, candidates for school board spend very little money on their elections and have relatively few volunteers to assist them (although this variable is nearly significant in the model). This "low-key" approach to school board campaigning might help explain why many factors normally related to candidate success in other types of races do not appear significant in the full model (aside from incumbency).

Christian Right candidates do not appear to benefit from at-large elections or partisan races, nor, more surprisingly, do they benefit from contextual factors such as region, community type, or percentage of evangelicals who live in the same counties as they do. Breaking down the data to examine Christian Right incumbents and nonincumbents also does not bring significant findings. Here, the data finding that Christian Right incumbents are not significantly less likely to win than non–Christian Right incumbents is of note, in view of the election results of conservative Christian incumbents who lost bids for reelection to school board in well-known cases in Kansas, New Hampshire, California, and Florida. Recall from chapter 1 that, in these notable cases, conservative Christians were elected as a majority to the board, only to be rejected by voters in their bids for reelection after making controversial decisions. The finding that non–Christian Right incumbents are not significantly reelected at higher rates than their Christian Right counterparts could suggest that conservative Christian candidates, once in office, are not necessarily likely to make decisions that lead to their dismissal in the next elections—or, that if they do, their local communities can live with such decisions. Here, examples from the case studies are telling. In Garrett County, several conservative Christians easily won their bids for reelection after serving one term on the board. (Two of the four opted not to seek reelection at the end of their terms.) And even in a more diverse county such as Fairfax, where countermobilization among groups opposed to the Christian Right was more heightened than in Garrett, one Christian Right incumbent (of two running for reelection), was successful. In both cases, conservative Christian board members made or suggested controversial policies that upset various members in the community, yet only one incumbent (the other social conservative in Fairfax County) paid the ultimate price—not being reelected. Chapter 6 more closely examines the governing styles of the conservative Christians who were elected to the two boards.

Chapter Six

The Christian Right as School Board Members: How Conservative Christians Govern

In 1992, Christian Right organizations and candidates became interested in the New York City school boards after the chancellor, Joseph A. Fernandez, supported a new "Children of the Rainbow" curriculum. Included in this curriculum, which taught elementary school students tolerance toward homosexuals, was the controversial book about lesbian parents, *Heather Has Two Mommies*. The fight regarding this curriculum culminated in Mr. Fernandez's resignation. It also sparked the decision of conservative Christians to run for seats on the thirty-two community school boards in New York City that set policy for more than 800 elementary and junior high schools (Wilcox 2000, 84). In 1993, conservative Christians were able to capture fifty of the city's 288 board seats, which the Christian Coalition and other Christian Right groups considered a major victory (Reed 1996). Yet three years later, the impact of conservative Christian board members was less dramatic than some people had hoped or others had feared, mainly because of the minority status of conservative Christians on the school board. On some community boards in New York City, conservative Christian board members were able to win modest victories such as budget reductions. Still, most conservative Christian board members were unable to make the sorts of changes that they would have liked, such as banning books that they deemed inappropriate for the classroom or teaching a "pro-American, Eurocentric" view of American history, in the words of one New York City Christian Right board member (Belluck 1996).

The case in New York is notable because it is one of the few times that the media covered how the Christian Right fared as a minority coalition on a school board. The Christian Right's experience as a minority here seems to confirm the assumption that conservative Christians have little impact in this scenario. Media attention instead has focused on the more controversial cases in which the Christian Right has assumed a majority on school boards (see, for example, Jones 1993; Brooks 1995; Wald 1995; Ammis 1996, B1). These cases demonstrate the willingness of newly elected Christian Right majorities to make major changes to school board policies. For example, in Merrimack, New Hampshire, a conservative Christian majority that was elected to the school board in 1994 voted to allow a moment of silence to begin the day in each school and approved a new abstinence-based sex education curriculum. Its most controversial action involved the passage of an antihomosexuality policy that stated the school district "shall neither implement nor carry out any program or activity that has either the purpose or effect of encouraging or supporting homosexuality as a positive life alternative" (Ammis 1996, B1). Another example is Vista, California, where in 1992 Christian Right board members passed a policy that allowed the teaching of creationism on par with evolution theory. One of the newly elected conservative Christian board members was an executive with the Institute for Creation Science, an organization that promotes teaching creationism as scientific theory. They also voted to turn down state grants that would have funded free breakfast programs for poor children, stating that children should eat breakfast with their parents instead and that the program "had more to do with welfare than education" (Granberry 1996, A21). In Florida, a conservative Christian school board majority in Lake County ordered all schools in its district to begin teaching in history courses that U.S. culture is superior to all others, while conservative Christian board members in Round Rock, Texas, dismissed the superintendent of their schools because he opposed prayer at high school football games.

A focus on these school boards leaves the impression that majority coalitions face few limitations in enacting their legislative agendas and that minority coalitions have little power to effect changes in policy. These situations are not necessarily representative, however, as cases involving majority and minority factions in other types of legislatures demonstrate. For example, the Republicans who took control of Congress after the 1994 elections were largely unable to initiate major changes in policy despite their majority status (see, for example, Marannis and Weisskopf 1996; Fenno 1997; Killian 1998; Rae 1998). Richard Fenno (1997) writes that the Republican revolution never occurred, in part, because of the Republican majority's lack of experience in governing, brought on by more than forty years as a minority party. Further, Fenno and Linda Killian (1998) contend that the Republican majority, particularly the newly elected freshman class, misread their mandate from the public. Rather than viewing their electoral success as the voter's rejection of the Democratic majority, the Republicans believed that their victory was an endorsement of the Contract with America, the Republican's campaign platform that outlined ten major policy proposals that Republican candidates pledged to uphold on their election to Congress. Only when these freshmen were socialized into learning about how to compromise, build coalitions, and listen to the views of the public did they become effective legislators, although, as Killian (1998) and Rae (1998) point out, a few of them never did.

Turning to minority factions, political scientists have long known that minorities can influence policy in legislatures by setting or shaping the agenda (Cobb and Elder 1983), whether these factions consist of interest groups (Walker 1991), congressional caucuses (Hammond 1998), or minority parties or coalitions in other types of legislatures, including city councils (Browning, Marshall, and Taub 1984). William Connelly and John Pitney (1994) write that, when Republicans were the minority party in the House of Representatives, on some occasions they effectively circumvented congressional rules (which the Democrats had used to block their participation) by appealing directly to the public with their national agenda. Charles O. Jones (1970), who wrote the definitive work on how minority parties in Congress can affect policy, also discusses this strategy. Jones argues that the minority party's role is not consistent over time—that external conditions such as public opinion and internal conditions such as minority party unity and organization help to determine the range of strategies available to the minority in congressional policymaking. In addition to agenda setting, Jones notes that a minority can affect policy through what he terms "consequential partisan opposition," including obstructionist behavior such as adding controversial amendments to bills to ensure their defeat. Two other strategies—constructive opposition, whereby a minority counters an existing policy with its on policy proposals, and innovation, whereby a minority initiates its own proposal—hinge on reaching the right audiences, such as the president or the public.

The earlier examples involving the election of Christian Right majority and minority school board factions would lead one to predict that Christian Right majority coalitions make major policy changes, such as the school boards in Merrimack and Vista, while Christian Right minority factions have little impact on school policy and procedures, as the case in New York City demonstrates. On the other hand, not all majority and minority factions face the same opportunities or constraints on their election to office, as certain political science literature on Congress and other types of legislatures demonstrate.

Do Christian Right school board members govern the same as non– Christian Right board members, or is their legislative behavior different? Are Christian Right board members likely to vote for or adopt major changes in school policy that correspond with the goals of the national movement, or are Christian Right board members likely to make few changes to school curriculum and procedures? The mixed findings in the two case studies, with respect to majority and minority governing coalitions in other legislatures, leaves little guidance in the way of predicting how Christian Right school boards members will govern.

Christian Right candidates fared differently in the two case studies analyzed for this study. In Garrett County, three conservative Christians were elected to the five-member board in 1994, joining another conservative Christian who was elected two years earlier (and who maintained her seat in 1996). Christian Right candidates did not fare as well in Fairfax County. Only two social conservatives were elected to the twelve-member board in 1995. Nevertheless, these two conservative Christians were usually joined by two fellow Republican board members to create a unified minority voting bloc on many policy-related issues.

This chapter relies on several sources of data to explore the impact of the Christian Right on the Garrett and Fairfax County school boards, including interviews, school board minutes, newspaper accounts of school board events, and participant-observations at school board meetings.[1] In light of the exploratory nature of these particular case studies, "impact" is not strictly defined. On the one hand, the study looks at attempts by Christian Right board members in both counties to propose and pass policies that correspond with the goals of the national movement, whether that includes, for example, making sex education more restrictive or promoting the use of phonics in elementary schools. On the other hand, impact is not limited to whether a policy is actually proposed or passed by the board. As the case study in Fairfax County will demonstrate, impact also means setting the school board's agenda and, through obstructionist behavior, limiting the ability of the more liberal school board majority to pass legislation. Although it is difficult to generalize about the governing opportunities and restrictions conservative Christian school board members face on the basis of these two examples, the case studies do offer some interesting perspectives on the subject and could offer new insight about the more general dilemma of governing.

Apart from learning more about the conditions that lead to effective governance, the findings from these cases also have implications for priestly versus prophetic religious politics. Recall from chapter 1 that priestly politics serve to legitimate government action, whereas prophetic politics are more critical in nature, with criticism toward politics steeped in biblical and moral precepts. As a majority faction on the school board in Garrett County, the Christian Right did enjoy some achievements while serving in office, serving in some capacity in a priestly role. Nonetheless, they were unable to enact widespread changes in school policies, in part because of their desire to merge their religious and moral values more closely with school board politics.

In Fairfax County, conservative Christian board members suffered their share of legislative defeats. At times, however, the minority coalition in Fairfax County successfully set the school board's agenda and shaped some aspects of its public policy. In essence, their status as a minority "freed" the social conservatives to use their prophetic voices, constantly challenging the status quo. In his book about religious lobbyists in Washington, D.C., Daniel Hofrenning (1995) argues that the prophetic perspective of these lobbyists led them to adopt an "outsider" strategy. Instead of seeking contact with political elites, which means compromise and bargaining, religious lobbyists remained distanced, focusing instead on outsider strategies such as mobilizing the grassroots and protesting. The important point here is that these lobbyists—religious conservatives and liberals alike—seldom have the ability to direct policy change, because of their minority status; however, by sticking to their religious principles, such lobbyists can sometimes transform the political agenda and change the nature and tenor of political debate. On many occasions in Fairfax County, social conservatives worked in the same capacity.

In many respects, as this chapter will discuss, the experiences of the conservative Christian board members in both Garrett and Fairfax Counties depart from what happened in places such as Merrimack, New Hampshire, or New York City. Findings from the case studies demonstrate that school boards with a Christian Right majority do not always make extreme policy changes without regard to the community's wishes and school boards with a Christian Right minority are capable of making substantive policy changes.

Garrett County: Christian Right Majority Learns Many Lessons

In Garrett County, Maryland, the religious and ideological motivation that inspired the newly elected board members to run for office also influenced many of their initiatives while serving on the board. Conservative Christian board members were unafraid to question policies or school events that offended their religious sensibilities. Nor were they afraid to question policies or proposals that threatened to weaken local control of school programs at the hands of the state and federal government. Nevertheless, the record of the Christian Right majority after four years in office yielded mixed results, at least with respect to establishing a new, conservatively based education agenda.

The conservative majority did achieve some success in terms of implementing new policy. The board approved a policy that would allow high school valedictorians to offer a prayer during their speeches at high school graduation. The board also made available to parents in 1997 an abstinence-based after-school program geared toward children in middle school. Several of their more controversial ideas, however, met resistance from school administrators, parents, and the local media, resulting in an often hostile relationship between the board and the education community and parents in Garrett County. Ultimately, the conservative Christian board members in the county might have realized that the biggest challenge for conservative Christians is not in getting elected to local office, but in governing.

The Christian Right majority in Garrett County did not initiate major changes to school policy for three reasons. First, the public served as a constraint on a number of their proposed actions. Public concern typically revolved around a perceived fear that the newly elected majority was instituting its religious beliefs at the expense of other voices in the county. Second, service on the school board and closer proximity to the daily workings of the schools gave newly elected board members a different view of education issues and policy. Such proximity and time spent on the board might have revealed to majority members that many education issues were far more complex than they may have been previously aware. Finally, differences among the conservative Christian school board members emerged regarding several issues, which had the effect of dividing the board and making policy changes more difficult.

After new board members were sworn into office in early January 1995, the Garrett County board made some immediate changes in the conduct of the monthly board meetings. The board voted to have each meeting begin with a prayer, led by ministers who were affiliated with the Mountain Top Ministerial Association (an association that also participated to some extent in the school board elections). The board also decided to tape each meeting and to publish more information about upcoming meetings in the local newspaper. Board members adopted a system of "holding" new suggested policies for a month to get community feedback and comments. The goal, according to one of the new Christian Right board members, was to "make it easier for the public who wants to be involved." The new Christian Right board members saw this development as a positive step, in part because they themselves felt that the previous board did not usually welcome their ideas and views.

The Battle over Outcomes-Based Education and School-to-Work Policies

This desire among board members to promote greater community involvement was fulfilled a short time after the board members took office, although perhaps not in the way the board members might have envisioned. One month after being sworn into office, the board's majority expressed concerns about the use of outcomes-based education (OBE) in the county's public schools. Sparked in part by the school administration's desire to switch to an "outcomes-based" system of grading physical education students in kindergarten through fifth grade (a move that the board rejected), the board decided to review OBE procedures already in use in the school system. This move met resistance from parents, teachers, and administrators, more than 100 of whom crowded the second school board meeting of the year to express their displeasure with the newly elected school board's actions.

The comments offered by board members, parents, and school administrators at this meeting revealed that all parties involved had different ideas of what OBE meant. The superintendent of schools explained to meeting participants that OBE, as it was used in the Garrett County schools and other public schools in the state of Maryland, was simply a series of goals for students to meet before passing to the next grade level or to graduate. At the time, Maryland law mandated that all schools must participate in the Maryland School Performance Assessment Program (MSPAP), which consists of a series of assessment tests in reading, writing, social studies, and mathematics.[2] The superintendent explained at the meeting his interpretation that the program places "values on a student's ability to think clearly, analyze and problem solve to meet the demands of the 21st century" ("Support and Criticism" 1995, A5).

Christian Right board members, however, voiced concerns about MSPAP. One believed that the assessment method required too much subjective grading by teachers. Another stated his concern that this method of teaching, geared toward getting students in the class to meet the desired outcomes, "gets away from the concrete measurement of facts, attempting to measure things that are very difficult to measure" ("Support and Criticism" 1995, A5). As an example, he read aloud a MSPAP social studies outcome from one grade level that said "studies will demonstrate attainment of a positive self-concept and empathy toward others in order to improve interaction among individuals and groups in our democratic society." This board member expressed his belief that the public might want a more traditional approach to teaching social studies and other subjects and that the board should try and work to reach such a goal "within the very real constraints of what we are mandated to do by the state" ("Support and Criticism" 1995, A5).

The non–Christian Right board member defended the use of OBE in the Garrett County schools through the MSPAP program. She said that business leaders are looking for graduates who can think critically, which is the "whole point" of the OBE approach ("Support and Criticism" 1995, A5). She also criticized Christian Right board members who expressed their belief that teaching methods under OBE no longer emphasize basic skills.

The views of the non–Christian Right board member, the school superintendent, and many parents in the audience who supported the MSPAP program ultimately served as a constraint for the conservative Christian majority who, despite their misgivings about OBE, voted to appoint an ad hoc committee to investigate how OBE related to the Garrett County schools. Rather than rushing to judgment, the board's majority appointed committee members (made up of parents and community leaders) to study and review the issue from different perspectives. This decision showed a willingness on the part of the Christian Right majority to listen to parents and administrators—a willingness that surprised many of the board's critics in the county, who had feared that the new majority would instigate major changes in policy on its election without considering the views of parents or educators.

The OBE committee reported its findings to the board in September 1995 and found that the central problem with OBE was terminology. The committee found that words used by professional educators such as "critical thinking" are often confusing and misrepresented. The committee offered their own definition of OBE as it was being used in Garrett County schools and found that many controversial issues that have come to be associated with OBE, such as the elimination of report cards or the emphasis on values and beliefs rather than academic facts, were not being implemented in the Garrett County schools. The committee's report recommended that Garrett County should not move toward incorporating any of these controversial items into the education system.

The committee also recommended that the local school system prepare a standard format to include specific content for each grade level program of study and make a "parent edition" of the syllabus available. The school board agreed to the committee's recommendations, demonstrating two things. First, the board majority was willing to address the public's concerns about this issue and even to incorporate the public's views as part of the task force to study OBE. Second, by agreeing to accept the task force's final recommendations, members of the Christian Right majority showed a willingness to withhold judgment about certain policies—even one as controversial to the Christian Right as OBE—until they had been more fully informed about its implementation in Garrett County.

OBE is one example of an education policy employed by the school system that was challenged by the board's conservative Christian majority. The county's involvement in a federally sponsored program called "school-to-work" also came under fire by the board majority in the summer of 1996. School officials came under criticism by the board when they sought to apply for a federal grant (along with two neighboring counties in western Maryland) to fund an expansion of the county's school-to-work program. This program had been funded up until that point in a more limited version by the county. School officials sought grant money because they lacked funds to expand the program to all the students who had expressed an interest in participating in it. The local school-to-work program in Garrett County, designed to arrange working experiences for students who choose particular career paths in schools, involved several businesses and work sites where selected students received hands-on experience after school and during the summer months.

The Christian Right majority questioned the administration's desire to apply for the federal grant money. Their main concern was that grant money provided by the federal government would come with "strings" attached—strings that would jeopardize the board's local control over the program. Another concern for the Christian Right majority involved the possibility that the county might be required to provide matching funds if they won the federal grant. One board member, who suggested that the grant would entail too much involvement by the federal government in the county schools, suggested that the administration should refrain from participating in the program entirely, an idea that frustrated many individuals in the community. Board members agreed to hold a special meeting to discuss whether the county should pursue the federal grant.

One parent who attended the meeting had served on a local labor market team that was involved with the school-to-work program. She also ran unsuccessfully for school board in 1996. According to her, part of the problem that Christian Right board members had with the program stemmed from their ignorance of it and their willingness to accept the criticisms of school-to-work brought on by Christian Right organizations such as Phyllis Schlafly's Eagle Forum. She recalled, "The board insisted that we weren't going to teach kids, that we were just going to certify them. They did not understand. Everything they brought [to the meeting], every bit of anti-school-to-work literature, I was holding in my hand from Phyllis Schlafly from the Internet. It was the same. . . . Sadly enough, they are just puppets. They are hearing it [from the Internet], and whatever they hear, it comes out of their mouths." This parent's concern is similar to the one raised about the OBE debate by the board's other critics—that the board's initial hostility toward education programs affiliated with the state government (or federal government, in the case of school-to-work) is often the result of a misunderstanding about what the program entails.

The special meeting about school-to-work drew a large crowd of interested parents and citizens. Local business leaders also attended the meeting in support of the grant pursuit. The four conservative Christian board members expressed concerns about the use of federal funds to finance the program. Each worried about the role that the board members themselves would play in implementing and overseeing it. The Maryland State Board of Education's assistant state superintendent for career and technology also attended the meeting and tried to allay the board member's fears about the program. She insisted that, although the grant required the establishment of "local labor market teams" to help coordinate the program with local businesses, the school board could decide how to manage these teams.

The meeting showcased tensions between the board's Christian Right majority and its lone moderate, who accused the board's majority of having the belief that the whole public education system is "out to do our children in" rather than to help them. She said the school-to-work program was another example of how the board majority mistrusted the school administrators and professional educators who worked on their behalf: "All these things that raise a red flag to you people—they just don't raise a red flag to me. I look at life in an entirely different way. I know that [the school administrators] would not deliberately start something that's going to damage our children" ("After Lengthy Discussion" 1996, A14). One conservative Christian board member responded to the comment by saying that the school's administrators needed to hear their concerns in order to make changes they felt were acceptable to the grant proposal.

Eventually, the Garrett County school superintendent suggested that the board accept the grant proposal with a condition that some of the language in it be changed. The superintendent suggested that the grant specifically state that students would be given the opportunity, but not forced, to participate in a career experience. The new language would also indicate that the board would be responsible for appointing the local market team members who would coordinate the program with area businesses. With the new language in the proposal, the board unanimously approved the administration's request to pursue the school-to-work grant.

Once again, this episode demonstrates that the community served as a check on the Christian Right majority when it initially pursued somewhat radical changes. Attempts by the board majority to engage in "priestly" politics, in which they sought to legitimate their decisions based on their own moral or religious precepts, were not acceptable to the community at large. Yet, somewhat surprisingly, in view of what has been written about other cases in which a school board has elected a majority of Christian Right members, the board's majority was willing to listen to the views of administrators, parents, and community leaders before making its final decisions about policies that it deemed suspicious, whether they relate to school-to-work or OBE. The debate about school-to-work and OBE also reveals that the board majority was willing to compromise about both issues, on learning of their greater complexity. The majority's previous knowledge about these policies was most likely shaped by the views of Christian Right organizations, such as the Christian Coalition and Eagle Forum, regarding the federal government's implementation of such programs. All four conservative Christian board members had been involved with the county's chapter of the Christian Coalition to some extent. These views were modified, however, once they learned more about how each program was actually being implemented in Garrett County.

Wellness Day Concerns

The Christian Right majority on the Garrett County school board did not restrict their review of school programs to those with ties to the federal or state government. Aspects of locally initiated programs also fell under scrutiny by the board, including Wellness Day, an annual daylong affair that takes place at Northern High School (one of two high schools in the county). The event is designed to raise awareness about the dangers of drugs and alcohol and to give students alternatives to using them. Students can attend as many as four seminars during the day, which are divided categorically into three sections: antidrugs and -alcohol, health and fitness, and entertainment. For example, students can learn how to perform CPR or how to become active in various community service projects.

Several weeks prior to Wellness Day in 1995, the principal of Northern High School mailed flyers that contained an agenda of events and guest speakers to school board members and other community leaders. One of the Christian Right board members became concerned about some of the topics included in this agenda. In particular, he voiced his objections to the school administration about a session that included a talk on astrology, as well as his concerns about seminars that featured acupuncture and massage therapy. He recalled, "I called the superintendent and asked for more information about those sessions. What was going to be taught? What would be done in the massage therapy class? . . . Originally, the impetus is religious. There are Buddhist views behind acupuncture. I asked are we going to be doing acupuncture on the kids? And what about this astrology thing? Are we going to be telling these kids that they ought to live their lives by the stars?" At the suggestion of the superintendent, the board member spoke directly to the principal and asked him if he would consider striking the seminar on astrology. The principal refused, saying that the topics of the seminars were initially chosen by several committees, parents, and students and then had to pass his desk for review and approval. In response, the board member announced that the board would hold a special session to have the astrology component of Wellness Day stricken, a move that the principal believed was beyond the board's authority.

The calling of the special meeting provoked an angry response from the editor of the local paper, who deplored the board member's "micro-management" and "outrageous behavior." The editorial also described the board majority's attitude as destructive: "They are suspicious and question, in a most negative way, every action of our educators. Instead of supporting our teachers and administrators, many of whom are outstanding, and giving them deserved credit for their education and experience, they distrust and intimidate them at every turn with their superior, holier-than-thou attitude, which, frankly, sickens us. The board members, not one of whom has a degree in education (most have no degree whatsoever), still don't understand their role on the elected board" ("Another Special Meeting" 1995, A1). The editor also argued that it was wrong for a board member to single out a staff person, in this case the principal of Northern High School, and challenge him on a particular program being held at the school.

The school board's special session, similar to the meetings involving OBE and school-to-work, attracted a large crowd. At issue for the board's Christian Right majority were the possible religious components of several of the seminars. The issue for the principal and his supporters, meanwhile, did not concern the "religious" aspect of astrology or the seminars—the principal and others viewed the session on astrology as entertainment only—but instead concerned the school board's rightful authority. The principal and many parents in the community believed that the school board had overreached its authority in threatening to strike *any* seminar from the Wellness Day event. For critics of the school board's majority, this special meeting was another example of the Christian Right board members not trusting school administrators to do their jobs. At the meeting, the principal was asked by the board to discuss the topics under scrutiny in greater detail. He pointed out to the board that they were not asking him questions that he had "not already asked [of event organizers]" ("Parents, Staff Incensed" 1995, A1). He explained that acupuncture was just one of several topics included in a chiropractic seminar and that astrology was included in a section simply for fun and amusement. He also defended a seminar on massage therapy, noting that the class covers basic massage techniques and that massage is a "highly regarded treatment" for many individuals. The principal noted that the program had won several state awards and was extremely popular with students and parents, adding, "We have never been questioned about the event. In fact, we have received nothing but praise" ("Parents, Staff Incensed" 1995, A1).

The board's only non–Christian Right member expressed her belief that the meeting was not only unnecessary but overstepped the bounds of the board if the proper policy had been followed in the selection of seminars to be presented for Wellness Day. She asked Northern High School's principal if in fact he had followed the proper policy, and he responded affirmatively.

Christian Right board members insisted that the meeting was being held only to get information about Wellness Day and was not intended to indicate that the board did not support the event. The board member who had first raised the issue about the astrology seminar, however, maintained his belief that the topics under consideration were not related to entertainment or health, as the event's supporters had argued. Rather, he reiterated his belief that the three components were religious. He expressed his desire to remove the astrology part of the seminar, in particular, because students might be "misled" by the program.

This board member's attempts to remove these three components from the Wellness Day program were unsuccessful, and the board reached a compromise with the school superintendent and the high school principal. The principal moved to make the astrology section available only to students whose parents gave their consent.

The board member who first raised questions about the components was unhappy with the outcome of the compromise and "would have preferred that the board take direct action to stop that session." He maintained that the astrology seminar was "akin to teaching religion" in the schools, adding that "there's no way [that] a minister would have been allowed to come in and say this is how you should live your life by the Bible." This board member's remarks are revealing in two ways. First, because the board member believed that astrology was not simply entertainment, but instead was a form of religion (and one that violated his own beliefs), his attempt to prevent the seminar from being offered by the school stemmed from his own personal religious convictions. Second, his comments about having a minister come in and speak about the Bible echo a popular theme among leaders of the Christian Right— that Christians, and the religion of Christianity more generally, often fall victim to discrimination in the United States. In this situation, from the point of view of the conservative Christian board member, the discrimination lies in the fact that the school finds it acceptable to include the "religion" of astrology as part of Wellness Day but not the religion of Christianity.

The debate about Wellness Day, as well as the two situations involving OBE and school-to-work, highlight some important findings about the Christian Right majority on the Garrett County school board. The Wellness Day controversy shows the willingness of the board majority to question events that somehow offend its religious sensibilities. This episode demonstrates that religion did not just inspire these conservative Christian board members to run for office, as indicated in chapter 3, but continued to influence their decision making once elected to the board. The board's intensive review of OBE and school-to-work, meanwhile, illustrates the board majority's suspicion regarding programs that have ties to the state and federal governments.

Moreover, the three situations are telling in that the board's conservative Christian majority did not get what it initially had wanted. Despite its skepticism about OBE and school-to-work, the board majority was willing to listen to the community and to school administrators and to become more knowledgeable about the issues before making any rash decisions about them. The public's involvement and attendance at meetings, according to one of the board's critics (who later ran unsuccessfully for school board in 1996), was an important key in keeping the Christian Right's impact from being too heavy-handed. He remarked, "It hasn't been as blatant, in large part, because we have a lot of public involvement. There have been numerous (especially the first two years the board was elected) board meetings where [the board majority] would have wanted to institute something that is really gross, and there were enough people at board meetings who raised their hands, saying, 'We don't want that,' and causing enough of a stink that it required them to go back and think and look and come up with a decent compromise." He adds that, if there had not been public involvement, "we could have seen some egregious examples" of drastic policy changes in the schools. In this way, the community served as an effective check against the board making radical changes to school policies and programs.

The majority's willingness to appoint task forces to study OBE or to reach a compromise on both the school-to-work proposal and on Wellness Day demonstrates that conservative Christian majorities do not always make radical changes to school policy. Rather, they sometimes take into consideration the views of the public or school administrators. Unlike the newspaper accounts of what happened with Christian Right boards in Vista, California, and Merrimack, New Hampshire, conservative Christian board members in Garrett County ultimately worked with the administrators and listened to other voices in the community, even though their initial actions provoked hostile reactions from their critics. Although some of the board's conservative Christian members might have wished for a different outcome in these three cases, as a majority they were still willing to seek compromise and listen to their constituents. The situations involving OBE and school-to-work also show that the board was willing to compromise once they considered new information about how these programs were being implemented in the Garrett County schools.

There is an additional reason that the Christian Right majority did not make the sorts of radical changes that their critics in the community had feared. As with many majority coalitions in government, important differences began to emerge among members of the Christian Right majority, at least with respect to certain issues. Several events illustrate the willingness of some Christian Right board members to depart from the "conventional" Christian Right point of view on education issues. Two examples, in particular, illustrate how the ideological and religious beliefs of some conservative Christian board members played out differently from their colleagues'.

The Majority Coalition Cracks: Textbook Adoption and Teacher Discipline

One example is in the area of textbook adoption. A major responsibility of school boards is to select textbooks and materials for the classroom, a task that yields a potentially enormous amount of influence on schoolchildren, depending on the content and tone of the books that are selected. Recall from chapter 1 the controversies generated by textbook selection in places such as Kanawha County, West Virginia. Christian Right leaders today often decry the liberal or "humanistic" bent of many textbooks that are used in the classroom. In Garrett County, the debate about the selection of textbooks for one course demonstrates that some Christian Right board members shared many of these same concerns. The debate, however, also showcased differences in opinion among the conservative Christians serving on the board.

In 1997, the board appointed a curriculum committee, as was customary, to review a series of textbooks to be used for an advanced placement U.S. history course. The final text recommended by the committee, *A People and a Nation*, was found to be offensive and too "liberally biased" by several of the conservative board members. Board members in December 1997 decided to add two other history books—reviewed but rejected by the committee—to be considered by the board on its final vote to approve a new text. These additional books, as well as the committee's selected text, were put on view to the public at the school board's office one month prior to the final vote in January 1998, to facilitate comments and feedback from the community.

The January meeting to discuss the book again brought out a significant crowd of parents and activists, most of whom were opposed to the board's actions regarding the textbook selection. Several parents spoke at the meeting, including one parent who believed that the action by the board to receive comments on the additional texts was distracting to the textbook committee process and that it undermined the committee's trust and expertise. One of the board members maintained that the board had every right to consider other alternatives to the recommended text and that a "necessary tension" exists between the public and elected officials and the administrative professionals.

Board members described their thoughts about the textbooks under consideration. One of the conservative Christians came to the meeting armed with two itemized pages of his case against the book that was selected by the committee. Among other criticisms, he believed that the book depicted Ronald Reagan in an unfavorable light and that there were too many references to women in history. He argued that the book, which he described as "liberally biased," led him to wonder "if the majority of citizens would want to spend tax dollars on the text." Another Christian Right board member indicated that the textbook did not emphasize enough factual knowledge but instead taught "social history." As an example, she said that Woodstock was depicted as "one big party" without any reference to the illegal drug abuse that occurred there.

Not all the conservative Christians were consistent in their disapproval of the text. One conservative Christian board member supported the text, despite his own differences in political leanings. He recounted his favorite class from high school, which he said was taught by a very liberal teacher. At the time, this board member had become a member of the John Birch Society while in high school. He recalled that he spent much of his time debating various issues with the teacher—an experience that made him "really think" and was great for the "learning process." He argued that it did not matter whether the textbook was balanced, because he believed that the goal in education is to have "worldly-wise children" and to leave it up to the teachers "to round things out." He said his greatest fear was not the views and materials expressed in *A People and a Nation*, but that a teacher would strictly "teach" the text.

The fourth Christian Right board member reserved his harshest judgment not for the textbook but for the parents who were critical of the board's actions. He was concerned about the hostility and "outrage" that parents in the community had expressed toward the board regarding their decision to make two additional textbooks available for public review and comment before the board made its final decision. He believed that making two additional textbooks available for review by the community in addition to the committee's recommended text fell in line with the board's general goal to promote greater public awareness and input by giving the community a wider range of options. He believed that parents could not really "have a say" if the board had simply selected what the committee recommended. In the end, this board member voted to adopt the recommended text because it appeared to enjoy the most support from the community.

Some critics in the community argued that the move to make these additional texts available for public review was intended to be a way for the board to legitimize their decision to refuse the committee's recommended text, if they made that decision. Whatever the motivation to make additional texts open to review, the board ultimately voted, by a three-to-two margin, to adopt the more liberal *A People and a Nation*. The textbook incident illustrates that Christian Right board members were not monolithic in their views. In this case, two conservative Christian board members were willing to let their views on ideology take a back seat to other concerns.

During the board's four-year tenure, other differences emerged among its majority members. Although each of the conservatives on the board held a faith in evangelical Christianity and shared many similar ideas about education policy, their views on education issues sometimes were affected differently by their religious beliefs. One incident that divided the conservative Christian majority involved a disciplinary action against a popular high school science teacher. Although three conservative Christians ultimately decided to dismiss the teacher, the incident serves as a further illustration of the differences of opinion that characterized, and at times fractured, the Christian Right majority.

The disciplinary action stemmed from the arrest of the science teacher for possession of marijuana. The teacher was immediately suspended by the board of education for misconduct in office, pending a formal hearing to determine whether she would be fired. Shortly before the hearing, the police dropped all formal charges against the teacher and a court ordered her to seek counseling. At the school board hearing, the teacher indicated that she was sorry for the incident, and she explained that she was no longer using the drug. Several individuals testified on her behalf, attesting to her dedication and skill as a teacher. Some school administrators from the high school indicated that it would be difficult to find another person with similar skills and competency to replace her.

The board was divided about whether to terminate her from the school system. Three of the conservative Christians on the board ultimately voted to have the teacher fired, for numerous reasons spelled out in a nine-page document written by the school board's attorney. Among other issues, the board majority noted that it had a partial policy dealing with employees' possession of illegal drugs or alcohol. The policy provides that employees convicted of possessing a controlled dangerous substance during or off school hours would be considered to have committed misconduct in office and would be subject to termination under state law. Although the formal charges against the teacher were dropped, the board believed that the "partial policy" was "not designed to limit the sanction a Board can bring with respect to use or possession of illegal drugs." The board believed that the teacher's credibility, if she were allowed to remain in the classroom, would be undermined when she attempted to teach a section on drug abuse in her biology classes, as mandated by state law.

The board majority was also disturbed by what they described as the teacher's "cavalier" attitude about the use of marijuana. Although the teacher admitted her regret about the incident at the hearing and said that she would not use the drug in the future, she also likened using marijuana to drinking beer and testified that she advised students in her biology classes that "it's just not worth it" to become involved with the drug. The board believed that her attitude about the drug would send the message that the use of drugs are "not worth it" because of the potential punishment that could result in their use, not because the use of drugs in and of themselves is immoral. The board wrote, "All these facts suggest that [the teacher] sees nothing immoral or inherently wrong in the use of marijuana, but believes, now, that she should not use marijuana as her 'choice' not because it is morally or inherently wrong, but only because it is against the law, and 'is just not worth it.' The Majority Board feels that this type of attitude is largely responsible for the ascendancy of drug abuse in the American experience and in the school systems in particular." The reference to morality in the written document suggests that the decision by the majority of board members to fire the teacher stemmed in part from their own religious convictions. The board also indicated in the letter that, had the facts been different, had the teacher recognized that the use of marijuana is "a far different thing than drinking a glass of beer," or had she testified that her actions were inherently wrong, the board's majority might have considered a sanction less drastic than dismissal.

The two other board members did not reach the same conclusion. Both board members interpreted the teacher's testimony differently than did the board majority and, in a dissenting opinion letter, indicated their belief that the teacher was truly sorry for the "shame and trouble she has caused her family." The two board members also noted that the defendant was an excellent teacher and a valued member of the staff at the high school where she taught.

Their dissenting opinion also had religious overtones, similar to the board's majority's decision. Instead of emphasizing the immorality of drug use, however, the minority chose instead to express the religious message of forgiveness. They wrote, "Those of us in society who have made mistakes and have been forgiven are extremely grateful, but we are also under an obligation to forgive others when they have fallen and seek our forgiveness. So with much prayer, a Christ-like heart, and a desire to do what is right, [we] cannot vote to terminate." The conservative Christian who sided with the board's moderate member in the decision and who also wrote the minority opinion is also a part-time pastor for his church in Garrett County. Several years later, he still maintained that his decision to forgive the teacher stemmed directly from his own experience as a pastor who preaches about the "power of forgiveness." Despite the teacher's dismissal, he recounts his actions in this incident as one of his most important achievements on the board.

This dissenting board member cited this incident as one that led him to no longer affiliate himself closely with the Christian Coalition. He said his "main problem" with the Christian Coalition and their dogma is that they subscribe to a "legalist" philosophy that calls for them to punish rather than forgive, or, in his words, leads the Christian Coalition to "shoot their wounded." This board member's thoughts about both the fired teacher and the "dogma" of the Christian Coalition reveal that religion influences his decision making in important ways, albeit in ways that differ at times from the other conservative Christians serving on the board. These differences among the conservative Christians on the school board, despite their shared faith in evangelical Christianity, had the effect of dividing the board and keeping it at times from moving toward a more conservative policy agenda.

The Christian Right majority in Garrett County showed a greater willingness than the Christian Right majorities in Merrimack, New Hampshire; Vista, California; Round Rock, Texas; or Lake County, Florida, to listen to the views of parents and administrators, perhaps because they believed that a local board should be open to the views of the public. Witness all of the initial changes made by the board that promoted greater community involvement and accountability. One parent activist (who ran unsuccessfully for the school board in 1996) said that the board's ideological and combative stance also "toned down" as they became more enlightened about how the schools operate in Garrett County. He stated, "The current board members have become more educated. When they first started, it was a Right Wing conservative Congress, Newt [Gingrich] was doing well, and I think that just everybody was feeling powerful. And we would stay at these board meetings until two in the morning, just trying to slow them down." The public's major effect on the board was to get board members to "slow down" and think about their proposed actions, causing some board members to learn that their preconceived ideas about such policies as OBE often did not match the reality of how the policies were being enacted in Garrett County. As a four-member majority on a five-member board, conservative Christians serving on the board had enough leeway to enact radical policy changes in the school system. Instead, the board's Christian Right majority spent much of their time listening to the concerns of their constituents and incorporating their ideas before making many of their final decisions. Ultimately, their experiences as elected board members might not have changed their religious beliefs. To a certain extent, however, their experiences altered the Christian Right board members' views about what types of policy changes would be good for the school system in Garrett County.

After their four-year terms ended in 1998, two of the conservative Christians decided not to seek reelection, citing personal reasons. The third board member elected in 1994, the same one who supported the high school biology teacher, was easily reelected to another term in 1998, joining the other conservative who had been reelected in 1996. Joining the board's moderate member in 1998 were two other nonconservative Christians, meaning that, for the first time in four years, the board did not have a Christian Right majority.

Fairfax County: Christian Right Minority Achieves Some Success

Unlike the case in Garrett County, the school board in Fairfax County did not have a majority of board members who were conservative Christians. After the county's first school board elections took place in the fall of 1995, only two social conservatives won seats on the twelve-member board. As a minority, the Christian Right faced certain obstacles in their desire to make board policy more conservative. Certainly, the Christian Right board members lost many hard-fought struggles.

Nonetheless, the conservative Christians on the board influenced board policy in three ways. First, the board minority was sometimes successful in setting the board's agenda, meaning that it often determined which issues the board would be debating (much to the chagrin of many of the board's more liberal members). Second, the board's minority was even occasionally success-ful in getting fairly conservative legislation passed by the school board. Finally, the Christian Right influenced policy by bringing the board's business to a standstill. In other words, the actions of the board's minority forced the board to spend more time dealing with issues that concerned the conservative Christian board members and stopped the board's more liberal majority from implementing or exploring new policy proposals.

How were the Christian Right board members successful on certain occa-sions despite their minority status? Their position as a minority on the board, in some sense, "freed them" to follow and argue their ideological views at board meetings. While this approach meant that they lost many battles, it also allowed the board's minority members to achieve limited success in two ways. First, when their arguments and pleas found favorable support among other political leaders in the county, as well as from some parents, the board's minority faction could get several of its initiatives passed by the board. Second, the arguments and amendments put forth by the board's conservatives occa-sionally served as an obstruction for the board's more liberal majority, often preventing the majority from passing additional legislation or considering new policies and programs. By remaining true to their prophetic voices, these members did, at least in some cases, effect change.

The actions of the board's minority members resulted in a bitterly divided school board. Although the school board elections were nonpartisan, recall from chapter 4 that both the Democratic and Republican Parties in Fairfax County endorsed candidates. A total of four Republicans and eight Democrats were elected to the board. While two of the Republicans can be considered "genuine" social conservatives, the two more moderate Republican board members sided with the conservative Christians on most policy-related votes, whether the votes concerned traditional conservative issues such as lowering the school budget or more ideological or even religious issues such as sex edu-cation. As was the case with the school board elections, partisanship defined and shaped much of the board's policy-related actions.

The Minority Loses: Student Information, Guidance Counselors, and Textbook Disclaimer

The partisan divisiveness of the board meant that many policy-related issues, ranging from budget matters to an amendment that would have eased restrictions on the establishment of charter schools in the county, ended in defeat for the board's conservatives. An "eight-four" split in voting among Democrats and Republicans became a common occurrence. For example, the parties were divided about the implementation of a new student information system during the school board's second year in office. The new system, which was supported by the board majority, would replace the outdated computer system used by the school to store various student records and would simplify scheduling, research, and data analysis for school administrators. Board Republicans were convinced that the new system, which would record much more information about students than the previous system, could potentially violate the rights of parents and families. One Christian Right board member expressed such concerns on her website, describing the new system as a "technology 'panacea' that threatens student and family privacy." (Many of the fears she expressed on her website and at board meetings echoed concerns raised by Christian Right organizations such as Phyllis Schlafly's Eagle Forum. Schlafly's group believes that data derived from such advanced computer data banks will eventually be used by the federal government for more sinister purposes beyond maintaining education statistics.) Despite these and other concerns raised by the conservatives on the school board, their motion to postpone the purchase of the system failed.

In another case, the board Republicans submitted a proposal that would limit what counselors could discuss with students without parental consent. Conservatives also sought to have parents sign a permission slip to allow their students to participate in sex education courses rather than having parents request to have their students "opted-out" of the courses, which was the current policy. By making the program "opt-in," the board conservatives hoped that parents would become more educated about the programs and ultimately choose not to have their children participate in them. On one occasion, board members revisited the issue of creationism, which was the defining issue of the 1995 school board elections. In the fall of 1996, parents of a student at a Fairfax County high school complained in a letter to the school board about a passage in their son's textbook that equated creationism with astrology, fad diets, and other forms of "pseudoscience." Board conservatives said the passage amounted to religious discrimination. One conservative Christian described the textbook's comparison of creationism to pseudoscience a "brazen and egregious attack on a group of people because of a benign characteristic called faith" (Ferrechio 1996, C5). This board member suggested putting a disclaimer in the book that condemned the book's language regarding creationism. This proposal, as well as the initiatives concerning guidance counselors and sex education, failed to pass.

These examples are part of a pattern that the conservative Christians often repeated. The board's minority members would challenge the Democrats' agenda at each turn or bring up their own amendments and initiatives, despite little chance of success. Although such defeats meant that the Republicans typically did not enact the types of policies they would have liked, their actions in challenging the Democrats had a more practical, obstructionist result. The Democrats on the Fairfax County school board say efforts by the conservative Christians to offer amendments and force votes distracted them from addressing issues that they believed were more substantive and important such as teacher training, classroom technology, and student behavior problems. In other words, conservatives on the board were "tangling up" the system by offering amendments and programs that had no hope of passage. According to one Democratic board member,

> Issues you wouldn't expect to have to fight about, you fight about. . . . So we were spending money and time, and we still are, because of things they put up. And the majority of parents are happy, and yet we have this group saying that we demand that you protect the rights of parents. And while you are spending money supposedly protecting the rights of parents, you're not helping children. And it seems to me that the goal should be to do what we can to help our children achieve, and I feel sometimes that they get in the way, and it is on issues that I wouldn't think to get in the way on.

Although some Democrats claimed to have respect for the convictions of the social conservatives on the board, their frustration with the conservatives' refusal to compromise made board meetings and actions more difficult. In this sense, the Republicans were successful in stopping the Democrats from enacting additional liberal programs and policies, by using a strategy that minority coalitions in other types of legislatures have used.

These defeats on the part of the conservative Christians also indicate that the board's minority was willing to stick to their conservative principles on a wide variety of issues, even though that meant that relationships between the two sides became strained. In a prophetic metaphor from the Bible, these conservative Christians could be described as serving on the board, but not being "of" the board. As one conservative Christian board member indicated, "There are eight of them and four of us, and the eight of them never speak to us. That's the problem. They need seven votes and they've got eight people and they can blow us off and they have. . . . I came to the realization that I don't care, it's not my fault. We're not running this board. When something goes wrong, I blame it on the majority. It is their fault! You guide us the way you want to [but] don't try and squelch my free speech because I have a message, which is getting out."

Despite the lack of communication between the majority and minority factions on the board, the Republicans refused to silence their conservative message and their criticism of board policy. Using a prophetic voice, and attaching their faith to a policy agenda, Republicans insisted that they were raising issues of importance to their constituents. Although one conservative Christian board member knew that many of his amendments would not pass, he argued that "nothing will ever change public education if you don't keep hammering away, if you don't keep it on the table." One of his proudest achievements was that the Republicans have been "consistent and clear" in their conservative message, and, in his opinion, this message was catching on. He stated:

> [We] are starting to get heard. [Three majority board members] are always responding to letters I am writing and comments that I am making. When they are responding, they are not leading. So, we are adrift. I've got my agenda and I've got my ideas and I don't respond to anyone. I throw them out, and people take them, and we keep driving on. And when you are responding, you are no longer leading. The person making the statements is in charge. So I think the four [Republican] people on the board have really guided us. The public sees that, and because of that, the majority of the board is angry with us.

This willingness *not* to compromise on the part of the board's Republicans meant that, in several cases, they effectively set the board's agenda.

Victories for the Minority Faction

One victory concerns the annual school budget. Despite losing the first budget battle in February 1996 (one month after being sworn into office), Republicans continued to call for additional cuts in the budget as a cost-saving measure. The board's conservatives also began to push for the hiring of a full-time independent auditor, who they believed would cut additional spending on programs that "underperformed." Democrats initially balked at the suggestion, but they announced plans to hire an independent budget consultant in an effort to save money by the end of the academic school year in 1996. The Democratic majority apparently changed their minds after receiving criticism from the community and county elected officials about the rising costs of education spending, a theme that the board's conservatives repeatedly hawked during their first year in office. In this instance, Republicans were able to achieve success by convincing other political actors and the public that the Democrats were not fiscally responsible.

The board's conservative Christians also achieved modest success in the area of "family life," or sex education. Republicans lost an initial vote on a series of family life education videos that were to be shown to classes in the fifth and sixth grade. Their biggest complaint was that absent from the videos was any depiction of parental involvement. Instead, the videos showed teenagers discussing sexual issues with older siblings, friends, or even aunts and uncles—but not parents. Republicans successfully filed a motion with the Family Life Education Committee—a group of parents and administrators appointed by the board to overview curriculum and policy proposals—to search for videos in the future that portray a supporting role of parents in the sexual development and maturation of children. The next year, board conservatives were successful in getting a version of a fifth- and sixth-grade family life education video edited for certain content. Conservatives argued that a section on tampons should be shown only to female students, while a section on male arousal should be restricted to the male students. (Although the board did agree to have the video edited, they rejected the conservatives' efforts to have the video shown only to seventh-grade classes as opposed to fifth-grade classes.) Another victory for board conservatives concerned a curriculum change that would have had family life teachers show a video to ninth- and tenth-grade classes instead of displaying a kit that contained condoms, diaphragms, and other contraceptives, which had previously been the practice. Despite the strong support of the Family Life Education Committee, which had endorsed the plan, the board voted eleven to one to keep the materials from being physically displayed to students. Each of these Republican-led initiatives enjoyed widespread support among parents in the community.

Similar to the school board in Garrett County, board members in Fairfax were faced with the chore of approving new textbooks, a responsibility that is rarely without controversy. The conservatives on the board lost several of their battles with regard to new textbooks, including a new language arts textbook approved by the board's majority that they believed was politically biased. (One conservative Christian said that the book approved by the school board, by an eight-to-four margin along party lines, contained a lack of positive role models and that the role models it did portray, such as Gloria Steinem and Spike Lee, were too liberal.) In other cases, however, the Republicans made headway regarding the choice of textbooks. In December 1998, the board approved two new series of elementary reading textbooks, among which was one that emphasized phonics as the dominant way to teach reading. Ultimately, the board approved an additional reading series along with the phonics-based

books that relied more on the "whole language" approach to reading instruction, leaving the final decision about which books to use up to the discretion of
individual elementary school principals. Most Democrats on the board argued
that phonics was just one of several teaching strategies employed by teachers to
teach children to read, although some did acknowledge that Fairfax schools
may have strayed too far from teaching phonics.

One of the conservative Christian school board members in Fairfax
County made the cause of phonics something of a crusade. Her efforts again
demonstrate the effectiveness of the board's minority in setting the school
board's agenda. She regularly posted articles and information about phonics
on her website and got permission to hold a town hall meeting about the
phonics debate, in May 1997, titled "The Keys to Reading: What Works?"
Critics claimed that the meeting was only partially successful. One speaker at
the meeting, invited by the Christian Right board member, said that reading
scores in Fairfax were very high already; however, the meeting led to the hiring
of a consultant to start a pilot phonics-based program in one of the county's
elementary schools. Persistence and organization were the keys to this conservative Christian's success in several areas. According to one Democratic member on the board,

> [This conservative Christian board member] is very well-organized, and she
> has friends who read and analyze every document that comes before the
> board cover to cover to find and highlight any possible thing they could dis-
> agree with. [She] is well prepared and well thought out and has kept the
> board occupied with things it would otherwise easily pass. She is also affect-
> ing the board by sponsoring new programs and trying to get us to pass new
> initiatives by getting programs that are already run by other people from the
> Christian Right or who are identified with the Christian Right. For example,
> in her town hall meeting about phonics, we enlisted the help of this Christian
> Right woman from Roanoke who specializes in phonics.

The woman from Roanoke was ultimately hired by the board to conduct
the pilot program, demonstrating another way that the Christian Right influenced the board on policy-related matters.

This board member's persistence also paid off in other curriculum areas,
including a controversial new grading policy implemented by school administrators at the beginning of the 1996–97 academic school year. The policy,
which applied to the county's middle schools, was designed to allow teachers
to assess a wider range of student skills. The new system had teachers grading
students on a four-point scale, as opposed to a scale ranging from 0 to 100. The
system also considered a student's health and home-life situation when grad-

ing homework assignments and weighed recent work more heavily in the final grade so that improvement during a semester would be counted. Critics argued that such a grading system would result in giving students less credit for completing homework assignments. School administrators maintained, however, that the plan offered parents a more complete picture of how their children were performing in school.

Republicans were immediately skeptical of the plan, arguing that the grading system could lower academic standards. One Christian Right board member argued that students would be less motivated to do their homework and that one goal of the school system should be "teaching kids a good work ethic" (O'Harrow 1997, B1). She posted an article on her website about other problems with the system, urging parents to attend school board meetings to show their support for returning to the older system of grading. Many teachers also complained that the new grading system was far more time consuming. By the fall of 1997, board members decided to address the controversial grading plan. One board Republican wrote to area business leaders seeking their support, discussing the same theme as his conservative Christian colleague. He wrote business leaders that their businesses "will be taking up the slack" if the "education system fails to educate or reinforce good work habits" (Benning 1997, V1). Board members eventually passed a motion made by the same conservative Christian board member who spoke out about phonics that allowed teachers to go back to grading on a 100-point scale and include all homework grades in a student's final grade.

The successes in the area of phonics and middle-school grading demonstrate that the conservative minority on the Fairfax County school board could be effective in certain policy areas. Both of these small victories correspond with the "back-to-basics" ideas touted by the Christian Right. The persistence of the conservative board members in these areas eventually led to the inclusion of these back-to-basics measures in the school curriculum.

Perhaps the successes enjoyed by the conservative Christian board members in Fairfax County are better understood if one considers their subject matter. The Republicans were particularly successful in policy areas that appealed to a broader audience than the Christian Right community alone. For example, the hiring of a full-time budget auditor resonated with local politicians seeking to reduce county spending on schools and in other areas. The Republican plan to allow teachers to return to a more traditional grading system appealed to both teachers and the business community. And the conservative changes made to some sex education videos enjoyed widespread support among many parents. It was not until the board's majority heard such criticism from other voices in the community that they were willing to listen to the

Republicans and implement their proposals. The conservative Christians were less successful in areas that were more controversial, such as their attempt to ease restrictions on charter schools or to limit the role of guidance counselors in the schools. Their efforts to insert a disclaimer in a textbook regarding creation science—an issue of religious bigotry in their minds—also failed.

The experiences of conservative Christian board members in Fairfax County mirror the experiences of the Christian Right in New York City to some extent. Christian Right board members in New York City were often unable to enact their agenda in the city's community school boards, largely because the public did not support their ideas and initiatives; however, the Christian Right was successful in New York shortly before the elections occurred in stopping the controversial Children of the Rainbow curriculum from being used in the schools. This curriculum, which depicted homosexuals in a positive light, was stopped largely because conservative Christians were able to influence and gain support among large sections of the public, not just their core constituency. Likewise, Republican board members in Fairfax County achieved partial policy victories in areas such as phonics, middle-school grading, and budget issues because such policies had broader appeal to constituencies other than Christian Right activists in the county. By reaching out and influencing large components of public opinion in Fairfax County on these issues, the Republicans were able to set the board's agenda as well as reach compromises with Democrats on particular matters.

One Democrat said compromise was also reached as a result of their frustration with the conservative board members' tactics. According to him, "What they do is tie you up on silly little issues. You find yourself putting all your resources into fighting these dumb battles and then they sneak in and are able to get more accomplished. . . . I think they have had a major impact on the school system. We tend to compromise with them too much." Democrats also believed that the Republicans' strategy of "tying up" the school board with actions and amendments that had little chance of passage affected the board in another way. The Republicans' persistence effectively prevented the more progressive board members from addressing other issues and putting new, possibly more liberal, policies into action.

Conclusion

How do conservative Christians govern at the school board level? In Garrett County, where conservative Christians make up a majority of the board, the

Christian Right suffered greater accountability to the public and was held responsible for both the successes and failures of the school system. In that respect, challenges by the community to the authority of the Christian Right board members were often more pronounced in Garrett County than in Fairfax County. Some events such as the furor about Wellness Day or OBE provoked reactions from the community that were similar to reactions that Christian Right board majorities in Vista, California, and Merrimack, New Hampshire, provoked in their school districts. Yet, for several reasons, the widespread, ideological changes that many critics of the Garrett County school board feared would occur during the Christian Right's tenure as the school board's majority faction did not materialize. First, in most situations, the conservative Christian majority listened to and addressed the concerns of school administrators and parents. Second, the "gung-ho" attitude of some of the more outspoken conservative Christians on the board was tempered after several years in office, as board members became more knowledgeable about how the school systems operated. Finally, differences among the conservative Christians, in terms of both policy positions and how religion influenced their views, proved that the Christian Right majority was not monolithic. In some cases, conservatives on the board were willing to side with the board's moderate member because their points of view did not match most of their Christian Right colleagues.

In Fairfax County, the stakes were lower for conservatives on the board. As a minority on the board, Christian Right board members were not necessarily held accountable by the public or local county officials for the successes or failures of the school board. Both Democrats and Republicans acknowledged that the relationship between the two sides was stormy. As one conservative Christian recounted, the Democrats needed seven votes to enact their policy preferences, and they had eight, leaving the board's conservatives with little say in many matters. Their status as a minority of the board, however, would prove to help conservative Christians in some ways. As a minority that did not have to compromise with the majority about most matters, Republicans were free to stick to their conservative principles and to criticize board Democrats repeatedly for what went wrong with the school system. Although they lost many battles, their unity and steady criticism of the board Democrats often garnered attention and gradually influenced some components of public opinion in the county. At times, when the conservatives' message reached the right audience, as was the case with the budget auditor and the middle-school grading policy, Democrats were forced to acknowledge and implement the Republicans' policy proposals.

Conservative Christian board members in both counties met with less success on issues that involved religion directly. In Fairfax County, Republicans made little headway in their attempt to insert a disclaimer in a science textbook that compared creationism with "pseudoscience." Although the conservative Christian board members in Garrett County did enjoy some policy success in the area of religion (most notably in starting their meetings with prayer and giving high school valedictorians the right to say a prayer in their speeches), their attempt to remove astrology and other topics that offended their religious beliefs from the Wellness Day program failed. In both cases, the Christian Right's concerns failed to generate much public support for their causes.

The case studies reveal how the context in which Christian Right board members find themselves affects their willingness and ability to change school board policy. In Garrett County, by and large a conservative county, board members faced opposition from the education community, many parents, and the local media when they considered enacting policy proposals that were deemed *too* conservative or radical. Even though some conservative Christians on the board in Garrett County wished to make more changes to policy than they did, as a majority their willingness to do so was often affected by the views of others in the community.

Had the Christian Right been a majority on the board in Fairfax County, one could speculate that they too would have had limits placed on their willingness to enact radical policy changes, considering the diversity of views held by residents and community leaders in Fairfax County. Conservative Christians, however, did not constitute a majority on the school board, and their status as a board minority typically resulted in the defeat of many of their policy proposals. Because the Republicans on the board in Fairfax County had little hope of enacting major policy changes, their strategy was to stick to their conservative message and hope to either influence public opinion in the county or stall the deliberative process so that Democrats would be unable to make many of their own changes to county education policy. Their persistence did yield some political payoffs, particularly in areas of education reform, which found broad support among several groups in addition to the Christian Right community.

In terms of the intersection of religion and politics, the cases demonstrate that conservative Christians are perhaps more effective as critics of the system in a minority setting than as policymakers with the authority to govern. Even in a conservative county such as Garrett, Christian Right board members, charged with the responsibility of making school board policy, found little success when they tried to employ their specific moral or religious agenda in a priestly manner, because such moves prompted hostility from the community. To their credit, these board members showed a willingness to listen to the voices and concerns of parents, teachers, and community leaders, perhaps because for so long their voices had been ignored by the administration in previous years. Meanwhile, conservative Christians serving on the Fairfax board were able to maintain their prophetic voices, criticizing the board majority on a routine basis. Bargaining is not an option for the true prophet, who criticizes society at large when its behavior does not correspond to his or her ideas of truth, justice, or morality. Because the conservative Christian minority in Fairfax was rarely in the position to bargain or compromise, they were free to stick to advocating their true beliefs, often informed by their religious principles. In the words of Hofrenning (1995), these Christian Right board members were able to maintain an "outsider" approach to politics. While such an approach led to few outright victories, it did allow the Christian Right minority to affect the tenor of the debate and to redirect the board's agenda. In either case, these findings demonstrate that perhaps political success comes easiest (if not often) for religious adherents when their voice is one among many that are heard, a finding that is consistent with our nation's pluralist heritage.

At the very least, the experiences of Christian Right school board members in both counties challenge many of the common perceptions about conservative Christians who govern at the school board level, which was developed in places as disparate as Vista, California, and Merrimack, New Hampshire. Governance by conservative Christians at the local level is far more complex. On the one hand, Christian Right board members do not always enact radical changes in local education policy simply because they have the capability to do so, as the case in Garrett County illustrates. On the other hand, conservative Christians who find themselves as part of a minority of a school board, as was the case in Fairfax County, are not always powerless to affect change. Legislators at any level of government—regardless of their majority of minority status—are often at the mercy of the environment in which they find themselves. Public opinion, budgetary constraints, and executive officials all influence the ability of elected officials to do their jobs.

Conclusion

The debate about the curriculum in public schools, according to Arthur Scheslinger, is "a debate about what it means to be an American" (1992, 17). In the opinion of Christian Right activists, that curriculum should respect and promote virtues and beliefs consistent with their worldview. A good American, they would argue, is one who leads a life steeped in traditional morality, in which prayer in school is preferred, creationism is the only explanation for the origin of humans, and patriotism is rooted in a belief in America's superiority to other cultures. The problem, however, is that this worldview is not necessarily shared by most Americans, particularly leading educators. The result of this clash in values has been that Christian Right leaders and organizations have been among the most preeminent critics of the public schools in the past two decades. In the 1990s, several of these groups made very public attempts to recruit like-minded activists to run for school board, turning school districts into local battlefields.

The Christian Right and School Board Elections

This book has analyzed the impact of the Christian Right on school board elections on a national scale. More specifically, it has studied the motivation, strategies, and electoral success of Christian Right school board candidates. In many ways, Christian Right and non–Christian Right candidates share common sources of motivation in their quest to seek school board office. First, there are relatively few socioeconomic differences between the two types of candidates, most of whom have income and education levels well above the national average. Candidates decide to run because serving on the school board is a good way to give something back to the community. Very few candidates indicate that their decision to run was completely self-motivated. Most were encouraged to run by friends, family members, community leaders, or—perhaps most important—current or past school board members. Finally, relatively few candidates, Christian Right or non–Christian Right, were actively mobilized by political elites such as interest group representatives or party leaders to run for school board.

Nonetheless, there are still some important differences in motivation that set Christian Right candidates apart from other candidates. Christian Right candidates are significantly more likely to indicate that returning schools to traditional values was a very important reason for running for school board. Conservative Christian candidates were also significantly more likely than non–Christian Right candidates to say that applying their religious or moral beliefs to school policy was important to their decision to run for office. This desire is further illustrated by the remarks of one conservative Christian candidates from Garrett County, who said that Christians "are instructed to be involved" in politics. Yet the case study research revealed that religion also matters to non–Christian Right candidates in some cases. Recall the moderate Episcopal candidate from Fairfax County who claimed that running and serving on the school board is akin to Jesus' commandment to "Feed my sheep" (or, as she claims, "teach my sheep"). Moreover, some other effects of religion are not isolated to Christian Right candidates. This study finds that regular church attendance—regardless of Christian Right status—is significantly related to whether candidates are encouraged by church members or ministers to run for school board.

By and large, and somewhat unexpectedly, Christian Right and non–Christian Right candidates run remarkably similar campaigns. Unlike campaigns for higher political offices, school board campaigns for both types of candidate are low key. Candidates running for school board spend little money on their races, have few volunteers working with their campaigns, and are most likely to campaign door-to-door. Perhaps most remarkably, very few Christian Right candidates report campaigning in churches and are no more likely to do so than non–Christian Right candidates. This finding calls into question the charge by critics of the Christian Right that their candidates engage in "stealth" techniques, meaning they avoid public events in favor of campaigning and mobilizing voters in conservative churches instead.

Another surprising finding was that the involvement of Christian Right organizations, most notably the Christian Coalition and Citizens for Excellence in Education, appears to be very limited on a national level. Although much attention has been given to the Christian Right's efforts to train and mobilize conservative Christian school board candidates, the involvement of these groups is not extensive. In fact, few school board candidates, regardless of whether they are a part of the Christian Right, receive direct assistance from interest groups or political parties, as both the survey and case study in Garrett County demonstrate. The election in Fairfax County is a notable exception, in which both interest groups and political parties were active in the campaigns, perhaps reflecting the large size of the school district and the very high socio-economic status of its residents.

Although there were many similarities between Christian Right and non–Christian Right campaigns in terms of their campaign strategies, differences still emerge. Though Christian Right candidates tended to avoid the hot-button issues endorsed by the movement such as sex education and outcomes-based education in their campaign platforms, they were significantly more likely than non–Christian Right candidates to run on more mainstream conservative issues also endorsed by the Christian Right such as increasing test scores and enforcing more discipline in the schools. Christian Right candidates refrained from making prophetic, overtly religious themes the center of their campaigns. Instead, for example, Christian Right candidates in Fairfax County ran on a united "back-to-basics" campaign theme emphasizing traditional teaching methods such as phonics. Christian Right candidates in Garrett County also emphasized academic concerns yet, at the same time, were the most likely to incorporate overtly religious themes in their campaigns, including the use of biblical scripture in their campaign ads, an appeal that worked in their conservative community.

The results of the survey demonstrate that, under most circumstances, Christian Right candidates are no more likely to win their elections than non–Christian Right candidates, even after controlling for various factors that could influence a candidate's electability. Similar to other elections in American politics, the advantage of incumbency is strong at the school board level. Even controlling for the religious context in which candidates live—in this case, looking at the percentage of evangelical adherents living in the county of residence of the respondents—has no impact on whether a Christian Right candidate is successful at the polls. Although it is impossible to gauge in the survey, the case studies reveal how Christian Right groups and ministerial organizations distributed voter guides and mobilized voters in sympathetic churches. Though this approach most likely helped the conservative Christian candidates to win in Garrett County, Christian Right candidates in Fairfax County also faced much greater countermobilization by groups and religious associations opposed to their agenda.

In terms of Christian Right activism, this study finds that the impact of Christian Right organizations is somewhat limited at the school board level. To paraphrase Mark Twain, once commentating about his death, fears of a Christian Right "takeover" of school boards are greatly exaggerated. There is simply little evidence to suggest that Christian Right candidates are trained by or receive consultation from Christian Right groups. For that matter, few candidates appear to receive much assistance, whether in the form of endorsements, campaign contributions, or training, from any type of interest group. Nor is there any indication that stealth campaigns are widespread among Christian Right candidates. Although such campaigns are admittedly difficult to uncover, particularly in survey research, it appears that Christian Right candidates campaign largely in the same ways as non–Christian Right candidates. In the case studies, particularly in Garrett County, Christian Right candidates were very open about their religious beliefs and ideas, to the point of including scripture in their campaign literature. The evidence here tells a more balanced story about elections involving Christian Right candidates.

The Christian Right as School Board Members

The two case studies profiled in this book give us a chance to look at the impact Christian Right school board candidates make once they are elected to school board. More generally, it affords the opportunity to examine the challenges that religious adherents face when elected to political office. As most Christian Right candidates discovered in these two counties, governing is very different from running a campaign. The Christian Right majority on the five-member board in Garrett County made some controversial decisions early in their term but avoided any widespread, ideological changes in the curriculum that their more progressive critics feared would happen. In many situations, conservative Christians on the board showed a willingness to listen to and respect the wishes of both parents and administrators. And several Christian Right board members sometimes sided with the board's moderate member, demonstrating that the Christian Right majority was not monolithic. This picture contrasts sharply with the Christian Right majority boards in places such as Merrimack,

New Hampshire, and Vista, California, which left the impression that such majorities are bent on a complete overhaul of school curriculum.

By contrast, the Christian Right minority on the twelve-member board in Fairfax County was free to stick to its conservative principles and to criticize repeatedly the more progressive majority on the board, because they had little hope of enacting widespread changes. Although they lost many battles, their unity with the two moderate Republicans on the board and their steady criticism of board Democrats often garnered enough attention to sway some components of public opinion in the county. The board conservatives even achieved some success on budget issues and grading policies, although they met with less success on issues that involved religion directly. Majority board members in Fairfax County also grew frustrated with the obstructionist tactics of the Christian Right members, which effectively kept some progressive policy ideas touted by the Democrats from coming to light.

Although these two cases may not be representative of most school boards that have Christian Right board members, they do offer some interesting lessons. First, the actions of a Christian Right board majority can be tempered by the attitudes of administrators and parents, if Christian Right board members are willing to have a dialogue with the community. Second, Christian Right board members are not necessarily monolithic, and divisions among the group over some issues can stop them from making substantial ideological changes to school curriculum and policy. In the case of Fairfax County, the lesson here is that the Christian Right as a minority faction on a school board can sway the board more to the right. Though they had little success with the more controversial platform issues of the Christian Right such as sex education and creationism, their criticism of the board's majority swayed public opinion enough on more traditional conservative issues that the board majority was forced to enact some of their initiatives.

The experiences of Christian Right board members both as a governing majority and as a minority coalition also illuminate the situations in which religious adherents are either effective or ineffective in the public arena. As noted in chapter 1, organized religion can serve as either a priestly or a prophetic voice in politics. Viewed in the light of priestly religious politics, the Christian Right majority learned early in their experience that attempts to make wholesale changes to board policy, in a sense to legitimate their brand of social policy, would be met with much resistance from the community. Had such members made many of the strong policy changes they initially proposed, the end result, most likely, would have been effectiveness in the short term only. Not only would they have jeopardized their relationship with many parents, teachers, and administrators, but they also would have likely jeopardized their chances for reelection. Instead, these members worked closely with the community at the expense perhaps of pursuing a more radical agenda. The case in Garrett County illustrates the difficulty of any community accepting the legitimacy of one "true" moral or religious vision, which is ultimately why the founders, in writing the establishment clause of the First Amendment, strove to guard against the dominance of any one religious voice in the public square.

Yet to say that religion should not have *any* voice in policy is also misleading. By guaranteeing the right of religious expression, the founders also seemed to be encouraging the influence of religion in society. Alexis de Tocqueville ([1835] 1956) wrote about the importance of religion, and churches especially, as mediating institutions in America that fostered democracy and protected citizens from an omnipotent government. There is a strong prophetic form of religious politics that has characterized America throughout its history—one whose criticism of the status quo is rooted in the search for truth and justice. The modest success of the Christian Right school board members in Fairfax County, in terms of steering the political agenda and obstructing the more liberal majority from enacting many of its policy goals, shows the sorts of situations in which this prophetic voice can be effective at the local level of government. Largely free from accountability by virtue of their minority status, conservative Christians on the board maintained their prophetic voice, constantly criticizing the decisions of the more liberal majority. At times, when their criticism found resonance with larger segments of the population, they were able to influence policy directly. This finding demonstrates that, when Christian Right activists work together with other factions within the community, they become more accomplished in local politics.

The Future of the Christian Right and School Boards

What does the future hold for school boards with respect to the Christian Right? In the past few years, the Christian Coalition and Citizens for Excellence in Education, arguably the two Christian Right organizations most active in trying to influence school board politics in the 1990s, have fallen on hard times. Funding for both groups has fallen, and the Christian Coalition has had to contend with not only the departure of most of their experienced, top-level employees, but also an embarrassing lawsuit from former African American employees charging the organization with racism. Meanwhile, Citizens for Excellence in Education and other Christian Right leaders and organizations have begun to promote homeschooling as the preferred alternative for chil-

dren of conservative Christians. Indeed, homeschooling has become an education phenomenon in the last decade, involving more than a million children
and spawning a new industry and counterculture geared at conservative
Christian parents (Stevens 2001; Talbot 2001). Further, critics of the movement argue that, once elected, the strong convictions of Christian Right board
members leave them without the sort of political skills necessary to succeed in
politics. According to David Berliner, Christian Right board members "may be
unable to compromise and to live with educational decisions reflecting a plu-
ralistic democracy keeping separate church and state" (1997, 381). To that end,
many argue that once Christian Right candidates are faced with such disap-
pointment, they will retreat back to their private lives and leave the political
arena.

This argument is similar to one made by pundits and scholars in the late
1980s, who argued that the Christian Right as a political movement was dead,
in light of its apparent lack of success in national politics. Instead, the movement transformed itself by the early 1990s, focusing more energy at cultivating
activism at the state and local level of government. Sara Diamond (1998)
argues that the movement's adaptability and vast resources, including the use
of multiple strategies by multiple groups, have helped make it one of the most
salient social movements in the United States.

There is no reason to suspect that Christian Right activism will slow down
at the grassroots level. While homeschooling appears to be growing, even promoted by Bob Simonds and other Christian Right leaders, most conservative
Christian parents will not be able to afford this option, so they will likely
remain concerned about the public schools. New cases involving church and
state and the public schools routinely appear in newspaper headlines. Among
other issues to arise since the beginning of the new century, debate rages about
the teaching of Bible history courses in public schools. The battle regarding
evolution is still present as well. In its most recent incarnation, Christian Right
activists are pushing for the inclusion of intelligent design theory in science
courses, which argues that the creation of life on Earth was not a random event
but rather the product of some greater power. In the wake of the Columbine
tragedy, Christian Right groups have promoted a new policy called "Hang
Ten," to try and place the Ten Commandments or similar documents in public schools. And in the summer of 2002, fierce debates about the role of religion
in the public schools emerged throughout the nation after two controversial
and seemingly contradictory federal court decisions were handed down. In the
Ninth Circuit, appellate judges voted that the recitation of the Pledge of
Allegiance in public schools was unconstitutional because it contains the
words "under God." Yet, one week later, the Supreme Court upheld the

constitutionality of an Ohio voucher program, which gives government grants to low-income parents to spend at private, parochial schools.

While such cases highlight an inherent tension between church and state in a very religious, yet diverse nation, they also tend to motivate and spur political activism among individuals who both support and oppose such policies. One approach, as this book has examined, is to seek election to school board. The Christian Right has had mixed success in terms of school board elections, just as it has had mixed success with respect to education policy at the state and national levels. But for movement activists, whose strong religious convictions draw them into the political battlefield, their successes and failures may be overridden by the theological beliefs that propel them to take political action in the first place.

Methodology

The Survey

I used the *Directory of Public and Elementary and Secondary Education Agencies* (1993–94), published by the U.S. Department of Education on CD-ROM, to generate a list of 300 school districts for the survey's primary sampling frame randomly. By using the entire list of school districts, the study can speak quite confidently about the generalizability of the survey results. The *Directory* lists 14,881 school districts in the United States. From this list, appointed school boards, "special" districts (such as those that monitor schools for the deaf and blind), and school districts having fewer than twenty-five students were excluded from consideration in the selection, which reduced the final primary sampling frame to 13,592.

To compensate for the fact that the majority of school districts had relatively few students compared with very large districts, I divided the sample into three groups on the basis of size. The smallest group was made up of districts of less than 2,000 students ($N = 6,627$, or 49 percent of all districts). Medium-size districts were those districts with between 2,000 and 9,999 students ($N = 6,275$ or 46 percent of all districts), and large districts were any districts with more than 10,000 students ($N = 690$, or 5 percent of all districts). I wanted to avoid a simple random selection that would have likely resulted in selecting more small districts and fewer large districts, which is problematic, in view of the fact that the largest districts serve more than 48 percent of all public school students in the United States. The 300 districts were then drawn randomly from these districts in a proportionate manner, with a total of 147 small school districts, 137 medium school districts, and 16 large school districts selected. The survey results are not weighted, because the districts were selected proportionately.

After the school districts were selected, each district was contacted and asked to mail or fax lists of all candidates (with their addresses) who ran in the most recent school board election held in their particular school districts. By law, candidates running for school board must list their home address when filing their candidacies to show that they are legal residents of the districts from which they run for office. The contact and follow-up process with these school districts took more than four months, from late August 1997 to December 1998. More than 91 percent of the districts ($N = 273$) responded by sending the names and addresses of citizens who had run in their most recent school board election. Three of the school districts (one in Nebraska and two in Vermont) conducted their school board elections at town hall meetings, and there was no formal filing process. These three districts were removed from the sample because no real "election" was held in these instances. Ultimately, the first wave of the survey was mailed to 1,220 former school board candidates. Eleven surveys were returned as undeliverable because the respondent had moved. After a second wave of mailings, 671 usable responses were received, for a response rate of 55 percent.

As indicated in chapter 2, 62 percent of respondents won their races, compared with 59 percent of nonrespondents, so it is likely that the survey is not biased with respect to whether the candidates lost their races. Nonrespondents appear, however, far more likely to have run in uncontested elections than respondents. In the thirty-one school districts in which no respondents returned any surveys, 52 percent ran unopposed, compared with 19 percent of survey respondents from the remaining 239 districts. In light of the fact that the survey asked many questions pertaining to campaigning, it makes sense that candidates who were unopposed would not be as interested in responding. (Appendix B contains a copy of the survey.)

Case Studies

The two cases featured in this book are counties in which conservative Christians now serve on school boards after heated school board campaigns. I conducted anonymous interviews of Christian Right and non–Christian Right candidates in the case studies. In Fairfax County, twenty-four of the thirty-five candidates who had run for the school board in the 1995 election agreed to be interviewed (a response rate of 69 percent). Focused interviews of these candidates, seven of whom are conservative Christians and seventeen of whom are not, took place from May 1997 to December 1997. A total of ten candidates ran for election in the 1994 and 1996 school board elections in Garrett County, seven of whom agreed to be interviewed for this study (a response rate of 70 percent). Four of the seven candidates interviewed are conservative Christians. Interviews of these seven candidates occurred in January and February 1998. (Appendix C contains a list of interview questions that were asked of all school board candidates in both Garrett and Fairfax Counties.)

In addition, the candidates completed a brief questionnaire (also in appendix C) that more systematically addressed the following issues: socioeconomic status; the benefits candidates derive from running for office; church membership, attendance, and activity; information about the school districts in which they ran; candidates' political background and attitudes, including party identification and information concerning interest group membership; and their attitudes about various education issues. Not all candidates were willing to complete the questionnaire: 83 percent of interview subjects in Fairfax completed the questionnaire, compared with 57 percent of the candidates in Garrett County.

I also interviewed citizens in both counties who closely monitor school board activities, such as parents, education activists, and local reporters who cover education issues, again anonymously. These interviews, as well as interviews with representatives from Christian Right groups and groups that oppose their agenda, give the study additional viewpoints about the impact of the Christian Right on school board policy in the two counties. Finally, news coverage of school board elections was also examined to determine what type of influence the Christian Right had on the elections from the standpoint of the local media.

Several strategies were used to gauge the impact of conservative Christians who were later elected to the school boards. First, throughout the course of the research for the study, I was a participant-observer and attended school board meetings regularly in Fairfax and Garrett Counties, from the spring of 1996 through the spring of 1998. I also analyzed newspaper coverage of the board meetings in both counties and reviewed coverage of school board events by local papers in Garrett County beginning with the first meeting at which newly elected board members took their office, in January 1995, until the school board elections in November 1998. I conducted a similar analysis for the school board in Fairfax County, where newspaper coverage was reviewed from January 1996 until December 1998. Finally, the official minutes of the school board meetings for both counties were analyzed roughly during this same time period.

Survey Instrument: The American University Survey of School Board Candidates

This survey asks you to share your opinions and experiences as school board candidates. All of your responses will be kept completely confidential. Your participation is greatly appreciated.

I would like to ask you questions concerning your decision to run for school board and your campaign. Please circle the appropriate response or write in the space allotted.

Q1. Is this the first time you have run for school board?
   1. Yes
   2. No * If no, please list the number of times you have run in the past: _____.

Q2. Briefly explain why you decided to run for school board.

Q3. Did any of the following people suggest that you run for school board? (CIRCLE ALL THAT APPLY)
   1. Current sitting board member
   2. Retired board member
   3. Friend or family member
   4. Community leader

    5. Representative from a local/national voluntary organization (e.g., chamber of commerce, Elks)
    6. Local or state politician or party official
    7. Fellow church, parish, or synagogue member
    8. Minister, priest, or rabbi
    9. Other(s) _____
    10. No one really asked me to run

Q4. In your campaign, which issues did you primarily stress? (CIRCLE ALL THAT APPLY)
    1. Tax and revenue issues
    2. Need for greater technology in schools
    3. Need for improving test scores and academic achievement
    4. Sex and health education
    5. Crime, drugs, and violence in the schools
    6. Need for construction and repair of school buildings
    7. Voucher programs
    8. Privatization of services and/or educational programs
    9. Outcomes-based education or other federal programs
    10. Discipline
    11. Character education
    12. Other(s) _____

Q5. People run for office for a variety of reasons. Some of those reasons are listed below. Please tell me if each of these reasons was very important, somewhat important, or not very important in your decision to run for school board by checking ($\sqrt{}$) the appropriate box:

	Very Important	Somewhat Important	Not Very Important
I found it exciting.	☐	☐	☐
I wanted to learn about politics and government at the local level.	☐	☐	☐
I wanted the chance to work with people who share my ideals.	☐	☐	☐
I wanted the chance to influence government policy.	☐	☐	☐

	Very Important	Somewhat Important	Not Very Important
I wanted the chance to further my job/professional goals.	☐	☐	☐
I wanted political experience because I might want to run for higher office one day.	☐	☐	☐
I wanted the chance to apply my religious or moral beliefs to education policy.	☐	☐	☐
I wanted the chance to be with people I enjoy.	☐	☐	☐
I wanted the chance to make the community a better place to live.	☐	☐	☐
I wanted the chance to return the schools to traditional values.	☐	☐	☐

Q6. Which of the following reasons were important in your initial decision to run for school board office? (CIRCLE ALL THAT APPLY)
1. There was an opening on the board.
2. I disagreed with a policy(s) that was recently passed by the board.
3. I had more free time than in the past.
4. I disliked the incumbent.
5. I had more money and resources to run than in the past.
6. Some individual or group asked me to run for the first time.
7. Other _____.

Q7. About how much did your most recent school board race cost?
1. Less than $1,000
2. $1,000–$5,000
3. $5, 001–$10, 000
4. $10,001–$20,000
5. More than $20,000

Q8. Did you run for office unopposed?
1. Yes
2. No

Q9. Which individuals and groups helped to finance your campaign? (CIRCLE
ALL THAT APPLY)
1. Family income/self-financed
2. Friends or supporters
3. Advocacy or political groups
4. Community groups or voluntary organizations
5. Church groups
6. Other(s) _____

Q10. Did you run for an at-large position or a single-member district position?
1. At-large position
2. Single-member district position

Q11. Was your election campaign partisan or nonpartisan?
1. Partisan
2. Nonpartisan

Q12. Various organizations often help candidates run for office through
endorsements, campaign donations, or by offering them various consultation or training services. Please place a check ($\sqrt{}$) next to the appropriate blanks to indicate if any of the following groups provided you with
any of these services. There are blank spots at the bottom so that you can
list groups that have not been listed that might have provided you with
similar services. Please leave blank if none of the organizations provided
you with these types of services.

Organization	Endorsement	Campaign Contribution	Consultation/ Training
Democratic Party	____	____	____
Republican Party	____	____	____
Other political party	____	____	____
National Education Association	____	____	____
American Federation of Teachers	____	____	____
National Women's Political Caucus	____	____	____
Christian Coalition	____	____	____
Citizens for Excellence in Education	____	____	____
State or local education organization	____	____	____
State or local political organization	____	____	____
Other	____	____	____

Q13. Where did you campaign? (CIRCLE ALL THAT APPLY)
   1. Shopping malls
   2. Candidate rallies or forums
   3. Churches, parishes, or synagogues
   4. Door-to-door
   5. Community meetings (Elk's/Jaycee's meetings, etc.)
   6. Candidate coffees or home meetings
   7. Through mailings to voters
   8. Other(s) _____

   *Of the above campaign sites, please indicate which one you considered the most important to your campaign: _____.

Q14. Please list the approximate number of volunteers that assisted you as you campaigned on a regular basis (EXCLUDING FAMILY): _____.

Q15. Where did you recruit these volunteers? (CIRCLE ALL THAT APPLY)
   1. Through my family or friends
   2. Business colleagues
   3. Community activists (for example, fellow PTA members)
   4. Church, parish, or synagogue
   5. They contacted me
   6. Other(s) _____

Q16. Which of the following words best describe the media's coverage of your campaign? (CIRCLE ALL THAT APPLY)
   1. friendly   6. accurate
   2. hostile   7. sufficient
   3. conservative bias   8. insufficient
   4. liberal bias   9. Other(s) _____
   5. inaccurate   10. There was very little media coverage

Q17. How important was media coverage to the outcome of your campaign?
   1. Not very important
   2. Somewhat important
   3. Very important

   Now I would like to ask you some questions concerning your political background and attitudes. Please circle or check the appropriate response.

Q18. How would you describe your general political views?
1. Very liberal
2. Liberal
3. Slightly liberal
4. Middle of the road
5. Slightly conservative
6. Conservative
7. Very conservative

Q19. Besides running for school board office, which political activities have you engaged in during the past two years? (CIRCLE ALL THAT APPLY)
1. Voted
2. Influenced another person's vote choice
3. Volunteered for a political campaign or party
4. Signed a petition
5. Donated money to a political candidate or party
6. Attended a political march or rally
7. Wore a political button, put a bumper sticker on car, put up a campaign sign in yard
8. Wrote a letter or contacted a public official about a political issue
9. Other(s) _____

Q20. Generally speaking, do you think of yourself as a Republican, a Democrat, an Independent, or member of another party?
1. Democrat   4. Other party _____
2. Republican   5. No party affiliation
3. Independent

Q21. Below is a list of various political and education organizations. Please place a check (√) next to the box marked "I Am a Member" to indicate if you are a member of any of these groups. If you are not a member of the group but you generally support the political positions that the group takes or the activities that the group sponsors, please place a check (√) in the box marked "I Support Positions/Activities of Group." If you are neither a member nor support the group's positions or activities, or are unsure, please leave blank. If you are a member or supporter of a group that is not mentioned, please indicate the name of the group(s) in the other spaces at the bottom.

Group	I Am a Member	I Support Positions/ Activities of Group	Group	I Am a Member	I Support Positions/ Activities of Group
National Education Association	☐	☐	National School Board Association	☐	☐
Local or state PTA	☐	☐	National Association of Christian Educators	☐	☐
Citizens for Excellence in Education	☐	☐	Chamber of Commerce	☐	☐
Sierra Club	☐	☐	American Federation of Teachers	☐	☐
Christian Coalition	☐	☐	National Organization for Women	☐	☐
AFL-CIO	☐	☐	Concerned Women for America	☐	☐
Eagle Forum	☐	☐	American Association for Retired Persons	☐	☐
Common Cause	☐	☐	Elks or other civic organization	☐	☐
League of Women Voters	☐	☐	B'Nai Brith or B'nai Brith Women	☐	☐
National Abortion Rights Action League	☐	☐	National Right to Life Committee	☐	☐
Focus on the Family	☐	☐	People for the American Way	☐	☐
EMILY's List	☐	☐	American Civil Liberties Union	☐	☐
WISH List	☐	☐	Other environmental group	☐	☐
Other education group	☐	☐	Other trade/ business group	☐	☐
Other profamily organization	☐	☐	Other: _____	☐	☐
Other: _____	☐	☐	Other: _____	☐	☐

Q22. Several issues and programs currently debated among public school administrators, boards of education, and teachers are listed below. Please indicate whether you strongly support, support, oppose, strongly oppose, or are neutral or undecided about these issues or programs by checking (√) the appropriate response below:

Issues/Programs	Strongly Support	Support	Neutral/ Undecided	Oppose	Strongly Oppose
Shifting from larger schools to alternative, off-site education programs aimed at helping troubled teens	☐				
Creating charter schools	☐	☐	☐	☐	☐
Voucher systems (including tuition tax credits) to pay tuition at private schools	☐	☐	☐	☐	☐
Multicultural programs that stress the history and culture of minority students	☐	☐	☐	☐	☐
Opening class with a prayer	☐	☐	☐	☐	☐
Reducing the number of students per classroom					
Abstinence-based sex education courses	☐	☐	☐	☐	☐
Opposing the mention of homosexuality in sex education or other courses	☐	☐	☐	☐	☐
Spending more on vocational-technical or "school-to-work" programs	☐	☐	☐	☐	☐
Granting parents greater rights through parental rights legislation	☐	☐	☐	☐	☐
Creationism being taught as an alternative theory to evolution in science courses	☐	☐	☐	☐	☐
Phonics used to teach reading in elementary schools	☐	☐	☐	☐	☐

Issues/Programs	Strongly Support	Support	Neutral/ Undecided	Oppose	Strongly Oppose
Adding a community service component to graduation requirements	☐	☐	☐	☐	☐
Outcomes-based education being used in your district	☐	☐	☐	☐	☐

Finally, this last set of questions requests some basic background information, including questions concerning your ethnicity, sex, occupation, income, and religion. Please circle the appropriate response or fill in the blank space.

Q23. What is your gender?
1. Female
2. Male

Q24. What is your ethnic background?
1. African American (not of Hispanic origin)
2. Asian American or Pacific Islander
3. Hispanic/Latino American
4. Native American
5. White/Caucasian (not of Hispanic origin)
6. Other _____

Q25. In what year were you born? _____

Q26. What was your approximate family income last year (before taxes)?
1. Less than $25,000
2. $25,000–$49,999
3. $50,000–$74,999
4. $75,000–$99,999
5. $100,000–$249,000
6. More than $250,000

Q27. What is the highest year of school that you have completed?
1. Some high school or technical training
2. High school graduate
3. Some college
4. College graduate
5. Postgraduate degree

Q28. What is your occupation? (If retired, what was your former occupation?)
1. Self-employed
2. Executive or management employee
3. Professional (law, medicine, finance, etc.)
4. Education (teacher, professor, administration)
5. Clerical or administrative support
6. Technician or related support occupation
7. Sales occupation
8. Not employed (spouse is primary breadwinner)
9. Employed part time
10. Other _____

Q29. What is your marital status?
1. Married
2. Single
3. Divorced
4. Widowed
5. Other

Q30. How many children do you have, and what are their ages? _____.

Q31. How would you characterize your community?
1. Rural
2. Suburban
3. Urban

Q32. How often do you attend religious services?
1. More than once a week
2. Once a week
3. Once or twice a month
4. Several times a year
5. Rarely, if ever

Q33. When attending religious services, what is the denomination of the church or synagogue you most frequently attend? Please be as specific as possible. If you attend a nondenominational church, are unsure of the denomination, or do not attend religious services, please indicate: _____.

Q34. Do you belong to or do you consider yourself a member of a church, parish, synagogue, or other religious institution?
1. Yes
2. No (SKIP TO NUMBER 36)

*If yes, how frequently are political issues or events (either pertaining to national, state, or local affairs) discussed in your church, parish, or synagogue?
1. Very frequently
2. Somewhat frequently
3. Hardly ever

Q35. Aside from attending services, in the past twelve months have you been an active member of your church, parish, or synagogue (for example, served on a committee, given time for specific projects, or helped organized meetings)?
1. Yes
2. No

Q36. Which of the following terms accurately reflect your religious beliefs? (CIRCLE ALL THAT APPLY)
1. Fundamentalist Christian
2. Pentecostal or Charismatic Christian
3. Evangelical Christian
4. Mainline Christian
5. Liberal Christian
6. Jewish Orthodox
7. Conservative or Reform Jewish
8. Traditional or conservative Catholic
9. Progressive or liberal Catholic
10. Born-again Christian
11. Ethical or secular humanist
12. Religious non-Christian
13. No religion/agnostic
14. None of these terms

Case Study Interview and Questionnaire

Interview Questions

1. Before you decided to run for office, how were you involved with Fairfax County Public Schools?

2. Who encouraged you to run for office? (Political party members; interest groups; other politicians; church members?)

3. Why did you decide to run for school board office? (Why not become more active in the PTA? Or do other forms of political activity?)

4. How did you prepare to campaign? (Attend any campaign training seminars? Read any manuals? Seek advice from individuals, the party, or interest groups?)

5. What was your campaign message or theme? What issues did you primarily stress?

6. Describe a typical week during the campaign season. What kinds of events did you plan?

7. What did you find most surprising about running for school board?

8. How would you characterize media coverage of the school board campaigns, in general, and of your campaign, in particular?

9. Do you believe the Pro-Family Movement (Christian Right) played an important role in the School Board elections in Fairfax County (or Garrett County)?

10. Now that the elections are over, is the Pro-Family Movement (Christian Right) still active in trying to affect school board policy?

11. Would you say that your decision to run for office was motivated in any way by your moral or religious convictions?

12. What role do you think religion should play in politics?

13. Is there anything you would like to add?

Author's Note: Questions 9 and 10 were asked of both Christian Right and non–Christian Right candidates. Because some Christian Right leaders believe that the term "Christian Right" is pejorative and often use the term "profamily" to describe their movement, I used that term when I interviewed Christian Right school board candidates. In other interviews with candidates who were not part of the Christian Right, I used the term "Christian Right" as opposed to "profamily."

Candidate Questionnaire

1. Generally speaking, do you think of yourself as a Republican, a Democrat, an Independent, or what?

2. Please list any political or educational groups of which you are a member. Please indicate your level of participation in these groups as well. (For example, are you a "dues-paying" member? Do you receive magazines or literature from these groups? Do you attend or have you attended meetings for these groups in the past? Have you ever held office for these groups?)

3. How would you describe your general political views?
   A. Very liberal   E. Slightly conservative
   B. Liberal   F. Conservative
   C. Slightly liberal   G. Very conservative
   D. Moderate/middle of the road

4. Besides running for school board office, which political activities have you engaged in during the past two years? (CIRCLE ALL THAT APPLY)
   A. Voted   E. Influenced another person's vote
   B. Volunteered for a political   F. Signed a petition
      campaign or party   G. Attended a political march or rally
   C. Donated money to a political   H. Other _____
      candidate or party
   D. Wore a political button,
      put a bumper sticker on
      car, put up a campaign
      sign in yard

5. Did you serve on the school board before the fall 1995 (1994 or 1996) elections? If yes, for how many years? _____

6. Approximately how much did your school board race cost? _____

7. Through which of the following sources did you raise funds for your campaign? (Circle all that apply)
   A. Family income/self-financed   E. Church groups
   B. Friends   F. Community groups or voluntary
   C. Fund-raisers   organizations
   D. Interest groups   G. Other(s) _____

8. Various organizations often help candidates run for office through endorsements or campaign donations or by offering them various consultation or training services.
   A. Please list the organizations that endorsed your candidacy:
   B. Please list any organizations that may have given you campaign donations:
   C. Please list any organizations that sponsored any candidate trainings that you may have attended or that may have provided you with any in-kind campaign services (i.e., political consultants, polling services, etc.):

9. People run for office for a variety of reasons. Some of those reasons are listed below. Please tell me if each of these reasons was very important, somewhat important, or not very important in your decision to run for school board by checking (√) the appropriate box:

Reason	Very Important	Somewhat Important	Not Very Important
I found it exciting.	☐	☐	☐
I wanted to learn about politics and government at the local level.	☐	☐	☐
I wanted the chance to work with people who share my ideals.	☐	☐	☐
I wanted the chance to influence government policy.	☐	☐	☐
I wanted the chance to further my job/professional goals.	☐	☐	☐
I wanted political experience because I might want to run for higher office one day.	☐	☐	☐
I wanted the chance to apply my religious or moral beliefs to education policy.	☐	☐	☐
I wanted the chance to be with people I enjoy.	☐	☐	☐
I wanted the chance to make the community a better place to live.	☐	☐	☐
I wanted the chance to return to traditional values.	☐	☐	☐

10. What is your current occupation or what kind of job experience do you have?

11. What is your educational background?

12. What is the date of your birth? _____

13. What is your marital status? _____

14. Do you have school age-children? If so, what are their ages, and do they attend public school?

15. How long have you lived in Fairfax (Garrett) County? _____

16. Are you a member of a church, parish, or synagogue? _____
    (If no, please skip to question 18)

17. If you are a church, parish, or synagogue member, please answer the following:
    A. What is the name and denomination of your church?
    B. Would you say that political events are often discussed in your church?
    C. On average, how often do you attend services?
    D. Aside from attending services, have you been an active member of your
       church, parish, or synagogue in the past twelve months (for example,
       served on a committee, given time for specific projects, or helped
       organize meetings?)

18. Which of the following terms accurately reflect your religious beliefs?
    (CIRCLE ALL THAT APPLY)
    A. Fundamentalist Christian   H. Traditional or conservative Catholic
    B. Pentecostal or Charismatic   I. Progressive or liberal Catholic
       Christian   J. Born-again Christian
    C. Evangelical Christian   K. Ethical or secular humanist
    D. Mainline Christian   L. Religious non-Christian
    E. Liberal Christian   M. No religion/agnostic
    F. Jewish Orthodox   N. None of these terms
    G. Traditional or reform
       Jewish

Notes

Introduction

1. Quoted in Steinberg (1999, A1).
2. In its annual (open-ended) poll asking Americans to name the most important problem facing the country, the Gallup organization found that education was ranked second behind morality in January 2001 (see Newport 2001).

Chapter 1

1. The aim of the legislation, known formally as Goals 2000: Educate America Act (1994), was to meet the following goals by 2000: "(1) All children in America will start school ready to learn. (2) The high school graduation rate will increase to at least 90 percent. (3) All students will leave grades 4, 8, and 12 having demonstrated competency over challenging subject matter in the core academic subjects. (4) U.S. students will be first in the world in mathematics and science achievement. (5) Every adult American will be literate and will possess the knowledge and skills necessary to compete in a global economy and exercise the rights and responsibilities of citizenship. (6) Every school in the U.S. will be free of drugs, violence, and firearms. (7) The Nation's teaching force will have access to programs for the continued improvement of their professional skills. (8) Every school will promote partnerships that will increase parental involvement and participation in promoting the social, emotional, and academic growth of children."
2. See, for example, Paul Burka's article about the Texas State school board's opposition to Goals 2000 (1998). For an interesting case study of Christian

Right opposition to outcomes-based education in Pennsylvania, see Boyd, Lugg, and Zahorchak (1996).

3. GOP congressional leaders endorsed the Christian Coalition's "Contract with the American Family" in May 1995, 100 days after Newt Gingrich began work legislating his party's Contract with America. Ralph Reed, the executive director of the Christian Coalition at the time, agreed not to disrupt the 104th Congress during its first 100 days with such divisive issues as school prayer in exchange for leadership support of the Christian Coalition's ten-point agenda in their own contract. Four of the ten issue agenda points in the Contract with the American Family concerned education issues. Besides endorsing a national parental rights act, the Christian Coalition's contract called for vouchers, the restoration of school prayer, and elimination of the Department of Education. For more on the Contract with the American Family, see Reed (1996).

4. Bible history courses have been offered in several public school districts in Florida, and other states are considering such proposals (Detwiler 1999; Tubbs 2001). As of this writing, however, People for the American Way has filed a lawsuit against such classes in one Florida county, citing constitutional concerns about church/state separation.

Chapter 2

1. The *Directory of Public and Elementary and Secondary Education Agencies* (1993–94), published by the U.S. Department of Education, provided the list of all 14,881 U.S. school districts. Appointed school boards, school boards that did not report student size, "special" school districts (such as schools for the blind), and school districts with fewer than twenty-five students were excluded from analysis. This brought the final primary sampling frame to 13,582.

2. The school districts represent a diverse cross-section of the nation, coming from thirty-nine different states. Regionally, the random selection of districts is as follows: Midwest (41 percent), West (27 percent), Northeast (19.5 percent), and South (12.5 percent). Finally, 65 percent of the school districts selected come from rural areas, 27 percent from suburban areas, and 7 percent from urban areas.

3. Although a 55 percent response rate for a "blind" survey after two waves is good, the response rate would have likely been higher if more candidates had not run for school board in uncontested races. Of the 273 school dis-

tricts in which surveys were mailed to recent candidates, candidates returned surveys from 242 districts. Of those thirty-one districts that yielded no returned surveys, however, 52 percent of candidates ran unopposed. For more information on how the survey was conducted, see appendix A.

4. The response rate among candidates in the two counties who agreed to be interviewed was 69 percent (31 of 45 candidates).

5. From the spring of 1996 through the spring of 1998, I regularly attended school board meetings in Fairfax and Garrett Counties. I also analyzed newspaper coverage from the local papers in Garrett County from January 1995 (when the conservative Christians first became a majority on the school board) until the school board elections in November 1998. Similar analysis was done for the school board in Fairfax County, where newspaper coverage was reviewed from January 1996 until December 1998. Finally, I analyzed the official minutes of the school board meetings for both counties during roughly the same time period.

6. Only one respondent identified himself as an Orthodox Jew. Because this person also identified himself as a Reform/Conservative Jew, he was grouped in the latter category.

7. Pentecostal Christians and Charismatic Christians generally share the same beliefs about the baptism of the Holy Spirit. Unlike Pentecostals, however, Charismatic Christians are located within already established religious traditions such as Lutherans, Methodists, and even Catholics (Smidt 1989).

8. For a more detailed treatment of the relationship between religion and attitudes about education issues, see Deckman (2002).

9. Moreover, ideology might hide some *indirect* effects of religion. Although space limits a more thorough examination of this point, path analyses show that many of the religious identities have a substantial impact when regressed on ideology as a dependent variable.

10. Both Christian Right and non–Christian Right candidates are members of churches at higher rates than the national average. According to the 1997 *Statistical Abstract of the United States*, 69 percent of Americans are members of churches, parishes, synagogues, or other houses of worship. This finding is not surprising, in light of the fact that research shows that the more involved an individual is in the community, through the schools, churches, or voluntary organizations, the more likely that he or she will be offered opportunities to become involved in politics (Verba, Schlozman, and Brady 1995).

11. The Catholic Church and the Christian Right have a complex relationship. In recent years, Christian Right leaders such as Ralph Reed have tried to make inroads with conservative Catholics to form political alliances about common issues such as abortion. Indeed, such significant Christian Right leaders as Pat Buchanan and Paul Weyrich are conservative Catholics. In terms of education policy, there are several policy areas in which the Catholic Church and the Christian Right are in agreement, such as support for education vouchers and tax credits. In the 1994 school board elections held in New York City, the Archdiocese of New York formed an unlikely union with Pat Robertson to help elect provoucher, conservative school board candidates, meeting with some success; however, although the Catholic Church and the Christian Right agree on some issues, they stand far apart on many social justice issues such as capital punishment, welfare, and other programs that benefit the poor. These differences have generally kept the Christian Right from recruiting as many Catholics to their ranks as they would like.

12. According to the *Statistical Abstract of the United States,* the median family household income was $34,076 in 1995 (1997, 160). In that same year, the education breakdown of the U.S. population for individuals over the age of twenty-five years was as follows: 18.3 percent had not finished high school; 33.6 percent were high school graduates; 17.3 percent had attended some college; 7.2 percent had an associate's degree; 15.8 percent had a bachelor's degree; and 7.8 percent had an advanced degree.

13. According to the U.S. Department of Commerce, in 1998—when the survey was conducted—about 56 percent of all American adults were married (U.S. Census Bureau 1999).

Chapter 3

1. One of the conservative Christian candidates made it clear that he is no longer a part of the Christian Coalition, although he was active in the group at the time he decided to run for school board in 1994.

2. One conservative Christian school board candidate in Garrett County served as the pastor of his church. He said that his decision to run for school board was largely self-motivated.

3. Although it is impossible to determine with this study's data, another theoretical possibility is that the political interests and actions of individual church members might actually politicize the church, rather than having

the church environment be responsible for politicizing individual members themselves.

4. Of the original thirty-seven candidates who filed as school board candidates, three dropped out for personal reasons; however, an additional candidate filed to fill one spot left vacant by a Republican candidate. Although the races were officially "nonpartisan," GOP party leaders did not want to leave the Democratic candidate in this particular district running unopposed and played a part in encouraging someone to replace this vacancy.

Chapter 4

1. It should be noted that Reed made a concerted effort in later years to avoid the use of military metaphors to describe his campaign philosophy after the Christian Coalition received much criticism for his statement. See his *Active Faith* (1996, 120).

2. This advertisement appeared in the November 3, 1994, edition of the Garrett County newspaper, the *Republican*.

3. Churches, as tax-exempt entities, are forbidden from endorsing or contributing to political candidates.

4. In Garrett County, the Christian Coalition did distribute voter guides to citizens. These guides, though not officially endorsing any candidates, most likely served as an effective way for Christian Right candidates to get part of their campaign message to voters. The distribution of these guides can be viewed, in some sense then, as a "soft-money" contribution. Data are not available as to the extent of the distribution or its cost to the organization. After research for this study was completed, the Christian Coalition split into two separate organizations, in 1999: Christian Coalition International, a non–tax-exempt political action committee that can legally endorse candidates and make contributions, and Christian Coalition of America, a tax-exempt group that focuses on voter education. This decision came after the Internal Revenue Service decided to deny the group's tax-exempt status because it deemed their voter guides overtly partisan (Goodstein 1999). As noted in chapter 1, this split represents the first in a series of missteps of the once powerful organization.

5. The vast majority of interest groups in the United States have a tax-exempt status by qualifying under 26 USCA 501(c)(3), one part of the United States code devoted to tax matters (Walker 1991). This tax status

202 Notes

allows contributors to interest groups to deduct their contributions from their personal taxes. Although section 501(c)(3) allows groups to educate citizens (including potential voters) on political matters, groups under this tax status are forbidden from participating in partisan matters, including endorsing or contributing to the campaigns of candidates for public office. Political action committees are formed with the express purpose of endorsing candidates and donating campaign funds. Political action committees, which fall under section 501(c)(4), are not tax exempt.

6. As was the case in Garrett County, Christian Right organizations (as well as more liberal groups) distributed voter guides to citizens in Fairfax County. These guides were mailed at the expense of the group that published them—not the candidates—and probably influenced the vote choices of some citizens.

7. During the 1995 elections, the Diocese in Northern Virginia was one of the most conservative in the United States. It was just one of two dioceses that did not allow girls to take part in the church service as acolytes (priest's assistants). Its bishop, John Keating, was known throughout the country for his outspoken, conservative views on political issues, including support for vouchers. Several Democratic candidates believed that his conservative views explained the church's actions in regard to the school board elections.

8. Of some surprise in the survey data is that a very small percentage (roughly less than 1 percent) of non–Christian Right candidates receive endorsements, contributions, and training from Christian Right organizations. A closer examination of these data reveals that a total of five non–Christian Right candidates made these claims. It is possible that these five respondents, all of whom claim to have been endorsed by or received contributions from Citizens for Excellence in Education, are mistaking Bob Simonds's organization for one with a similar name. The non–Christian Right candidate who was trained by the Christian Coalition is a supporter of the group, though not a member, nor does this individual share a majority of Christian Right positions on education issues.

9. There is recent evidence, however, to suggest that such claims on the part of the Christian Coalition in the past have been overstated. One former Christian Coalition official claims that the organization knowingly printed guides that it knew would never be distributed and that state affiliates ended up recycling many of them after the elections (Goodstein 1999).

10. See Rozell and Wilcox (1996) for a case study of Christian Right political activism in Fairfax County (chapter 6). The chapter details the Christian

Right's involvement with local party politics. The case study demonstrates that conservative Christian activists and social moderates have bitterly struggled about who should lead the Republican committee since the early 1980s.

11. This point was made during many of the one-on-one interviews with various school board candidates in Fairfax County.

Chapter 5

1. Quoted in Shogren and Frantz (1993, A1).

2. It is difficult to assess accurately the number of individuals in the United States who closely identify with the Christian Right. Instead, many analysts look at the primary constituency of the Christian Right—evangelical Christians—to give a rough estimate, realizing that some evangelicals do not share the same beliefs and that Christian Right identifiers are sometimes conservative Catholics and mainline Protestants (Rozell and Wilcox 1997). Evangelicals make up slightly more than one-quarter (27 percent) of the U.S. population (Wald 1997), although their ranks are growing.

3. A single-member district is any school district election in which only one member is elected from a region or district within the school district. In a few cases from the study, candidates run in elections that are regionally divided, yet often include two or more seats from each region. Those types of races, as well as the more typical at-large structure, are coded as at-large.

4. The data, collected by the Glenmary Research Center (1990), can be found in the American Religion Data Archive (www.arda.tm/archive/CMS90ST. html). The data contain statistics by county for 133 Judeo-Christian church bodies, providing information on both the number of churches and church members and adherents.

5. Using the coding scheme for religious affiliations and traditions developed by Kellstedt, Green, Guth, and Smidt (1996), I coded each individual church listed in the Glenmary Data as evangelical or nonevangelical.

6. An ecological fallacy, as defined by Nachmias and Nachmias, is when a distortion occurs due to relationships being "estimated at one level of analysis (e.g., collectivities) and then extrapolated to another level (e.g., individuals)" (1987, 57).

7. In light of the reduction of the sample size due to consideration of just nonincumbents and some missing data, the full model analyzing success

of school board candidates for nonincumbents including all twenty-four variables was untenable and resulted in a model that was no longer significant. Therefore, I controlled for both the variables that most closely approached theoretical significance in the original model (number of volunteers) and those that were most theoretically compelling, such as region, community type, percentage of evangelical church members by county, and open seat status.

Chapter 6

1. For information about the Garrett County school board, I relied on archived editions of the county's only weekly newspaper, the *Republican*. I analyzed each week's edition, beginning with the first weekly edition of the paper in January 1995 until early February 1999 for coverage of school board events. Coverage was also supplemented with the *Cumberland News-Times*, a regional paper that covers political events in four counties in western Maryland, including Garrett County. The main source of newspaper information about the Fairfax County school board came from the *Washington Post* and the *Washington Times*. I searched these two papers using the online computer system LEXIS/NEXIS from January 1, 1996, until February 28, 1999. The search retrieved any newspaper stories that contained the words "Fairfax County school board."

2. As of 2001, the state of Maryland made county participation voluntary with the MSPAP test as many educators believed there were problems with the test. As of this writing, the state was developing an alternative to the test in order to meet the criteria established by the No Child Left Behind Act, passed by the federal government in 2002, which mandates that each state require students to pass yearly exams before entering the next grade from fifth to eighth grade.

References

"After Lengthy Discussion." 1995. *Republican.* February 5: A14.

Allen, Mike. 1996. "Conservatives Lobby for Parental Rights." *New York Times.* January 15: 10.

American Family Association (Fairfax County Affiliate). 1995a. "Media Fails to Identify the Real 'Stealth Candidates' for Fairfax County School Board." Press release, November 3.

———. 1995b. "Media Looks for Smoke Where There Is No Fire." Press release, October 15.

American Library Association. 2000. "Banned Books Week." www.ala.org/bbooks/challenge.html [accessed December 18, 2002].

Ammis, Tammy. 1996. "Outside Influence Denied." *Union Leader.* May 12: B1.

"Another Special Meeting. . ." 1995. *Republican.* October 19: A4.

Ansolabehere, Stephen, and Alan Gerber. 1994. "The Mismeasure of Campaign Spending: Evidence from the 1990 US House Elections." *Journal of Politics* 56 (4): 1106–18.

Arocha, Zita. 1993. "The Religious Right's March into Public School Governance." *School Administrator* October: 8–15.

Barone, Michael, and Grant Ujifusa. 1993. "Virginia." *The Almanac of American Politics, 1994.* Washington, D.C.: National Journal.

Belluck, Pam. 1996. "Conservative School Board Gains Turn Out to Be No Revolution." *New York Times.* April 26: B2.

Benning, Victoria. 1997. "School Officials Take Aim at Grade Policy: Board Member Enlists Business Community." *Washington Post.* October 9: V1.

Berkeley, George E., and Douglas M. Fox. 1978. *80,000 Governments: The Politics of Subnational Government.* Boston: Allyn & Bacon.

Berliner, David. 1997. "Education Psychology Meets the Christian Right: Differing Views of Children, Schooling, and Learning." *Teachers College Record.* 93 (3): 381–417.

Box-Steffensmeier, Janet. 1996. "A Dynamic Analysis of the Role of War Chests in Campaign Strategy." *American Journal of Political Science* 40 (2): 352–71.

Boyd, William L., Catherine A. Lugg, and Gerald L. Zahorchak. 1996. "Social Traditionalists, Religious Conservatives, and the Politics of Outcomes-Based Education: Pennsylvania and Beyond." *Education and Urban Society* 28 (3): 347–65.

Brooks, A. Philip. 1995. "Moderates Resurge in School Districts." *The Austin American-Statesman.* June 26: B1.

Browning, Rufus P., Dale Rogers Marshall, and David H. Taub. 1984. *Protest Is Not Enough: The Struggle of Blacks and Hispanics for Equality in Urban Politics.* Berkeley: University of California Press.

Brudney, Jeffrey L., and Gary W. Copeland. 1984. "Evangelicals as a Political Force." *Social Science Quarterly* 65: 1072–79.

Burka, Paul. 1998. "Disloyal Opposition." *Texas Monthly* 26 (12): 116–23.

Carleton, Don E. 1985. *Red Scare! Right Wing Hysteria, Fifties Fanaticism, and Their Legacy in Texas.* Austin: Texas Monthly Press.

Cassie, William, and David A. Breaux. 1998. "Expenditures and Election Results." In *Campaign Finance in State Legislative Elections,* edited by Joel A. Thompson and Gary F. Moncrief, 99–114. Washington, D.C.: CQ Press.

Christian Coalition. 2001. "Christian Coalition of America Announces Plan for Activist Training Schools across the Country." Press release, April 18. www.cc.org/becomeinformed/pressrelease042001. html [accessed December 13, 2002].

Cistone, Peter J., ed. 1975. *Understanding School Boards: Problems and Prospects.* Lexington, Mass.: Lexington Books.

Citizens for Excellence in Education. 2001. "Dr. Robert Simonds." www. nace-cee-org/ceepresident.html [accessed August 1, 2001].

Clabaugh, Gary K. 1974. *Thunder on the Right: The Protestant Fundamentalists.* Chicago: Nelson-Hall.

Clarkson, Frederick. 1998. "Texas School Board Showdown." *In These Times.* July 26:16.

Cleaver, Cathleen A., and Greg Erkin. 1996. "Parental Rights: Who Decides How Children Are Raised?" *Family Policy.* Washington, D.C.: Family Research Council.

Clevenger, Ty. 1995. "Lawmaker's Hopes Are Dashed Fast." *Washington Times.* November 3: C4.

Cobb, Roger W., and Charles D. Elder. 1983. *Participation in American Politics: The Politics of Agenda-Setting.* Baltimore: Johns Hopkins University Press.

Cohen, Michael. 2002. "Implementing Title I Standards, Assessments, and Accountability: Lessons from the Past, Challenges for the Future."

Prepared for the Will No Child Be Truly Left Behind? The Challenges of Making the Law Work conference sponsored by the Thomas B. Fordham Foundation. February 13.

Colletta, Paolo E. 1969. *William Jennings Bryan*. Vol. 3: *Political Puritan: 1915–1925*. Lincoln: University of Nebraska Press.

Connelly, Jr., William F., and John J. Pitney, Jr. 1994. *Congress' Permanent Minority? Republicans in the U.S. House*. Lanham, Md.: Rowman and Littlefield.

Conway, M. Margaret. 1991. *Political Participation in the United States*, 2d ed. Washington, D.C.: CQ Press.

County and City Databook, 1994: A Statistical Abstract Supplement. 1994. Washington, D.C.: U.S. Department of Commerce.

Cremin, Lawrence A. 1980. *American Education: The National Experience, 1783–1876*. New York: Harper & Row.

Deckman, Melissa M. 2002. "Holy ABCs! How Religion Affects Attitudes about Education Policies." *Social Science Quarterly* 83 (2): 472–87.

Deighton, Lee C., ed. 1971. *Encyclopedia of Education*. Vol. 8. New York: Free Press.

Detwiler, Fritz. 1999. *Standing on the Premises of God: The Christian Right's Fight to Redefine America's Public Schools*. New York: New York University Press.

Diamond, Sara. 1998. *Not By Politics Alone: The Enduring Influence of the Christian Right*. New York: Guilford Press.

Dobson, James. 2002. "Complete Marriage and Family Home Reference Guide." www.family.org/docstudy.solid/a0015102.html [accessed December 18, 2002].

"Ebey Story." 1953. *The Nation*. September 26: 242. Quoted in Don Carleson. *Red Scare! Right Wing Hysteria, Fifties Fanaticism, and Their Legacy in Texas*, 219. Austin: Texas Monthly Press, 1985.

Family Research Council. 2002. "Family Research Council Applauds Supreme Court Decisions in School Voucher, Drug Testing Cases." Press release, June 17. www.frc.org/get/p02f05.cfm [accessed December 18, 2002].

Fenno, Richard. 1997. *Learning to Govern: An Institutional View of the 104th Congress*. Washington, D.C.: Brookings Institution Press.

Ferrechio, Susan. 1996. "Text's Creationism 'Attack' Causes Fairfax School Flap." *Washington Times*. November 11: C5.

Gabler, Mel, and Norma Gabler. 1985. *What Are They Teaching Our Children?* Wheaton, Ill.: Victor Books.

Gaddy, Barbara, T. William Hall, and Robert J. Marzano. 1996. *School Wars: Resolving Our Conflicts over Religion and Values*. San Francisco: Jossey-Bass.

Galst, Liz. 1994. "The Right Fight." *Mother Jones.* March/April: 58–59.

Garcia, John A. 1979. "An Analysis of Chicano and Anglo Electoral Patterns in School Board Elections." *Ethnicity* 6: 168–83.

Gatewood, Jr., Willliam B. 1966. *Preachers, Pedagogues, and Politicians: The Evolution Controversy in North Carolina, 1920–1927.* Chapel Hill: University of North Carolina Press.

Gierzynski, Anthony, and David Breaux. 1991. "Money and Voters in State Legislative Elections." *Legislative Studies Quarterly* 16 (2): 203–17.

Gilbert, Christopher. 1993. *The Impact of Churches on Political Behavior.* Westport, Conn.: Greenwood Press.

Glenmary Research Center. 1990. *Churches and Church Membership in the United States, 1990.* Mars Hill, Ga.: Glenmary Research Center.

Goodstein, Laurie. 1999. "Coalition's Woes May Hinder Goals of Christian Right." *New York Times.* August 2: A1.

Granberry, Michael. 1996. "New Vision for Vista Schools." *Los Angeles Times.* March 14: A21.

Green, John C., and James L. Guth. 1993. "From Lambs to Sheep: Denominational Change and Political Behavior." In *Rediscovering the Religious Factor in American Politics,* edited by David C. Leege and Lyman Kellstedt, 177–98. Armonk, N.Y.: M. E. Sharpe.

Green, John C., James L. Guth, Corwin E. Smidt, and Lyman A. Kellstedt. 1996. *Religion and the Culture Wars: Dispatches from the Front.* Lanham, Md.: Rowman and Littlefield.

Green, John C., Mark J. Rozell, and Clyde Wilcox, eds. 2000. *Prayers in the Precincts: The Christian Right in the 1998 Elections.* Washington, D.C.: Georgetown University Press.

Guth, James L. 1983. "The Politics of the Christian Right." In *Interest Group Politics,* edited by Allan J. Cigler and Burdett A. Loomis, 60–83. Washington, D.C.: CQ Press.

Guth, James L., and John C. Green. 1991. *The Ballot and the Bible Box: Religion and Politics in the 1988 Elections.* Boulder, Colo.: Westview Press.

Hammond, Susan Webb. 1998. *Congressional Caucuses in National Policy-Making.* Baltimore: Johns Hopkins University Press.

Henry, Tamara. 2002. "Parents Say Textbook Reads Like Recruitment." *USA Today.* March 4: 6D.

Herrnson, Paul S. 1995. *Congressional Elections: Campaigning at Home and in Washington.* Washington, D.C.: CQ Press.

Hofrenning, Daniel. 1995. *In Washington But Not of It: The Prophetic Politics of Religious Lobbyists.* Philadelphia: Temple University Press.

Holland, Robert. 1994. "Outcome-Based Education: Dumbing Down America's Schools." *Family Policy.* January. Washington, D.C.: Family Research Council.

Honderich, Ted, ed. 1995. *Oxford Companion to Philosophy.* New York: Oxford University Press.

Horstman, Barry M. 1992. "Christian Activists Using 'Stealth' Campaign Tactics: Conservative Religious Groups Try to Capitalize on Gains Using Methods Shielded from Public Views." *Los Angeles Times.* April 5: A1.

Huckfeldt, Robert, and John Sprague. 1995. *Citizens, Politics, and Social Communication: Information and Influence in an Election Campaign.* Cambridge: Cambridge University Press.

Hudson, Kathi. 1993. *Reinventing America's Schools: A Practical Guide to Components of Restructuring and Non-Traditional Education,* rev. ed. Costa Mesa, Calif.: National Association of Christian Educators/Citizens for Excellence in Education, 1:66. Quoted in Fritz Detwiler, *Standing on the Premises of God: The Christian Right's Fight to Redefine America's Public Schools,* 190. New York: New York University Press, 1999.

Hunter, James Davison. 1991. *Culture Wars: The Struggle to Define America.* New York: Basic Books.

Jacobson, Gary C. 1992. *The Politics of Congressional Elections,* 3d ed. New York: HarperCollins.

Jelen, Ted G. 1987. "The Effects of Religious Separatism on White Protestants in the 1984 Election." *Sociological Analysis* 48 (1): 30–45.

———. ed. 1989. *Religion and Political Behavior in the United States.* New York: Praeger.

———. 1991. *The Political Mobilization of Religious Belief.* New York: Prager.

Jelen, Ted G., Corwin Smidt, and Clyde Wilcox. 1993. "The Political Effects of the Born-Again Phenomena." In *Rediscovering the Religious Factor in American Politics,* edited by David Leege and Lyman Kellstedt, 199–215. Armonk, N.Y.: M. E. Sharpe.

Jewell, Malcolm, and David Breaux. 1988. "The Effect of Incumbency on State Legislative Elections." *Legislative Studies Quarterly* 13 (4): 495–514.

Jones, Charles O. 1970. *The Minority Party in Congress.* Boston: Little, Brown.

Jones, Janet L. 1993. "Targets of the Right: Public Schools—and School Boards—Are under Attack from the Religious Right." *American School Board Journal* 180 (June): 22–29.

Jordahl, Steve. 2002. "'Banned Book Week' Decried." *Family News in Focus.* www.family.org/cforum/fnif/news/a0022426.html [accessed December 18, 2002].

Jorstad, Erling. 1970. *The Politics of Doomsday: Fundamentalists of the Far Right.* Nashville, Tenn.: Abingdon Press.

Kazee, Thomas A. 1994. "The Emergence of Congressional Candidates." In *Who Runs for Congress? Ambition, Context, and Candidate Emergence,* edited by Thomas A. Kazee, 1–22. Washington, D.C.: CQ Press.

Kellstedt, Lyman A., John C. Green, James L. Guth, and Corwin E. Smidt. 1996. "Grasping the Essentials: The Social Embodiment of Religion and Political Behavior." In *Religion and the Culture Wars: Dispatches from the Front,* edited by John C. Green, James L. Guth, Corwin E. Smidt, and Lyman A. Kellstedt, 174–92. Lanham, Md.: Rowman and Littlefield.

Kellstedt, Lyman A., and Corwin Smidt. 1993. "Doctrinal Beliefs and Political Behavior: Views of the Bible." In *Rediscovering the Religious Factor in American Politics,* edited by David Leege and Lyman Kellstedt, 177–89. Armonk, N.Y.: M. E. Sharpe.

Killian, Linda. 1998. *The Freshmen: What Happened to the Republican Revolution?* Boulder, Colo.: Westview Press.

Kosmin, Barry A., and Seymour P. Lachman. 1993. *One Nation under God: Religion in Contemporary American Society.* New York: Crown Trade Paperbacks.

Lane, Robert E. 1959. *Political Life: Why People Get Involved in Politics.* Glencoe, Ill.: Free Press.

Larson, Edward J. 1989. *Trial and Error: The American Controversy over Creation and Evolution.* New York: Oxford University Press.

Leege, David C. 1993. "Religion and Politics from a Theoretical Perspective." In *Rediscovering the Religious Factor in American Politics,* edited by David C. Legee and Lyman Kellstedt, 3–25. Armonk, N.Y.: M. E. Sharpe.

Leege, David C., and Lyman Kellstedt, eds. 1993. *Rediscovering the Religious Factor in American Politics.* Armonk, N.Y.: M. E. Sharpe.

Leege, David C., Joel A. Lieske, and Kenneth D. Wald. 1991. "Toward Cultural Theories of American Political Behavior: Religion, Ethnicity and Race, and Class Outlook." In *Political Science: Looking to the Future,* vol. 3: *Political Behavior,* edited by William Crotty, 193–238. Evanston, Ill.: Northwestern University Press, 193–238.

Lienisch, Michael. 1997. "Organizing Opportunities: Opportunity Structures in the Anti-Evolution Movement." Paper presented at the 1997 Annual Meeting of the American Political Science Association, Washington, D.C.

Lugg, Catherine. 2000. "Reading, Writing, and Reconstructionism: The Christian Right and the Politics of Public Education." *Educational Policy* 14 (5): 622–38.

Maisel, L. Sandy, Walter J. Stone, and Cherie Maestas. 2001. "Quality Challengers to Congressional Incumbents: Can Better Candidates Be

Found?" In *Playing Hardball: Campaigning for US Senate*, edited by Paul Herrnson, 12–34. Upper Saddle River, N.J.: Prentice Hall.

Maraniss, David, and Michael Weisskopf. 1996. *"Tell Newt to Shut Up!"*: *Prizewinning Washington Post Journalists Reveal How Reality Gagged the Gingrich Revolution*. New York: Simon & Schuster.

Marsden, George. 1993. "The Religious Right: A Historical Overview." In *No Longer Exiles: The Religious New Right in American Politics*, edited by Michael Cromartie, 1–23. Washington, D.C.: Ethics and Public Policy Center.

Marshall, Jennifer. 1995. "Goals 2000: The Case for Repeal." *Family Research Council Insight Report*. March. Washington, D.C.: Family Research Council.

Marshall, Jennifer, and Eric Unsworth. 1995. "Freeing America's Schools: The Case against the U.S. Education Department." *Family Policy*. Washington, D.C.: Family Research Council.

Martin, William. 1996. *With God on Our Side: The Rise of the Religious Right in America*. New York: Broadway Books.

Mayhew, David. 1974. *Congress: The Electoral Connection*. New Haven, Conn.: Yale University Press.

McCurley, Carl, and Jeffrey J. Mondauk. 1995. "Inspected by #1184063113: The Influence of Incumbents' Competence and Integrity in US House Elections." *American Journal of Political Science* 39 (4): 864–85.

McKinney, William. 1998. "Mainline Protestantism 2000." *Annals of the American Academy of Political and Social Sciences* 558 (July): 57–66.

Meier, Kenneth, and Joseph Stewart, Jr. 1991. "Cooperation and Conflict in Multiracial School Districts." *Journal of Politics* 53 (4): 1123–33.

Michaelson, Johanna. 1989. *Like Lambs to the Slaughter*. Eugene, Ore.: Harvest House Publishers.

Moen, Matthew C. 1989. *The Christian Right and Congress*. Tuscaloosa: University of Alabama Press.

———. 1992. *The Transformation of the Christian Right*. Tuscaloosa: University of Alabama Press.

Nachmias, David, and Chava Nachmias. 1987. *Research Methods in the Social Sciences*, 3d ed. New York: St. Martin's Press.

National Center for Education Statistics. 1995. *The Directory of Public Elementary and Secondary Agencies (1993–1994)*. Washington, D.C.: United States Department of Education.

National Council on Bible Curriculum in Public Schools. n.d. "Course Objective: The Bible as History and Literature." www.netmender.net/client/bibleinschools/objective [accessed December 18, 2002].

Newport, Frank. 2001. "Morality, Education, Crime, Dissatisfaction with Government Head List of Most Important Problems Facing Country

Today." *Gallup News Service.* February 5. www.gallup.com/poll/releases/pr10205.asp [accessed December 18, 2002].

O'Harrow, Robert. 1997. "Middle School Grading System Encounters Resistance in Fairfax; Mass Teleconference Held to Reassure Teachers." *Washington Post.* January 22: B1.

Olson, Mancur, Jr. 1965. *The Logic of Collective Action: Public Goods and the Theory of Groups.* Cambridge, Mass.: Harvard University Press.

Owens, John R., and Edward C. Olson. 1977. "Campaign Spending and the Electoral Process in California, 1966–1974." *Western Political Quarterly* 30: 493–512.

Page, Ann L., and Donald A. Clelland. 1978. "The Kanawha County Textbook Controversy: A Study of the Politics of Lifestyle Concern." *Social Forces* 55 (1): 265–81.

"Parents, Staff Incensed with BOE Members of Questioning NHS Event." 1995. *Republican.* October 26: A1.

Parker, Barbara. 1979. "Your Schools May Be the Next Battlefield in the Crusade against 'Improper' Textbooks." *American School Board Journal* 168 (6): 21–26.

Rae, Nicol C. 1998. *Conservative Reformers: The Republican Freshmen and the Lessons of the 104th Congress.* Armonk, N.Y.: M. E. Sharpe.

Reed, Ralph, Jr. 1994. *Politically Incorrect.* Dallas: Word Publishing.

———. 1996. *Active Faith: How Christians Are Changing the Soul of American Politics.* New York: Free Press.

Reich, David. 1995. "Fighting the Right on Local School Boards." *World,* November/December: 16–21.

Riemer, Neal, ed. 1996. *Let Justice Roll: Prophetic Challenges in Religion, Politics, and Society.* Lanham, Md.: Rowman and Littlefield.

Rippa, S. Alexander. 1976. *Education in a Free Society: An American History,* 3d ed. New York: David McKay Co.

Robinson, Ted, and Robert E. Englund. 1981. "Black Representation on Central City School Boards Revisted." *Social Science Quarterly* 62 (3): 495–502.

Rosenau, James N. 1974. *Citizenship between Elections: An Inquiry into the Mobilizable American.* New York: Free Press.

Rosenstone, Steven J., and John Mark Hansen. 1993. *Mobilization, Participation, and Democracy.* New York: Macmillan.

Rothenberg, Stuart, and Frank Newport. 1984. *The Evangelical Voter: Religion and Politics in America.* Washington, D.C.: Free Congress Research and Education Foundation.

Rozell, Mark J., and Clyde Wilcox. 1996. *Second Coming: The New Christian Right in Virginia Politics*. Baltimore: Johns Hopkins University Press.

Salisbury, Robert H. 1980. *Citizen Participation in the Public Schools*. Lexington, Mass.: Lexington Books.

Schlafly, Phyllis, ed. 1984. *Child Abuse in the Classroom*. Alton, Ill.: Pere Marquette Press.

———. 1993. "What's Wrong with Outcome-Based Education?" *Phyllis Schlafly Report* 26 (October): 1–3.

———. 1994. "Big Brother Education, 1994." *Phyllis Schlafly Report* 27 (10): 3.

———. 1997. "School to Work at Goals 2000." *Phyllis Schlafly Report* 30 (April): 1–7.

———. 2002. "Will New Education Law Leave Every Child Behind?" *Education Reporter* 191: 1.

Schlesinger, Arthur M. 1992. *The Disuniting of America*. New York: W. W. Norton.

Sellers, Patrick J. 1997. "Fiscal Consistency and Federal District Spending in Congressional Elections." *American Journal of Political Science* 41 (3): 1024–41.

Shibley, Mark A. 1998. "Contemporary Evangelicals: Born-Again and World Affirming." *Annals of the American Academy of Political and Social Sciences* 558 (July): 67–87.

Shogren, Elizabeth, and Douglas Frantz. 1993. "School Boards Become the Religious Right's New Pulpit." *Los Angeles Times*. December 10: A1.

Sigelman, Lee, and Stanley Presser. 1988. "Measuring Public Support for the New Christian Right: The Perils of Point Estimation." *Public Opinion Quarterly* 52 (4): 325–37.

Sikkink, David. 1999. "The Social Sources of Alienation from Public Schools." *Social Forces* 78 (1): 51–86.

Simonds, Robert. 1993. "What's Wrong with the Public Schools?" From *Parental Concerns,* report # 25. Costa Mesa, Calif.: National Association of Christian Educators/Citizens for Excellence in Education.

———. 1995. *President's Report. June*. Costa Mesa, Calif.: National Association of Christian Educators/Citizens for Excellence in Education.

———. 1998. *President's Report. January*. Costa Mesa, Calif.: National Association of Christian Educators/Citizens for Excellence in Education.

———. 2002. *President's Report. February*. Costa Mesa, Calif.: National Association of Christian Educators/Citizens for Excellence in Education.

Simpson, John H. 1983. "Moral Issues and Status Politics." In *The New*

Christian Right: Mobilization and Legitimation, edited by Robert C. Liebman and Robert Wuthnow, 188–207. New York: Aldine.

Sinclair, Don. 1996. "'Stealth' Candidates from the Right." *Christian Social Action.* January: 28–31.

Smidt, Corwin. 1989. "'Praise the Lord Politics' Politics: A Comparative Analysis of the Social Characteristics and Political Views of Evangelical and Charismatic Christians." *Sociological Analysis* 30: 53–72.

Smith, Christian. 1998. *American Evangelicalism: Embattled and Thriving.* Chicago: University of Chicago Press.

Smith, Oran P. 1997. *The Rise of Baptist Republicanism.* New York: New York University Press.

Statistical Abstract of the United States. 1997. Washington, D.C.: U.S. Department of Commerce.

Steinberg, Jacques. 1999. "School Districts in Kansas Split over Evolution Ruling." *New York Times.* August 25: A1.

Stevens, Mitchell L. 2001. *Kingdom of Children: Culture and Controversy in the Homeschooling Movement.* Princeton, N.J.: Princeton University Press.

Stewart, Jr., Joseph, Robert E. Englund, and Kenneth J. Meier. 1988. "Black Representation in Urban School Districts: From School Board to Office to Classroom." *Western Political Quarterly* 41 (4): 287–305.

"Support and Criticism of 'Outcomes-Based Education' Voiced at BOE Meetings." 1995. *Republican.* February 23: A5.

Taebel, Delbert. 1977. "Politics of School Board Elections." *Urban Education* 12 (2): 153–66.

Talbot, Margaret. 2001. "The New Counterculture." *Atlantic Monthly.* November. Posted on website: www.newamerica.net/articles/article.cfm?pubID==599&T2=Article [accessed August 20, 2002].

Tocqueville, Alexis de. 1956 [1835]. *Democracy in America.* Edited and abridged by Richard J. Hefner. New York: Penguin Books.

Townley, Arthur J., Dwight B. Sweeney, and June H. Schneider. 1994. "School Board Elections: A Study of Citizen Voting Patterns." *Urban Education* 29 (1): 50–62.

Tubbs, Sharon. 2001. "The Bible without Religion." *St. Petersburg Times.* July 5: 1D.

Tucker, Harvey J., and Ronald E. Weber. 1987. "State Legislative Election Outcomes: Contextual Effects and Legislative Performance Effects." *Legislative Studies Quarterly* 12 (4): 537–53.

United States Census Bureau. 1999. "Married Adults Still in the Majority,

Census Bureau Reports." Press release, January 7, 1999. www.census.gov/ Press-Release/www/1999/cb99-03.html [accessed February 2, 1999].

United States Department of Education. 1993. *The Directory of Public and Secondary Education Agencies.* Washington, D.C.: U.S. Department of Education.

———. 1994. *Goals 2000: Educate America Act.* Washington, D.C.: U.S. Department of Education.

———. 2002. No Child Left Behind Act of 2002: Reauthorization of the Elementary and Secondary School Act Legislation and Policies. www.ed.gov/ offices/oese/esea [accessed December 18, 2002].

Upperman, James E., Joan L. Curcio, Jim C. Fortune, and Kenneth E. Underwood. 1996. "Options for Everyone." *American School Board Journal* 183 (1): 31–35.

Vail, Kathleen. 1995. "Conservatively Speaking." *American School Board Journal* 182 (12): 30–32.

Verba, Sidney, and Norman H. Nie. 1972. *Participation in America: Political Democracy and Social Equality.* New York: Harper & Row.

Verba, Sidney, Kay Lehman Schlozman, and Henry E. Brady. 1995. *Voice and Equality: Civic Volunteerism in American Politics.* Cambridge, Mass.: Harvard University Press.

Wald, Kenneth. 1995. "Florida: Running Globally and Winning Locally." In *God at the Grassroots: The Christian Right in the 1994 Elections,* edited by Mark J. Rozell and Clyde Wilcox, 19–46. Lanham, Md.: Rowman and Littlefield.

———. 1997. *Religion and Politics in the United States,* 3d ed. Washington, D.C.: CQ Press.

Wald, Kenneth, Dennis E. Owen, and Samuel S. Hill. 1990. "Political Cohesion in Churches." *Journal of Politics* 52: 197–215.

Walker, Jack L. 1991. *Mobilizing Interest Groups in America: Patron, Professions, and Social Movements.* Ann Arbor: University of Michigan Press.

Wallis, Jim. 1995. *The Soul of Politics: Beyond "Religious Right" and "Secular Left."* San Diego, Calif.: Harcourt Brace.

Warner, R. Stephen. 1988. *New Wine in Old Wineskins: Evangelicals and Liberals in a Small-Town Church.* Berkeley: University of California Press.

Wilcox, Clyde. 1992. *God's Warriors: The Christian Right in Twentieth-Century America.* Baltimore: Johns Hopkins University Press.

———. 2000. *Onward Christian Soldiers: The Religious Right in American Politics,* 2d ed. Boulder, Colo.: Westview Press.

Wills, Garry. 1990. *Under God: Religion and American Politics.* New York: Simon & Schuster.

Wilson, James Q. 1973. *Political Organizations.* New York: Basic Books.

Wolfinger, Raymond E., and Steven J. Rosenstone. 1980. *Who Votes?* New Haven, Conn.: Yale University Press.

Wynsma, J. R. 1997. "Education Reform: The HELP Scholarships Amendment of 1997." *NeoPolitique.* www.neopolitique.org/Np2000/Pages/Essays/Articles/dec97-help.html [accessed December 13, 2002].

Yang, John E., and Laurie Goodstein. 1997. "Reed Stepping Down as Christian Coalition Leader: Political Consulting Is Next for Organizer Reed." *Washington Post.* April: A6.

Ziegler, Harmon L., and M. Kent Jennings. 1974. *Governing American Schools.* North Scituate, Mass.: Duxbury Press.

Zingarelli, Mark. 1994. "God's Country." *Mother Jones.* March/April: 50–57.

Index

Note: Page numbers followed by a "t" indicate tables in the text.